DEFINITION IN THE CRIMINAL LAW

In recent years, a number of key terms of the criminal law have seemed to defy definition. Scepticism over the possibility of defining basic concepts and identifying general principles has been voiced by both judges and academic commentators. The condition of the criminal law raises broad issues of theoretical interest, but also touches on practical concerns such as proposals for reform made by the Law Commission, the campaign for codification, and the requirement of legality under Article 7 of the ECHR, given greater prominence since the implementation of the Human Rights Act 1998.

This book undertakes an investigation of the role and scope of definition within the criminal law set within a wider examination of the nature of legal materials and the diversity of perspectives on law. It offers a fascinating account of how the rules and principles found within legal materials provide practical opportunities for responding to, rather than merely following the law. This opens up a richer notion of legal doctrine than has been acknowledged in earlier representations of the workings of legal rules and principles. It also leads to a rejection of some of the established views on the roles of judges and academics, and provides the incentive for a more rigorous assessment of the serious challenge made by a 'critical' perspective on the criminal law.

The intimate connection between the use of legal materials and the practice of definition is explored through a number of detailed studies. These deal with some of the apparently intractable problems concerning the definition of theft, and changes to the definition of recklessness culminating in the recent decision of the House of Lords in *R v G*. Theoretical insights on the different features of the process of definition and a remodelling of culpability issues are combined to question the conventional intellectual apparatus of the criminal law. The approach developed within the book offers a more realistic appraisal of the feasibility of reform, and of expectations for the principle of legality within the criminal law.

Definition in the Criminal Law

ANDREW HALPIN

·HART·
PUBLISHING

OXFORD AND PORTLAND OREGON
2004

Published in North America (US and Canada) by
Hart Publishing
c/o International Specialized Book Services
5804 NE Hassalo Street
Portland, Oregon
97213-3644
USA

Hart Publishing is a specialist legal publisher based in Oxford,
England. To order further copies of this book or to request a list of
other publications please write to:

Hart Publishing, Salters Boatyard, Folly Bridge, Abingdon Rd,
Oxford, OX1 4LB Telephone: +44 (0)1865 245533
Fax: +44 (0)1865 794882
email: mail@hartpub.co.uk
WEBSITE: http://www.hartpub.co.uk

British Library Cataloguing in Publication Data
Data Available

ISBN 1-84113-071-0 (hardback)

Typeset by Olympus Infotech Pvt Ltd, India, in Palatino 10/12 pt.
Printed and bound in Great Britain by
MPG Books Ltd, Bodmin, Cornwall

Preface

Some books are organised like a Teutonic banquet. This book adopts the more modest organising principles of a Russian zakouski, spreading out on the table such a variety of hors d'oeuvres that everyone will find something to their taste. I hope that anyone with an interest in the law, whether or not they are concerned particularly with the criminal law, whether or not they have reflected previously on the process of legal definition, will find something of interest in its pages.

My own interests in writing this book have been advanced and broadened by the kindnesses of a number of persons. I am grateful for the encouraging comments offered by Andrew Ashworth, Stanley Yeo and Jeremy Horder, when the project was at an early stage. Progress was assisted by comments from, or discussions with, Kit Barker, Charles Debattista, Peter Sparkes, Oren Ben-Dor, Stuart Macdonald, Neil Duxbury, Jim Evans, Dennis Patterson, William Twining, Andrew Jefferies and Alan Newman. I am grateful to them all.

I am particularly happy to acknowledge the support provided by the British Academy and Leverhulme Trust in the award of a Senior Research Fellowship for the academic year 2002–03 during which most of the work on the book was undertaken.

Richard Hart, Jane Parker and Mel Hamill at Hart Publishing have provided the friendly, intelligent and efficient support which continues to distinguish the Hart publishing enterprise. I am also grateful for the support provided in numerous other ways by Ken Emond at the British Academy, Joy Caisley in the Hartley Library, and Aloma Hack in the School of Law.

I remain grateful to Dorit, Rafael, Daniel and Avital for helping me to focus on more important issues, and to Sergei and Rachel Tarassenko for combining Russian insights with French hospitality.

I have used in chapters 3 and 4 material previously published in the following articles: 'The Appropriate Appropriation' [1991] *Criminal Law Review* 426; 'The Test for Dishonesty' [1996] *Criminal Law Review* 283; and 'Definitions and directions: recklessness unheeded' (1998) 18 *Legal Studies* 294.

Contents

1

The Use of Legal Materials

INTRODUCTION

THE CONDITION OF the law attracts the attention of a number of parties, and arouses their passions in different ways. If we permit some caricature, the judge charged with applying the law complains about the difficult state of the law which makes the judicial role so burdensome, but considers that only the judicial mind, honed by practical experience, is capable of dealing effectively with the complexities faced in the law. The orthodox academic commentator bemoans the incoherent state of the law, to which unreflective judicial responses have made a major contribution, and considers that only a rigorous application of rational principle can redeem the law. The reformer acknowledges the historical mess that the law is in, and even-handedly recognises both judicial and academic disagreements that have contributed to this state, but optimistically believes that through an iterative process of draft and discussion a consensus can eventually be reached so as to provide a stable foundation for the law.[1] The heterodox academic commentator, on the other hand, views the state of the law with pessimism, seeing within its failings an indictment of the conventional premises of the law, and offers in their place a radical reassessment of the directions the law should take.

In juxtaposition to the pessimism of the heterodox commentator, there exists a natural alliance between the middle two perspectives. Both the orthodox academic commentator and the reformer share what Ian Dennis, borrowing from William Twining, has referred to as 'optimistic rationalism'.[2] Perhaps the only impediment to the steady flow from

---

[1] With regard to this, consider the Law Commission's abandonment of their project for reforming the law of consent on the ground that 'no consensus emerged'—Law Commission No 274 (HC 227, 2001), *Eighth Programme of Law Reform* 44. For discussion, see Paul Roberts, 'Philosophy, Feinberg, Codification, and Consent: A Progress Report on English Experiences of Criminal Law Reform' (2001) 5 *Buffalo Criminal Law Review* 173, 209ff. Roberts notes (at 187 n23) the Law Commission's avoidance of 'political' issues.

[2] Ian Dennis, 'The Critical Condition of Criminal Law' (1997) *Current Legal Problems* 213, 214. A particularly strong manifestation of this condition is to be found in EC Clark, *An Analysis of Criminal Liability* (Cambridge, Cambridge University Press, 1880; reprinted, Littleton, CO, Fred B Rothman & Co, 1983) 110: 'A time may, it is hoped, be coming, when such legal rules

commentary to reform is the additional dimension of optimism required by the latter. The commentator need only be optimistic about his or her own powers of rationality. The reformer needs to be optimistic about the ability of rational discussion among a number of participants to reach a consensus on the desired state of the law.

There also exists a less obvious alliance between the first and last of these perspectives, those of the judge and the heterodox scholar. Both of these display scepticism towards the enterprise of producing a formal scheme of law as academic treatise (or reforming code). To a certain extent the divergence of perspective is as much about focusing one's scepticism on different targets as it is about focusing one's attention on different aspects of the subject matter. Nevertheless, the complexity of the subject matter may, in part at least, account for the condition that the law is in, and for the variety of perspectives taken on it. Certainly, the condition of the law is a product of the nature of legal materials and the use that has been made of them. In this chapter I shall attempt to show that these materials are more complex in nature than has been acknowledged, and their corresponding use more varied. As a way into the subject I shall concentrate on the perspectives of orthodox academic commentators and the judiciary, though only as a means of arriving at a more general picture of legal materials.

THE RESORT TO PRINCIPLE

It is easy enough for academics to be sceptical about the condition of the law and the part played by judges in bringing it about. The English criminal law provides a particularly glaring example. Peter Glazebrook came to the conclusion that it has deteriorated significantly in the hundred years between the ends of the nineteenth and twentieth centuries.[3] Adrian Briggs, in his comment on the House of Lords decision in *Moloney*, extended the time frame to a thousand years in his acerbic assessment of the level of sophistication reached by the common law.[4] Whereas Briggs

---

may be brought into a form as exhaustive as we believe their mathematical congeners to be; and when criminal law generally will receive little, if any, addition from later cases, because a new point can scarcely arise.'

[3] Peter Glazebrook, 'Still No Code! English Criminal Law 1894–1994' in Martin Dockray (ed), *City University Centenary Lectures in Law* (London, Blackstone Press, 1996). Judicial efforts within the criminal law in the United States do not receive a better press. George Fletcher, 'The Fall and Rise of Criminal Theory' (1998) 1 *Buffalo Criminal Law Review* 275, 282, unfavourably contrasts these with judicial achievements in tort law: 'The fact is that stripped of their power and their judicial robes, these authors of opinions in the criminal law have very little to say. They stand to Cardozo's reflections on risk in *Palsgraf* as doggerel stands to poetry.'
[4] Adrian Briggs, 'Judges, juries and the meaning of words' (1985) 5 *Legal Studies* 314, 319.

pointed to the refusal of the judges to define basic terms,[5] others have condemned the readiness of the judiciary to redefine basic terms, a criticism captured in Andrew Ashworth's evocative image of the appellate judges playing a piano accordion.[6]

The scepticism expressed by the judges themselves seems in part defensive. Judges cannot be blamed for a failure to consistently define the basic terms of the criminal law if it is in the nature of those terms to defy comprehensive definition. More interestingly, this scepticism goes on the offensive in suggesting that the nature of the basic terms of the criminal law is such as to require a specialist function to be performed by the judiciary in applying these terms to specific cases. Lord Goff has refined this judicial scepticism in his stimulating attempt to present a demarcation of academic and judicial roles in developing the law, delivered as the 1983 Maccabaean Lecture.[7] Although other judges have not addressed the topic with the dedication of Lord Goff, the view he expresses clearly springs from a common judicial sentiment that the job to be done in judging particular cases cannot be performed by the simple reliance on a body of legal materials, no matter how much academic endeavour has been expended on their formulation and arrangement.

Sir Robert Megarry, for example, had in 1969[8] previously provided the core of Goff's position in stating what Basil Markesinis describes as 'the prevalent position ... that judges and academics were performing *entirely different tasks.*'[9] In relation to the criminal law in particular, the entrenched view of a specialist judicial function is evident in the judicial hostility of the nineteenth century towards the proposals for codifying the criminal law.[10] More recently, it is a straightforward matter to find

---

[5] *Ibid* at 318.

[6] Andrew Ashworth, Editorial [1986] *Criminal Law Review* 1, 1–2. Glazebrook, above n 3, at 7, refers to the 'seven conflicting and confusing House of Lords decisions' on intention (to which could be added several from the Court of Appeal); and, at 9–10, comments on the need for three House of Lords cases to settle a point on the law of theft. Dennis, above n 2, at 226, points to three legal meanings for recklessness in the aftermath of *Caldwell* ((i) *Cunningham*, (ii) *Caldwell*, (iii) modified *Caldwell* for rape), which multiplied subsequently to include (iv) recklessness as gross negligence in *Adomako* and (v) a softer form of *Caldwell* in *Reid* contrary to the hardline approach in *Elliott v C*—prior to the House of Lords' decision in *R v G* (for detailed discussion, see ch 3 below).

[7] Robert Goff, 'The Search for Principle' (1983) 69 *Proceedings of the British Academy* 169.

[8] *Cordell v Second Clanfield Properties* [1969] 2 Ch D 9, 16–17. Megarry's analysis of the difference stresses the susceptibility of the author (academic) to preconceptions, and the advantage conferred on the judge by his having to deal with the detailed facts of a contested case. The strict demarcation between functions of author/academic and judge is all the more marked for being made in relation to one person performing both functions, himself.

[9] Basil Markesinis, *Comparative Law in the Courtroom and in the Classroom: The Story of the Last Thirty-Five Years* (Oxford, Hart Publishing, 2003) 36. Markesinis himself argues for a cooperative venture between judges and academics.

[10] See Keith Smith, *Lawyers, Legislators and Theorists* (Oxford, Clarendon Press, 1998) 138, 147, 171–72, 368. Goff, above n 7, at 172–74, shows scepticism towards the value of codification, concluding that 'the best code is one which is not binding in law.'

judicial dicta reinforcing the role of making a judgment on the particular facts of the case, at the expense of developing a general understanding of the law.[11]

Given the strength of this judicial sentiment, it is worth considering in detail the arguments that Lord Goff provides in expounding his view of the specialist judicial function. Even if the current trend is for judges to be more appreciative of academic sources,[12] a study of Goff's demarcation of academic and judicial roles is capable of illuminating both roles, as well as how they might interrelate. Central to Goff's thesis is the distinction between general ideas and specific judgments. Crudely put, academics deal with ideas and judges provide judgments on particular facts.[13] However, in order to elaborate his view of the judicial function, Goff

[11] We can restrict ourselves to examples taken from the topics mentioned in n 6 above. On intention, see Lord Scarman in *Hancock and Shankland* [1986] 2 WLR 357, 364–65: 'I am, however, not persuaded that guidelines of general application, albeit within a limited class of case, are wise or desirable. ... Guidelines, if given, are not to be treated as rules of law but as a guide indicating the sort of approach the jury may properly adopt to the evidence when coming to their decision on the facts.' On appropriation in theft, see Lord Keith in *Gomez* [1992] 3 WLR 1067, 1080: 'The actual decision in *Morris* was correct, but it was erroneous, in addition to being unnecessary for the decision, to indicate that an act expressly or impliedly authorised by the owner could never amount to an appropriation.' On recklessness (or gross negligence), see Lord Mackay in *Adomako* [1994] 3 WLR 288, 297: 'Personally I would not wish to state the law more elaborately than I have done. In particular I think it is difficult to take expressions used in particular cases out of the context of the cases in which they were used and enunciate them as if applying generally.'

[12] For a general picture, see Neil Duxbury, *Jurists and Judges: An Essay on Influence* (Oxford, Hart Publishing, 2001) ch 5. Duxbury (at 104–05) sees Goff's Maccabaean Lecture as being a welcome break with the past, including the position of Megarry, but this is based mainly on the aspect of Goff's lecture which allows room for academic involvement, rather than the aspect which demarcates how far that involvement should go. Duxbury hints at grounds for scepticism on this (at 105) and indicates it may fall to the receptivity of the individual judge (at 105–06). More than this, it may depend on the receptivity of the individual judge to particular academic sources in a particular case. Contrast Goff's own responses in *Kleinwort Benson v Lincoln City Council* [1998] 4 All ER 513, 541–43 (which Duxbury cites) and in *Hunter v Canary Wharf* [1997] 2 WLR 684, 697 (which contrasts sharply with the response of Lord Cooke in the same case). Some indication of the continuing increase in judicial openness to academic sources is given in a Westlaw search of 2001–2 cases in UK-RPTS-ALL DataBase for 'academic writing' or 'academic literature'. This reveals 29 cases (discounting multiple citations and false positives where the sources are not providing academic views of the state of the relevant law), ranging across a wide variety of subject matter, where the academic sources are treated without denigration or qualification, often in the same breath as judicial sources. The significance of the total is enhanced by the fact that the search does not include references to individual academic authors. This possibly shows an improvement on the picture presented from 1999 materials by Michael Zander, 'What precedents and other source materials do the courts use?' (2000) 150 *New Law Journal* 1790, though without reaching the greater use of academic sources in America and Germany that Zander reports. For a wider survey, including discussion of the deterioration of judicial-academic relations in the United States, see William Twining, Ward Farnsworth, Stefan Vogenauer and Fernando Tesón, 'The Role of Academics in the Legal System' in Peter Cane and Mark Tushnet (eds), *The Oxford Handbook of Legal Studies* (Oxford, OUP, 2003).

[13] Goff, above n 7, at 170–71.

weaves around this crude distinction the development of legal principle. Both judge and academic may contribute to the development of principle, but do so in a manner reflecting their own preoccupations: the judge by reacting to fact-situations and then generalising from those reactions; the academic by ruminating on fundamental ideas so as to provide a coherent framework or philosophy into which the particular fact-situations can be fitted.[14] Although Goff sees the two roles as complementary, he stresses the dominance of the judicial role, so as to remain open to assessing unforeseen fact-situations unrestricted by theoretical preconceptions.[15]

There is a danger of this view of the judicial function degenerating into an apologetic for the judicial hunch. Indeed, Goff's application of his view of the judicial function to the problems of defining murder,[16] cited not only his Maccabaean Lecture but also his subsequent dictum epitomising the judicial function as 'an educated reflex to facts'.[17] It was this latter remark that fuelled Glanville William's response in suggesting that it would be necessary to separate those judges with correct hunches from those that suffered from 'defective hunching abilities'.[18] However, in the Maccabaean Lecture itself Lord Goff takes some pains to avoid the suggestion that he is licensing judicial discretion.

Goff's more careful argument turns on his view of principle. Legal principles are taken to avoid the rigidity of rules on the one side, and the dangers of untrammelled discretion on the other side.[19] In tackling the first evil, Goff identifies four pitfalls that may befall the exposition of legal

---

[14] *Ibid* at 184–87.

[15] *Ibid* at 186–87. For contrary arguments advancing the priority of the academic, see generally, RC van Caenegem, *Judges, Legislators and Professors: Chapters in European Legal History* (Cambridge, Cambridge University Press, 1987) 53–65, 96–101; and more particularly regarding the criminal law, Finbarr McAuley and J Paul McCutcheon, *Criminal Liability: A Grammar* (Dublin, Round Hall Sweet & Maxwell, 2000) xii. A somewhat softer approach to the judicial-academic relationship is apparent in a lecture given by Lord Goff three years after his Maccabaean Lecture, 'Judge, Jurist and Legislature' (1987) 2 *Denning Law Journal* 79, 92–94—in part due to the jurist being coopted on the side of the judge against the dangers of codification, and in part due to Goff taking a cooperative line on the uses of comparative law such as espoused by Markesinis, above n 9. A completely different insight on the contrast between academic and judicial approaches to the criminal law, respectively tending to adopt liberal or social values to the same fact situation, is offered by Andrew Ashworth, 'Interpreting Criminal Statutes: A Crisis of Legality?' (1991) 107 *Law Quarterly Review* 419, 447. Ashworth's recognition that 'values of both kinds do and should form part of criminal law doctrine' is made as a step to insisting that the judicial choices that will be required should be made in a transparent manner—a view endorsed by Lord Hutton in *B v DPP* [2000] 2 WLR 452, 473.

[16] Robert Goff, 'The Mental Element in the Crime of Murder' (1988) 104 *Law Quarterly Review* 30.

[17] *Ibid* at 30–31. The dictum is taken from *Smith v Littlewood's Organisation Ltd* [1987] AC 241, 280. Cp 'informed and educated judgment' in Goff, above n 7, at 183.

[18] Glanville Williams, 'The *Mens Rea* for Murder: Leave It Alone' (1989) 105 *Law Quarterly Review* 387, 391–92.

[19] Goff, above n 7, at 181.

principle: seeking elegance at the cost of recognising an untidy complexity of qualifications and exceptions; aiming for completeness at the cost of allowing for future developments; embracing universals at the cost of recognising the nuances of context; and (what may be regarded as the culmination of these errors) 'the dogmatic fallacy' in seeing law in terms of rules rather than principles.[20] In tackling the evil of untrammelled discretion, Goff invokes the qualities of 'clearly recognizable principles', of 'systematic legal principle'.[21] However, Goff's position between these two perils is made more complex, and less secure, due to the fact that within his Maccabaean Lecture he uses the word principle in four distinct ways.[22]

THE USES OF PRINCIPLE

(i) Principle as a Weak Formula of General but not Universal Application

It is this use which is employed by Goff, in the passages noted above, to distinguish the tentative scope of principle from the rigid application of rule. Principle here is taken to express an important consideration which, all other things being equal, will govern the outcome of the case. However, since all things are not always equal, it may be that the case in question will throw up a further consideration which will make the principle inapplicable. The same tentative connotation is found in the phrase, 'agreement in principle', and is exemplified in the abstract quality of human rights principles.[23]

---

[20] *Ibid* at 174–77.

[21] *Ibid* at 182, 184.

[22] The four uses of principle are not peculiar to Goff, as I hope the discussion that follows indicates. Each of them may be discerned, though not fully articulated, in Neil MacCormick's discussion of principles, *Legal Reasoning and Legal Theory* (rev edn, Oxford, Clarendon Press, 1994) ch VII. MacCormick focuses on use (ii) (eg, at 156–57), but not without being aware of the contestability of principles used in this way (eg, at xi).

[23] See Andrew Halpin, *Rights and Law – Analysis and Theory* (Oxford, Hart Publishing, 1997) 116–23, 159–74. There is not agreement within the literature on what is meant by principle, nor on how principle is to be distinguished from rule. Some variations are discussed in John Braithwaite, 'Rules and Principles: A Theory of Legal Certainty' (2002) 27 *Australian Journal of Legal Philosophy* 47, 50–52. Part of the problem may be the failure to recognise the different uses of principle, and the different combinations of those uses that may arise in practice, which I seek to discuss in the present chapter. Braithwaite (at 47 & 78 n104) clarifies his own characterisation of principles, as 'unspecific or vague prescriptions', to make the point that for him the key feature of principle is not found in a contrast between specific and general, but between specific and vague; ie, it is possible for general prescriptions to be either precise or vague. I make a similar point (*op cit*) in distinguishing abstract rights from both particular concrete rights *and* general concrete rights. However, in stressing the tentative feature of principle in use (i), and in taking the abstract quality of human rights principles as a paradigm, I hope to avoid the suggestion that the vagueness of principle is simply a matter of semantic vagueness (we may know what freedom of expression means in a particular case,

(ii) Principle as the Underlying Rationale for Requiring Particular Conduct

This use of principle produces a different contrast with rule in that the principle is now seen as the rationale for the rule, so that, as Goff indicates, we may 'seek behind the rule for the principle'.[24] Treating rules as the rougher practical formulations of principle provides an explanation for why the need to make an exception to a rule is sometimes overwhelming.[25] Sir James Fitzjames Stephen went so far as to suggest that the basic technique for reforming the criminal law was to identify places in the law where an existing rule failed to give effect to the underlying principle and then to change the rule to avoid the dislocation with principle.[26] Goff himself seems to be open to such an approach, in suggesting that 'the principle when identified can surely be formulated in such a mannner as to avoid the worst injustices flowing from the rule.'[27]

Although this use of principle may seem to account for particular instances of exceptions to rules, it cannot provide a comprehensive underpinning for the law, nor the basis for a programme of law reform, for a number of reasons. First, it is not always clear and uncontroversial just what principle a rule serves. The history of the law is peppered with instances of laws being enacted as a result of political compromise, expediency, and even inattentiveness; rather than through univocal assent to a single principle.[28]

Secondly, even where there is agreement on the underlying principle for a particular rule, effective law reform has often been achieved by blatantly ignoring that principle through the use of fiction,[29] or even boldly rejecting both rule and any underlying principle together.[30]

yet still decline to recognise the instantiation of the right there). I consider below how semantic vagueness may affect rules as much as principles. I hope also to avoid confusing the tentative feature of principle in use (i) with the potentially contestable nature of value in use (iii) or even of rationale in use (ii), although, as we shall see, in certain combinations of the use of principle there may be a connection between these phenomena.

[24] Goff, above n 7, at 177.
[25] For some classic examples, see Fernando Atria, *On Law and Legal Reasoning* (Oxford, Hart Publishing, 2001) 12–13.
[26] Sir James Fitzjames Stephen, *A History of the Criminal Law of England*, III (London, Macmillan & Co, 1883; reprinted New York, NY, Burt Franklin, 1973) 347–48.
[27] Goff, above n 7, at 177.
[28] A point discussed in Andrew Halpin, *Reasoning with Law* (Oxford, Hart Publishing, 2001) 68–70 and n 35, in relation to legislative intent, and more generally by NE Simmonds, 'Bluntness and Bricolage' in Hyman Gross and Ross Harrison (eds), *Jurisprudence: Cambridge Essays* (Oxford, Clarendon Press, 1992) 12–20.
[29] Sir Henry Maine, *Ancient Law* (10th edn with Introduction and Notes by Sir Frederick Pollock, London, John Murray, 1920) ch II; Lon Fuller, *Legal Fictions* (Stanford, CA, Stanford University Press, 1967).
[30] A possibility recognised by Goff, above n 7, at 177–78, though somewhat tempered by his describing the rejection of exisiting legal principle as a process of 'reformulation' or 'development' of principles by the judges. Excessive judicial reformulation of principle is strongly criticised by Hobhouse LJ in *Perret v Collins* [1998] 2 Lloyd's Rep 255, 258 (see further n 73 below).

Thirdly, again assuming general recognition of what the underlying principle might be, there still remain problems in relying on principle as rationale, as a basis for developing the law, due to the characteristic of principle as a weak general formula, noted in use (i) above. In particular, the relatively easy process of recognising the *absence of any rationale* for the application of a rule in a given case (there could be no reason for applying a rule designed to prevent violence accompanied by bloodshed to a barber who accidentally nicks his client's throat[31]), is not symmetrical to the difficulty in ascertaining whether the *presence of a rationale* should be determinative of a particular case. For example, the promotion of freedom of expression is a reason to allow publication of an article criticising a politician, but this still leaves open the issue of whether the damage to the politician's reputation is a strong countervailing reason to prohibit it. How do we decide on whether the existing fair comment rule of the law of defamation is too harsh or too lenient by reference to its underlying principle? The picture is complicated further when it is recognised that a single abstract principle, such as the principle of freedom of expression, is itself capable of being supported by a variety of potentially conflicting and contestable rationales.[32]

Fourthly, the indeterminate and contestable nature of principle just noted leads to the recognition of a distinct role for rules in the law, which is not exhausted by any link to an underlying principle. Although the precise nature and scope of legal rules may themselves be controversial matters, it is clear that the rigidity of legal rules is perceived as a virtue. Even if rules are formulated in a crude and overbroad manner, this may be just what is required in order to ensure clarity and efficacy in attaining some social objective, which would be diminished by a requirement to implement principle.[33] For example, a law prohibiting the possession of handguns by members of the public seeks to reduce the use of guns in

---

[31] Following Pufendorf, as cited by Atria, above n 25, *loc cit*. Pufendorf's hypothetical dealt with blood-letting for medical purposes, but was based on an original case involving shaving a judge. For the history, see Jim Evans, 'Questioning the Dogmas of Realism' [2001] *New Zealand Law Review* 145, 155.

[32] See Tom Campbell, 'Rationales for Freedom of Communication' in Tom Campbell and Wojciech Sadurski (eds), *Freedom of Communication* (Aldershot, Dartmouth, 1994), discussed in Halpin, above n 23, at 169. The recognition of multiple and potentially conflicting rationales for a principle undermines the primary role given to a monolithic principle in the work of Ronald Dworkin. See, eg, his 'In Praise of Theory' (1997) 29 *Arizona State Law Journal* 353, 356: 'one principle or another provides a better justification of some part of legal practice.'

[33] See, eg, Frederick Schauer, *Playing by the Rules: A Philosophical Examination of Rule-Based Decision Making in Law and in Life* (Oxford, Clarendon Press, 1991), and Larry Alexander and Emily Sherwin, *The Rule of Rules: Morality, Rules, and the Dilemmas of Law* (Durham, NC, Duke University Press, 2001). The 'semantic autonomy' of rules proposed by Frederick Schauer as a means of accounting for the way rules work has been criticised by Mark Tushnet, Review of Schauer's *Playing with the Rules* (1992) 90 *Michigan Law Review* 1560, and by Timothy Endicott, *Vagueness in Law* (Oxford, OUP, 2000) 18–19, for placing too heavy a reliance on the language used by rules divorced from the realities of the lives of rule users. Alexander and

committing crimes, not by relying on a principle requiring gun owners to behave responsibly in the use and storage of their weapons but by enacting a strict rule which prohibits any use of the guns by private individuals. In such circumstances the ideal practice of the law cannot be determined by reference to its underlying rationale.[34] The explicit purpose of the rule is to prevent all possession of handguns by members of the public. If this is achieved, it will encompass but exceed the rationale of reducing the use of guns in committing crimes. This quality of ruleness has to be recognised as governing the appropriate scope of a rule, alongside the rationale that might be identified as the reason for having the rule in the first place.[35]

(iii)   Principle as the Expression of Value Rather than Personal Preference

This use of principle carries connotations of objectivity and authority, as opposed to subjective inclination and self-interest. It is found in the phrases 'a man of principle', and 'a matter of principle'. It is this use that Goff draws on to argue against the view that judges are developing the law through personal whim or discretion. So Goff opposes 'clearly recognizable principles' to discretionary relief,[36] and 'systematic legal

Sherwin take a more modest view of what can be achieved by rules, but still emphasise their key characteristic of bluntness as a practical response to the imperfections of the human condition.

[34] See Firearms (Amendment) Act 1997, amending Firearms Act 1968, s 5. For another example, see the requirement that a contract for the sale of land has to be in writing under s 2 of the Law of Property (Miscellaneous Provisions) Act 1989. When the details of this provision came to be interpreted in *Commission for the New Towns v Cooper (GB) Ltd* [1995] Ch 259, the rule was interpreted as requiring 'a greater degree of formality' (per Stuart-Smith LJ at 287E), rather than by reference to the underlying rationale of preventing fraud or avoiding ambiguity (which in certain circumstances might be met *without* such a high degree of formality).
[35] The virtue of rigidity is not absolute. The quality of ruleness may be overdone, where it does not simply exceed the desired rationale but overrides other pertinent considerations. This was held to have occurred in s 41 of the Youth Justice and Criminal Evidence Act 1999, by the House of Lords in *R v A (No 2)* [2001] UKHL 25; [2002] 1 AC 45: the provision in s 41 amounted to a rule prohibiting reference to a complainant's sexual history in rape trials that failed to allow for the defendant's right to a fair trial protected by Article 6 of the European Convention on Human Rights. Empowered by the Human Rights Act 1988, s 3(1), the House of Lords read into s 41(3)(c) a discretion for the trial judge to permit evidence of previous sexual history where the fairness of the trial required it. The rigidity of s 41 has also been taken to have overridden relevant general principles of the law of evidence. For further discussion, see Di Birch, 'Rethinking Sexual History Evidence: Proposals for Fairer Trials' [2002] *Criminal Law Review* 531. For a contrary view, arguing that a rigid rule excluding sexual history evidence in most cases is required to avoid the use of unacceptable sexual stereotypes influencing the exercise of judicial discretion, see Jennifer Temkin, 'Sexual History Evidence—Beware the Backlash' [2003] *Criminal Law Review* 217. The debate is continued by Di Birch, 'Untangling Sexual History Evidence: A Rejoinder to Professor Temkin' [2003] *Criminal Law Review* 370.
[36] Goff, above n 7, at 182.

principle' to personal judgement.[37] Similar appeals to this use of principle have been made more recently by Sir John Laws,[38] among others.[39]

(iv)   Principle as a Broad Synthesising Conception

This use of principle serves to create an open category permitting a general issue (or a cluster of issues) to be raised across a wide variety of factual situations. The use of such broad synthesising conceptions may be regarded as a mark of progression to modern sophisticated legal systems, from the more concrete provisions of primitive law. They enable a vast array of complex factual situations to be governed by a single legal provision, and provide opportunity for the law to develop in ways not initially contemplated at the point the synthesising conception is introduced into the law.[40] Goff applies this use of principle to two major developments in English law, the recognition of general principles of negligence and unjust enrichment.[41] In relation to the second example, Goff demonstrates how this use of principle allows for the avoidance of technicalities associated with separate heads of recovery and opens up a 'cross-fertilization of ideas'.[42]

[37] *Ibid* at 183–84.

[38] In the Ganz Lecture in Public Law delivered at Southampton University in November 1997, 'The Limitations of Human Rights' (subsequently published in [1998] *Public Law* 254) Sir John Laws argued that judges may be trusted to interpret the rights of the ECHR, because in so doing they are only performing their traditional function of dealing with objective principles of law. In his 'Judicial Review and the Meaning of Law' in Christopher Forsyth (ed), *Judicial Review and the Constitution* (Oxford, Hart Publishing, 2000), delivered as a paper at a conference in May 1999 at the Cambridge Centre for Public Law, Laws develops a detailed view of legal principle which 'confines the judge's own views in a strict and objective context' (at 189). For comment on Laws' views, see Halpin, above n 28, at 58 nn76 & 79.

[39] For an example of this use of principle by an American judge to defend collegiate development of the law, see Harry Edwards, 'Collegiality and Decision Making on the D.C. Circuit' (1998) 84 *Virginia Law Review* 1335. A response to Edwards is made by Richard Revesz, 'Ideology, Collegiality, and the D.C. Circuit: A Reply to Chief Judge Harry T. Edwards' (1999) 85 *Virginia Law Review* 805. For historical precursors, see the discussion of the approach to principle taken by Sir Frederick Pollock, and the influence of Lord Mansfield, in ch 4 of Neil Duxbury, *Frederick Pollock and the English Juristic Tradition*, forthcoming (Oxford, OUP, 2005). A strong antidote to the reassuring blandishments of principle is provided by Stanley Fish, *The Trouble with Principle* (Cambridge, MA, Harvard University Press, 1999): 'the vocabulary of neutral principle can be used to disguise substance so that it appears to be the inevitable and nonengineered product of an impersonal logic' (at 4).

[40] See Peter Birks, 'The Early History of Iniuria' (1969) 37 *Tijdschrift voor Rechtsgeschiedenis* 163, 164–65, for discussion of the development of the Roman delict *iniuria* from a specific provision on assault to an 'abstract organising principle'. For further discussion of how such an abstract organising principle assists in the development of both the classical Roman law and modern common law, see his *Harassment and Hubris: The Right to an Equality of Respect*, the Second John Maurice Kelly Memorial Lecture (Dublin, Faculty of Law, University College Dublin, 1996).

[41] Goff, above n 7, at 179–80.

[42] *Ibid* at 180. For recent discussion of this use of the principle of unjust enrichment, see Kit Barker, 'Understanding the Unjust Enrichment Principle in Private Law: A Study of the

THE SEARCH FOR PRINCIPLE

I have taken the trouble to distinguish these four different uses of principle, and gone to some lengths to demonstrate that principle cannot be relied upon in the second use to produce an exhaustive framework for the law, in the belief that these matters have a wider significance than their relevance to the assessment of Goff's lecture. Multiple usage of the word principle, slippage between the different uses, and presumption as to the theoretical weight that principles can bear, are not confined to Goff's lecture, and are exploited in arenas beyond the law and legal theory. For example, the connotation of objective value in use (iii) is readily mixed with the practical characteristic of lacking universal application in use (i) by statesmen and politicians, who wish simultaneously to take upon themselves the credit, and to divest themselves of awkward burdens associated with embracing human rights principles. However, my detailed examination of these matters is primarily motivated by the view of their importance to illuminating the nature of legal materials.

Wherever principle is invoked, as an analytical construct or as a rhetorical device, it would be helpful to clarify precisely which use of principle is in play at any particular time. This could be achieved by insisting on the appropriate synonym being employed on each occasion. Although it is easy to slip, perhaps unconsciously, between the different uses of principle, it is more difficult to avoid confronting the differences that may emerge when switching the discussion from a weak formula, to an underlying rationale, or an objective value, or a broad synthesising conception, and so on.

This is not to say that a single principle cannot be found in more than one use. We may find, for example, that an objective value (iii) does provide the rationale (ii) for a particular law and that it has only been articulated at the level of a weak formula (i)—and hence all three of these uses inhere in our speaking of principle X. However, we cannot presume this to be the case whenever a principle is mentioned.

Moreover, even when each of these three uses applies in the case of principle X, there is still reason to discriminate between them. Otherwise the connotations of different uses may inappropriately merge with one another, and even conceal a connotation from a use that is present on the occasion in question. For example, we take the principle of freedom of expression as a case where each of the three uses just discussed applies. Then we take the objective connotation of use (iii) together with the role of rationale performed in use (ii), so as to reach the conclusion that the principle provides an exhaustive basis for the particular law under

Concept and its Reasons' in Jason Neyers, Mitchell McInnes and Stephen Pitel (eds), *Understanding Unjust Enrichment* (Oxford, Hart Publishing, 2004).

consideration. We are led to think that the connotation of objectivity leaves no room for subjective preference in determining the extent to which the law can be relied upon to put into effect its underlying rationale. In adopting this argument, we forget that we have also employed the principle in use (i) as a weak formula, which indicates that some further exercise of judgement* is required in order to determine whether the tentative (even presumptive) pull of the principle should be realised in a particular concrete case.

Arguably, just such a confusion of usage is relied upon to support the argument that the constitutional protection of freedom of expression does not leave open the possibility of prohibiting hate speech. At the heart of the argument is the concern that if hate speech is constitutionally unprotected, then this leaves open to those in authority the power to determine what is and what is not hate speech, and hence what speech is protected. In order to maintain the objective value of freedom of speech against incursions based on the subjective preferences (or convenience) of those in authority, it is therefore necessary to protect all speech without an exception for hate speech. Essentially the same argument resurfaces in the doctrine of viewpoint neutrality, once it is acknowledged that some sort of restraint on freedom of speech will be required in order to protect other legitimate interests. By requiring the restraint to be neutral among viewpoints, the semblance of the objective value of freedom of speech is maintained: no subjective discrimination against one form of speech is permitted; the restriction, since it applies equally to all forms of speech, is not regarded as a restriction on what kind of speech is acceptable.[43] In any event, clarifying the different uses of principle forces out into the open just what is at stake in such controversies. The First Amendment of the US Constitution states that 'Congress shall make no law … abridging the freedom of speech, or of the press'. It is one thing to say that this constitutional provision enshrines the principle of freedom of expression, but quite another to work out exactly what this entails.

The first point that needs to be clarified is whether we are taking the legal provision as amounting to a principle in use (i), a weak formula

---

* I adopt a convention of using the spelling of 'judgement' to indicate an exercise of general practical reason, reserving 'judgment' for a formal decision of a court.

[43] For general discussion in favour of the position against prohibiting hate speech, see Nadine Strossen, 'Liberty and Equality: Complementary, Not Competing, Constitutional Commitments' in Grant Huscroft and Paul Rishworth (eds), *Litigating Rights: Perspectives from Domestic and International Law* (Oxford, Hart Publishing, 2002). There was some movement from this position by the Supreme Court in the recent case of *Virginia v Black*, No 01-1107, 7 April 2003. The fineness of the argument on viewpoint neutrality is illustrated in the oral argument before the Supreme Court in that case (11 December 2002), where the respondents argued that a Virginia statute banning cross-burning 'with the intent to intimidate' violated the First Amendment, whilst conceding that a statute with a general prohibition on the use of words or symbols intended to intimidate would be valid (http://www.supremecourtus.

requiring further judgement to be exercised as to its precise scope, or, as a rigid rule requiring that no speech shall be curtailed on any occasion.[44] In either case, we may also be adopting the legal provision as a principle in use (iii), as enunciating an objective value, but we need to be clear which of the two possible combinations applies.

The combination of (iii) but not (i) provides us with a legal provision that amounts to a rigid rule upholding the value of freedom of speech. We shall consider an illustration of this shortly. By contrast, the First Amendment illustrates the combination of (iii) and (i), providing us with a legal provision in the form of a weak general formula upholding the value of freedom of speech. It should be stressed that the weakness of the First Amendment does not lie in its lacking the tenacity to protect freedom of speech in the face of strong opposing interests, but relates to the technical form in which it is expressed. As a weak formula rather than a rigid rule, it asserts the value of freedom of speech without providing a precise account of the occasions on which it will be appropriate to protect speech. The question then arises, as to how the principle is capable of still enshrining the value of freedom of speech when judgment may be made in a particular case that speech should be curtailed. The short answer to this is that the further judgement as to the scope of the principle must be undertaken in the light of respecting freedom of speech as a value, not simply as an inconvenience that can be discarded at whim. The need to judge between competing values, or principles in use (iii), will remain until such a time as it is possible to draw up precise rules indicating the exact scope of all such principles. Since this requirement has not been met in any historical or contemporary code or body of law, our practice of principle necessarily involves finding that one of a number of competing values does not hold on particular occasions. This does not thereby discredit as a value the value that the principle expresses. It merely underlines that our grasp

gov/oral_arguments/argument_transcripts/01-1107.pdf). The reality is that in both the cases of the Virginia statute specifically focusing on what the petitioner described as 'especially virulent intimidation', and of the hypothetical statute with a general provision against intimidatory expression, a further judgement has been made to determine that the principle of freedom of speech should not be realised in a number of particular cases.

For wider doubts about the neutrality of 'viewpoint neutrality', and also comment on how 'the chill factor' argument (which was also aired in *Virginia v Black*) confuses the nature of an abstract right (or principle), see Halpin, above n 23, at 159–65. And for judicial support for the need to chill speech in certain cases, see the recent Privy Council decision, *The Gleaner Company and Stokes v Abrahams* [2003] UKPC 55 at [72] *per* Lord Hoffmann.

[44] Atria, above n 25, at 98–99, makes the point that a legal norm may not bear on its face its identity as either a rule or a principle, and suggests that the distinction 'is not a classification of legal *norms*, but a typology of *legal reasoning*'. Certainly, in some cases it may be open to the court to decide whether to take the particular norm before it as a rule or principle, though in other cases it will be apparent from the context which of the two is appropriate. See further, n 103 below.

of values is not so finely grained as to carry with it a detailed understanding of every instantiation of every value.[45]

Further issues emerge to be clarified when we focus on use (ii). Perhaps the legal provision, combining uses (i) and (iii), expresses its own rationale and so also amounts to a principle in use (ii). At first glance, the First Amendment would appear to express the self-evident rationales of freedom of speech and freedom of the press, or by implication freedom of expression in general. However, as has been noted,[46] it is possible for the principle of freedom of expression itself to be based on a number of different rationales.

We can accommodate this observation in two ways. We could say that freedom of expression provides a general rationale for the legal provision, but that a number of particular rationales fit under this heading, and, moreover, that there exist tensions or even conflicts between these sub-rationales. The image here is of a general classification whose members compete amongst each other, like a criterion set for candidates for a prize. This imposes restrictions on who may enter (eg, authors who have published their first novel in the previous calendar year) but does not grant to each candidate the same measure of success. Only they are allowed to compete, but compete they must for a prize that only one will win. According to this view, freedom of expression as *a general rationale* opens up consideration of a number of *sub-rationales* which must satisfy the general criterion of providing a reason to make the protection of speech valuable. It does not, however, provide *the rationale* that will account for the existence of the legal provision, and enter into the process of judging whether a potential instantiation of that provision should be upheld. Obviously, which sub-rationale is selected will materially affect the discussion of when it is appropriate to uphold a particular instantiation of the principle of freedom of expression.

The alternative way of accommodating the phenomenon of further rationales is to deny that the apparent rationale, freedom of expression, is the true rationale. In other words, we treat this as a case of mistakenly taking principle in use (ii) when we only have a principle in use (i), whose true rationale is to be found elsewhere. This form of explanation may appeal to sceptics who regard the apparent rationale on the face of the principle to be a rhetorical ploy concealing a more sinister motive for having the principle recognised by the law. For example, it could be questioned whether the principle of freedom of contract (use (i)) truly serves a rationale of freedom of contract (use (ii)), rather than promoting the efficient exploitation of economic power. In order to meet such scepticism,

[45] See Halpin, above n 23, at 120–22.
[46] See n 32 above, and accompanying text.

it is necessary to distinguish uses of principle with the combination of
(i) but not (ii), from the combination of (i) and (ii).

However, where the legal provision is regarded as a principle in uses
(i), (ii) *and* (iii), the former way of looking at things seems more helpful.
For the recognition that the principle expresses a value, in use (iii), implies
that there is a rationale in some way connected to that value. To promote
something as a value is to provide a rationale for promoting it. Nevertheless, this switch in analysis does not stifle the sceptical voice. As we
have seen, the principle operating as a general rationale leaves room for a
number of competing sub-rationales to direct the scope of the principle. It
is, accordingly, still possible for the principle to be invoked with a rhetorical impact on those who would subscribe to one sub-rationale, whilst
deviously being employed in the service of a competing sub-rationale. So,
for example, we could regard the principle of freedom of contract as
expressing a value, and providing a rationale (uses (i), (ii) and (iii)), yet
recognise the value as sufficiently open as to be linked to a general
rationale, which can exploit support for the principle from those who
wish to promote the autonomy of contracting parties as the sub-rationale,
whilst implementing the principle so as to promote economic efficiency
as a conflicting sub-rationale.[47]

The connections between these three different uses of principle, and
the relationship between rules and principles, can be explored further by
returning to an earlier point in the discussion. We noted the importance
of distinguishing whether we have a principle in use (i), or a rigid rule, in
the context of upholding the value of freedom of speech. In the case where
we do not have a principle in use (i) but instead a rigid rule, we may still
have that rule expressing a principle in use (iii), and also have the principle
in use (ii) as its rationale. Where we have this combination of (ii) and (iii)
but not (i), the importance of considering whether the principle acts as a
general rationale, and, if so, what the competing sub-rationales might be,
becomes less significant. Since the legal provision has been accepted as a
rigid rule, it may be implemented as such without concern as to its precise
underlying rationale. For example, the rule upholding the principle (use
(iii)) of freedom of speech by Members of Parliament by granting them
an absolute immunity from liability for defamation for statements made
during parliamentary debates, may be considered to have as a general
rationale the principle of freedom of speech (use (ii)), but it will not be

---

[47] Roger Brownsword, *Contract Law: Themes for the Twenty-First Century* (London,
Butterworths, 2000) 52–53, discusses the contested nature of freedom of contract, 'the inter-
pretation of which turns on the particular ethical base from which the interpreter begins.'
The contestability extends to competing views of what is required by autonomy, or economic
efficiency, as much as being between these two as alternatives. See further, Hugh Collins,
The Law of Contract (4th edn, London, Butterworths, 2003) 20–35, 282–83.

necessary to enquire further as to which particular sub-rationale may be operating. To the extent that it has been accepted that the provision applies as a rigid rule, debate as to its scope is redundant and hence enquiry into its particular sub-rationale unnecessary.

This might suggest a crisp distinction between rules and principles, and the way they operate, but this would be erroneous. The distinction between the protection of freedom of speech under the rigid rule of parliamentary privilege and the weak general formula of the First Amendment does not furnish a standard test for the operation of rules and principles. We have already seen from our exploration of the different uses of principle that there is not a single model for principle. We should also be reluctant to accept a uniform model for rules. There are, in particular, three features of the way rules operate in the law that militate against a simplistic model for rules: semantic imprecision, structural positioning, and allowance for exceptions.[48]

The simplistic model of a rule, which arises in the example of protecting freedom of speech that we have just considered, depends on there being a fairly straightforward way of identifying factually the instantiations of the rule. In the case of statements made during debates in Parliament, this is a relatively easy task since the potential reference points for this phrase are extremely limited, though what is covered at the margins of parliamentary privilege by 'proceedings in Parliament' is not so clear.[49] The model assumes we can assemble a general class of instances covered by the rule, and takes the rule to operate by providing immunity to any statement that falls within that class. The model accordingly works to the extent that the content of the rule possesses semantic precision. It will break down when we find rules within the law that lack semantic precision. Although what amounts to semantic imprecision opens up another area of heated controversy, it is undeniable that some legal rules lack semantic precision for a number of reasons. Their content may be particularly complex, or vaguely understated, or require the application of contestable standards.[50]

---

[48] For far more detailed discussion of the factors which cause departures from the simplistic model, see the helpful treatment of 'problematic readings' of rules in ch 6 of William Twining and David Miers, *How To Do Things With Rules* (4th edn, London, Butterworths, 1999). The scope of the discussion by Twining and Miers extends to matters dealt with towards the end of the present chapter, in considering how legal materials are used in deciding a particular case.

[49] See Colin Munro, *Studies in Constitutional Law* (2nd edn, London, Butterworths, 1999) 219–23; Ian Loveland, *Constitutional Law, Administrative Law and Human Rights: A Critical Introduction* (3rd edn, London, Butterworths, 2003) 243–46.

[50] It is not necessary for present purposes to work out a particular view of what causes semantic imprecision in the law (for some efforts to do so, see Halpin, above n 28), merely to recognise its existence. Flesh can be put on the loosely collected causes of semantic imprecision provided here, by considering a single example. The definition of theft in ss 1–6 of the Theft Act 1968 includes within its terms illustrations of the particularly

In such a case, the simplistic model with its two straightforward steps, identifying instances of the general class covered by the rule and then dealing with each instance in accordance with the outcome provided by the rule, has to be interrupted by a preliminary enquiry as to what falls within the general class. At this point, the operation of the rule seems particularly close to the operation of principle, for the preliminary enquiry sorts out what the rule applies to in a manner that appears not dissimilar to the further judgement required to sort out where the principle applies. Moreover, both processes may explicitly invoke the rationale of the rule/principle, and, if necessary, provide argument as to what the rationale is as well as how it governs the particular case. It may appear then that the difference between a principle, and a rule lacking semantic precision, is a difference of form rather than a difference of substance.

To test this hypothesis, let us consider more closely the operation of the principle of freedom of expression as contrasted with the operation of the rule prohibiting theft, which, under English law, exhibits a variety of types of semantic imprecision.[51] We have already considered how recognition of the principle of freedom of expression as possessing a general rationale in use (ii) may open up discussion as to which particular sub-rationale should be influencing the further judgement in use (i) needed to determine whether a particular instantiation of freedom of expression should hold. How does this process differ from the process involving discussion of the purpose or rationale behind the legal rule providing a definition of theft, in order to settle the semantic imprecision of a term in that definition, and by so doing determine whether a particular instance should be held to be a case of theft?

Discussion of the rationale for a rule, and how it might affect our understanding of the words constituting the rule, are commonplace practices. Where the rule is in statutory form, as it is in the English definition of theft, seeking the rationale for the rule is nothing more than a conventional exercise in statutory interpretation, adopting the purposive approach to provide an understanding of the statutory text. Even with a common law definition, the exercise of seeking the rationale for the rule within the discussion of earlier cases is a normal step towards resolving what the rule means. The process is illustrated in a House of Lords case concerned with the meaning of 'appropriation' in the definition of theft.[52] Lord Steyn rejects a narrower definition of appropriation on the basis of his view of the rationale for the rule prohibiting theft: because this would

---

complex ('appropriation'), the vaguely understated ('intention to permanently deprive'), and a contestable standard ('dishonestly').

[51] See previous note.
[52] *Hinks* [2000] 3 WLR 1590.

'place beyond the reach of the criminal law dishonest persons who should be found guilty of theft.'[53] Steyn presumes a rationale for the rule that is capable of dealing with the defendant's 'dishonest and repellent conduct' in the case before him, in taking the victim 'for as much as she could get'.[54]

The operation of both rules and principles seems to permit reflection on the rationale for a legal provision in order to determine whether it applies in a particular case. There is, however, a difference on the surface of these two processes. In the case of a rule suffering from semantic imprecision, we reflect on the rationale for the rule in order to resolve the meaning of its terms, but once having done that the simplistic model for the operation of a rule kicks in. Having identified this as an appropriation (of another's property dishonestly made with the intention of permanently depriving the other of it), the outcome provided by the rule necessarily follows. We have a case of theft. There is no room for further judgement in relation to all the circumstances of the case as to whether we should still hold this to be a case of theft, as is open to us in the process of applying a principle in use (i). We might, for example, reflect on the rationale for the principle of freedom of expression and take it to be the promotion of open political debate, but from this it does not necessarily follow that we have legal protection of freedom of speech in the case before us. We are still required to exercise judgement as to whether what amounts to freedom of speech in this case is to receive legal protection, in the face of countervailing interests to reputation, national security, etc.

Differences in the surface contours of these processes may be summarised as follows. In the case of a legal provision amounting to a rule, the application of the rule is a matter of fixing the content of the rule's subject matter, and then applying the legal outcome provided by the rule to anything that falls within that subject matter. In the case of a legal provision amounting to a principle, the application of the principle is a matter of fixing the content of the principle's subject matter, and then considering whether the law should apply the outcome provided by the principle to anything that falls within that subject matter, in the light of other factors.

Whether these really amount to differences in substance depends on whether the sort of judgement involved in classifying something as a member of the rule's subject matter is different to the sort of judgement made in considering whether what falls under a principle's subject matter should be treated in accordance with the principle in the light of other

---

[53] *Ibid* at 1600.
[54] *Ibid* at 1599, 1593. The defendant was the primary carer of a person with limited intelligence, whom she persuaded to lavish upon her a number of gifts amounting to a value of around £60,000.

factors. It is not necessarily the case that there will always be the same answer to this question. Obviously, it is possible in dealing with the question whether something bears a meaning required to classify it under a rule, to be conscious of and affected by the consequence of so classifying it. It is not difficult to find examples of this happening in the case law. A striking example is provided by the Court of Appeal's decision that the conduct of a farmer in using fields for farming over a period of years did not amount to adverse possession, conscious that the consequence of finding it to be so would operate the rule under the Limitation Act 1980, s 15(1), granting him title to development land worth several million pounds.[55]

Since the outcome determined by the rule reflects what the law has judged to be the appropriate result of such an event in all the circumstances, the decision to place something under a rule effectively amounts to buying into that judgement, and the decision not to do so equally amounts to opting out of it. In either case, determining what falls under the rule amounts to making the judgement indirectly, by retroactive proxy, which still remains to be made directly in the case of deciding whether a particular instantiation of a principle should be upheld in all the circumstances, or not.

The second feature of rules which cannot be accommodated within the simplistic model of their operation is the way that the structural positioning of a rule within a system of rules, which provides the wider environment in which that rule operates, may affect what the rule can achieve. The outcome of following one rule can be completely altered by subsequently taking into account the operation of another rule within the same system of rules. So, for example, the rule requiring a contract for the sale of land to be in writing in order to be valid, appears to provide an outcome of making it impossible to acquire an interest in land by an agreement that does not comply with this formality. However, if we also take note of the rules permitting an interest in land to be acquired by part-performance of an agreement, or through proprietary estoppel, or under a constructive trust, then the outcome may be changed completely. Which rule governs the outcome will depend on the relative structural position it holds within the system of rules. In the example considered, it will depend on at least one of the rules of part-performance, proprietary estoppel, or constructive trust, retaining priority over the rule of contractual formalities,[56] rather than the other way round.

---

[55] The Court of Appeal's interpretation of 'possession' was held to be too strained by the House of Lords, who decided, despite the outcome, that the rule should properly be applied in this case. See *Pye (JA)(Oxford) Ltd v Graham* [2001] EWCA Civ 117; [2001] 2 WLR 1293; [2002] UKHL 30; [2002] 3 WLR 221. Lord Steyn's reasoning in *Hinks* (text at nn 52–54 above) also seems to follow this pattern.

[56] The issue was so decided by the Court of Appeal in *Yaxley v Gotts* [1999] 3 WLR 1217. This case nicely illustrates the difference between the second and third of the three features

In fixing the relative priorities of different rules within the system, there is again the opportunity for the sort of judgement to be made which resembles the further judgement required to determine whether a particular instantiation of a principle holds in all the circumstances. And here too, there is the possibility for that judgement to be made on the basis of what rationale is taken to underlie the rule whose relative priority is in question.[57]

The similarity in the processes of reasoning becomes even more marked if we expand the environment from a system of rules to a system of rules and principles, and consider the need to resolve the priority in a case of a rule conflicting with a principle. The most celebrated example of this is the American case of *Riggs v Palmer*,[58] which had to decide whether a rule of succession or the principle that no man should profit from his own wrong should take priority in determining whether a grandson could inherit from the grandfather he had murdered. Looked at from the side of the competing principle, it is a matter of deciding whether the principle in use (i) should be instantiated in this case, with the possibility of also delving into the principle as rationale in use (ii). Looked at from the side of the competing rule, it is a matter of deciding the structural positioning of the rule within the system of legal norms, as either dominant over or subordinated to the principle being considered. Yet these are two sides of the same argument, and cannot, therefore, sensibly be regarded as involving totally different reasoning processes.[59]

The third feature of rules which takes them outside the simplistic model is one that we have already commented on in passing. This is the

---

I am discussing. Although it may be common to refer loosely to the impact of one rule taking priority over another as creating an exception to the subordinated rule, the recognition of the dominant rule in such a case does not deny the integrity of the subordinate rule. A valid contract for the sale of land must still be in writing, the priority given to proprietary estoppel or constructive trust simply means that a valid contract is not required in order to transfer ownership in the land. By contrast, a pure exception, such as was being considered in *Buckoke v GLC* (n 62 below), threatens the integrity of the rule: the rule requiring vehicles to stop at a red light does not apply to a fire engine answering an emergency call. There is also what may be described as a hybrid case, where instead of having a single rule and then rejecting it in the exceptional case, we are presented with a rule and another norm whose contents do not merely require prioritising but conflict in such a way that to prioritise the other norm over the rule defeats the integrity of the rule. An example is provided in n 103 below.

[57] [1999] 3 WLR 1217, 1243, per Beldam LJ: 'I do not think it inherent in a social policy of simplifying conveyancing by requiring the certainty of a written document that unconscionable conduct or equitable fraud should be allowed to prevail.'

[58] 115 NY 506, 22 NE 188 (1889). The case gained prominence through being used by Ronald Dworkin, *Taking Rights Seriously* (London, Duckworth, 1977) 23, to illustrate his distinction between rule and principle.

[59] The argument was decided in *Riggs v Palmer* by a majority judgment in favour of the principle, the dissenting judgment of Gray J giving priority to the rule. The fact that assessing the structural positioning of a rule involves the same sort of argument as determining the weight of a principle does much to devalue Ronald Dworkin's 'logical distinction' between

exception illustrated by Pufendorf's barber, discussed in an earlier section, where the exception to the rule is so outrageous as to defeat any plausible rationale that could be imagined for the rule. In fact, for a completely uncontestable exception of this kind, the requirement is stricter. Bearing in mind the quality of ruleness that, as we have noted, cannot be reduced to the rationale of the rule,[60] for an incontrovertible exception of this kind to be accepted it must be the case that there is no conceivable rationale for having the case follow the rule *and* no conceivable advantage in nevertheless sticking to the rule in this case so as to avoid problems in dealing with other cases. Even if there is general agreement on the first point, there may be room for disagreement on the second.[61] In popular discourse such disagreement is displayed in an accusation of legalism by one party against another, and an accusation of irresponsible behaviour as a retort by the other. In more formal legal argument there may still be disagreement over this point.[62]

In the light of this more extensive discussion of rules and principles, it becomes impossible to draw a strict distinction between them, such as might be suggested by taking principle in use (i) and contrasting it with the simplistic model of a rule. The fuller discussion of uses (i)–(iii) of principle, and of the three features of rules which challenge the adequacy of the simplistic model, allow us to locate rules and principles in a broader picture of the process of moving from the looser identification of values or important considerations towards the determination of specific disputes. This process has a core element of making a judgement as to the appropriate way to handle points of conflict, but that judgement may need to be exercised at further stages along the process, where the points of conflict

---

rule and principle (above n 58, at 24). For further discussion, see Raimo Siltala, *A Theory of Precedent: From Analytical Positivism to a Post-Analytical Philosophy of Law* (Oxford, Hart Publishing, 2000) 52.

[60] Text accompanying n 35 above.
[61] Atria, above n 25, at 47, appears to neglect the second factor (the quality of ruleness). In discussing an example from Fuller, he treats the rule merely as 'the universalisation of substantive reasons' and takes the glaring exception to be evident to all on the grounds that 'no substantive reason is served by fining the first man'. Fuller's example of the rule making it an offence 'to sleep in any railway station' (first discussed by Atria at 13) can be regarded for the sake of argument as possessing a rationale, or rationales, which would require the offence to cover tramps seeking a night's kip in the station waiting room; and, that no conceivable rationale would require the offence to cover a respectable, weary traveller who dozes off while waiting for a delayed train. Nevertheless, the quality of ruleness may require us to find an offence committed in that case, just so as to avoid the rule being unable to regulate other troublesome cases, such as the impoverished student who deliberately breaks his journey at a station with a warm and comfortable waiting room late at night, and waits there for the morning train to avoid the cost of a room for the night.
[62] A notable example is the difficulty Lord Denning had in deciding whether a fire engine could be treated as an exceptional case in breaching the requirement to stop at a red traffic light when answering an emergency call—*Buckoke v GLC* [1971] Ch 655, 668.

become more refined.[63] Moreover, this core element of judgement may be required to fix the extent of rules as well as the scope of principle.

We may take as a standard illustration of this process the movement: from (1) principle, as the judgement that a particular value should be respected; to (2) the judgement that that value should be upheld in a particular class of case, and hence the generation of a general rule governing that class of case; to (3) the judgement that the rule should be interpreted to cover a specific case within its class. However, at each stage of judgement it is possible for the underlying value or other rationale to be contentious, for the principle, rule, or even the determination of a specific case. Hence the standard illustration just given cannot be relied upon as an exhaustive model for the working of rules and principles. In particular, it may happen that the application of a principle in a particular case, where there is a strong consensus as to how the value it expresses should prevail in the circumstances, is more determinate than the application of a rule suffering from severe semantic imprecision. Indeed, in complex situations John Braithwaite has convincingly argued that binding principles taking priority over non-binding rules may be the best way of achieving a consistent approach, *provided that those operating the principles participate in 'shared sensibilities'*.[64]

So far within this section I have avoided discussing use (iv) of principle, principle as a broad synthesising conception. One reason for the delay is that this use does not fit so tidily with the combinations of uses (i)–(iii) and the associated discussion of rules and principles, but another reason is that this use of principle can be viewed with greater clarity once the varied usage of both rules and principles has already been appreciated. From this we can make a general observation that the function of legal materials is to raise questions as well as to provide answers. For the varied usage of rules and principles has led us to a broader picture, of the process of moving from the looser identification of values or important considerations towards the determination of specific disputes. This process relies not simply on answering questions but also on posing the questions that need to be answered. Furthermore, we have seen that the core element of judgement required by this process may have to be

---

[63] By speaking of conflict here I do not mean to suggest that the role of the law is always to resolve conflict, and to ignore the part it plays in coordinating harmonious arrangements. However, even in performing the latter role, the law deals with potential points of conflict: this is the legal manner to arrange the sale of your house, to avoid any dispute if the purchaser should change his mind, or to avoid any problems for the purchaser if his ownership is disputed by a third party.

[64] Braithwaite, above n 23. The possibility of sensibilities not being shared requires a more complex analysis, such as I attempt for rights in chs V & VI of Halpin, above n 23. The recognition that sensibilities are not always shared leads to the conclusion that law suffers from an inherent incoherence, as reached in Halpin, above n 28.

undertaken by reflecting on what is the issue to be addressed, since in both rules and principles the underlying value or other rationale may be contentious.

The clearest location of this phenomenon discussed so far is in the recognition of a general rationale, which opens up the *question* of which sub-rationale should be selected to provide the reason for recognising something as valuable, and, in turn, can be used in the process of determining where exactly the thing valued should be given protection. The broad synthesising conception in use (iv) of principle replicates the work of a general rationale on a wider scale. Whereas the general rationale may invite consideration of how a particular legal provision, such as the protection of freedom of speech in the First Amendment, should be evaluated and enforced, a broad synthesising conception permits the law to raise questions about the value and potential enforcement of interests across a wide area of conduct.

This can be seen in the two examples provided by Goff. The principle of negligence, once recognised as a broad synthesising conception by the law, permits the law to raise the questions whether one person has failed to take sufficient care in his conduct, and whether a person whose interests have been harmed by that lack of care should be given a legal remedy, across an almost unlimited range of human conduct. In this respect, the most important part of Lord Atkin's speech in *Donoghue v Stevenson* is not the neighbour test,[65] but the neighbour question: 'Who then, in law, is my neighbour?'[66] The answers provided by the law to the question assist in developing the doctrine of the tort of negligence. However that doctrine develops, it does so not by exposition of a core idea of negligence hidden in the depths of legal understanding, but by providing answers to a central question posed in legal materials. Moreover, the answers may vary considerably as the question is raised in relation to different types of conduct, or within different sets of circumstances, such as is seen, for example, in the treatment of negligent misstatements, or the occurrence of economic harm, or nervous shock. The coherence of legal doctrine within the tort of negligence cannot, accordingly, be achieved by reflection on a core idea but by systematically raising the central question over a variety of situations, and then producing answers and sorting the answers obtained, in a consistent manner.[67]

---

[65] [1932] AC 562, 580: 'You must take reasonable care to avoid acts or omissions which you can reasonably foresee would be likely to injure your neighbour.'
[66] *Ibid*. The neighbour 'test' in fact contains the latent question as to what amounts to reasonable care, as does Atkin's tentative answer to the neighbour question, in terms of persons who ought reasonably to be in contemplation. The difficulties faced by the courts in finding an adequate formulation for this test, and the contradictory attempts made over the years to do so, provide further evidence to support the contention that the courts are mistakenly seeking to formulate a test when they are actually framing a question.
[67] For further discussion, see Halpin, above n 23, at 138–59.

Similarly with unjust enrichment, there is not a core idea which is uniformly applied in all situations.[68] Acknowledging the principle of unjust enrichment as a broad synthesising conception permits the law to ask whether one person has been unjustly enriched at the expense of another, and whether the other should receive some sort of remedy, across a variety of situations where the law would otherwise be silent in its response.[69] Again, although the answers may vary in different situations, treating the principle of unjust enrichment as a central question raised across those different situations opens the law up to development in a far more flexible manner than the attempt to fit each situation under an appropriate established rule.[70] On the other hand, this very flexibility may promote uncertainty and controversy in the law, particularly where there is disagreement as to what stage the law has reached in the process of movement from the loose identification of values or other important considerations to the determination of specific disputes.

This problem is exacerbated when the recognition of principle in use (iv) has been historically preceded by the law only permitting recovery under a restricted number of heads of liability, as is the case with both negligence and unjust enrichment. It may then be unclear whether the status of a general rule within a body of legal doctrine relates to the later period of the law where the synthesising conception has been recognised, or to the earlier more restrictive period.[71] If formed in the later period, the rule amounts to a refined expression of the law that governs a class of situations, which has emerged by collating the answers produced in response to the central question posed by the principle in use (iv). If derived from the earlier period, it amounts to the law's response to a class of situations constituted by an obsolete category created by the old head of liability, which obstructs the free response that might otherwise be made to the central question.[72]

---

[68] Barker, above n 42, text following n 60: 'the various rules which the principle mediates all address the same *question* about the actionability of gains in private law' (emphasis added).
[69] The unjust enrichment question was raised, and answered affirmatively by Lord Goff in the House of Lords, in *Kleinwort Benson v Lincoln City Council* [1998] 3 WLR 1095, 1113–14, to overcome the law's previous unresponsiveness to mistakes of law.
[70] Goff, as quoted at n 42 above; Barker, above n 42.
[71] The importance of this point is recognised for both negligence and unjust enrichment by George Klippert, 'The Juridical Nature of Unjust Enrichment' (1980) 30 *University of Toronto Law Journal* 356. Klippert speaks of a move from a mere unifying principle to a principle as a basis of liability. His 'unifying principle' represents a common underlying rationale for the discrete heads of liability; ie, a principle in use (ii) serving as the rationale for a number of separate legal rules. His depiction of a principle in use (iv) as a principle providing 'a basis for liability' is perhaps less helpful nomenclature than 'broad synthesising conception', for it suggests that the principle operates as a basis of liability in a similar way to a rule. It fails to capture the central question posed by a principle in use (iv), and the distinctive process of responding to that question and then enunciating rules from the responses given.
[72] *Ibid* at 372, 374–76.

Even where it is clear that the general rule has been recognised subsequently to the acknowledgment of the principle in use (iv), and amounts to an expression of the law's considered response to the question it poses, the temptation may be overwhelming to revert back to the principle. This permits the central question to be addressed afresh as a means of overstepping an unwelcome rule, but brings with it inconsistency in the development of legal doctrine.[73]

Given the enormously varied and complex usage of principle that we have documented, and the opportunity for creative participation in the process of resolving how principles are to apply, it may seem that the search for principle is more like a game of hide and seek, where those doing the searching are permitted to change the location of the prize. The question posed at the beginning of our investigation of principle remains to be answered. How does this affect the possibility of a specialist judicial function?

JUDICIAL AND OTHER FUNCTIONS

It will be recalled that prior to commencing the investigation of principle, an apparently simple distinction had been noted as the basis for asserting a distinctive role for the judiciary. Judges, it was suggested, have the capacity for dealing with particular fact-situations, whereas academics deal with ideas. Moreover, the propensity of academics to ruminate on and cherish ideas, it was thought, might create preconceptions which would act as obstacles to reaching the appropriate judgment in specific cases.[74] When it comes to a discussion of principle, the complementary roles for judge and academic allowed by Goff seem to follow this simple distinction. Academics sit in their armchairs musing on interesting ideas. Judges sit in court and select any of these ideas that might actually be useful in propounding a principle to decide the case before them.[75]

One aspect of the broader picture of legal materials that has emerged from the discussion of rules and principles above, is that there is not a clear division of labour between the refinement of general ideas and the determination of particular fact-situations. It should by now be apparent

---

[73] For further discussion, see Halpin, above n 23, at 149–56, and, above n 28, at 160. Clear judicial warning against this phenomenon is provided by Hobhouse LJ in *Perret v Collins* [1998] 2 Lloyd's Rep 255, 258. Although in seeking to protect established 'clear criteria' from 'subjective assessments ... uncertainty and anomaly', Hobhouse speaks of preserving the 'fundamental principles of the law of negligence', it is clear that these 'principles' amount to what I have referred to here as general rules formed from the law's response to the principle of negligence in use (iv).

[74] See n 8 above (Megarry), and text at nn 13–15 above (Goff).

[75] See n 15 above, and text accompanying.

that the general ideas of the law, whether expressed in rules or principles, may sometimes pose questions rather than provide answers. It should also be clear that the scope of these ideas, again whether expressed in rules or principles, may sometimes be tentative. It follows that the determination of fact-situations will sometimes be needed in order to refine general ideas adopted by the law, or to clarify the scope of these ideas. A process also flows in the opposite direction, whereby fact-situations are determined in accordance with the ideas adopted into the law. Sometimes this may amount to a formal process of deduction, where the ideas are sufficiently refined and their scope sufficiently fixed in order to clearly dispose of the fact-situation in question. Sometimes this may amount to a weaker influence, where the adoption of the idea in the law serves to raise an issue that would otherwise have been off the agenda, and the response to that issue in determining the fact-situation is what disposes of the case. Recognition of this dynamic interplay between the development of ideas and the determination of particular fact-situations makes it difficult to accept the simple distinction put forward as the basis for a distinctive role for the judiciary, and brings into question the peculiar capacity for dealing with fact-situations attributed to judges.

The simple distinction seems to place the thinking of academics at a level at least once removed from the determination of practical issues in the court. Hence there is perceived to be a danger in approaching fact-situations with academic ideas ('preconceptions') that are not sensitive to the particular facts of a case. The licence academics sometimes allow themselves in developing ideas about a subject without concerning themselves with the details of its practice, may be a legitimate cause for concern. Fernando Atria has recently remarked on the oddity that Neil MacCormick appears to have provided 'the only one, self-avowedly positivist work in which the discussion of decisions given in *actual* cases plays a crucial methodological role'.[76] More caustically, Ronald Dworkin has accused contemporary positivists of engaging in theoretical work so totally removed from the realities of practice that it is comparable to scholastic theology.[77] Indeed, there may even be a kind of conceit in some academic circles which considers that the ability to reflect on the law at a level purified from the humdrum concerns of actual cases, implies a higher level of intellectual endeavour. Acknowledgment of this conceit may account for the need felt not to apologise in the preface of a theoretical work on the criminal law, for 'the substantial use of hypotheticals and, perhaps more than is usual in works of this kind, of material commonly found in criminal law textbooks.'[78]

[76] Atria, above n 25, at 184.
[77] Ronald Dworkin, 'Thirty Years On' (2002) 115 *Harvard Law Review* 1655, 1679.
[78] William Wilson, *Central Issues in Criminal Theory* (Oxford, Hart Publishing, 2002) vi.

However, the suggestion that all academic work is liable to the charge of operating without any concern for the details of practice is clearly absurd. Even if the charge can be made to stick for certain theoretical works, the simple distinction noted above requires it to apply to academic works of a totally different character. Notably, as voiced by Megarry, we would have to accept that his own work as an author propounds ideas which fail to concern themselves with the niceties of particular fact-situations.[79] It is difficult to categorise Megarry's writing on the law of real property as work indulging in theoretical excess, unconcerned with the details of practice.

A more plausible explanation for Megarry's desire to keep distinct his roles as author and judge is his reluctance in performing the latter role to be bound by his views previously published in the former role. This can be regarded as a matter of personal advantage, allowing the judge-author two bites at the cherry, or, more seriously, as a matter of constitutional propriety to indicate that when sitting as a judge he is open to argument rather than closed by his previously published views, so avoiding any accusation of judicial prejudice, or even preventing any legitimate expectation arising as to how he might dispose of the issue in a future judgment.[80] In either case, this only speaks of the revisability of published views. This in itself does not mark out a different function for the academic/author, but simply points to a difference in setting and outcome for the judicial role. The fact that a judge's view of the law as applied to a case before him brings about a binding judgment for the parties, does not mean that only judges think about the law at the level of determing particular fact-situations. Academic commentary is replete with discussion of actual and hypothetical fact-situations, and even those awaiting judgment; and on occasion judges will express themselves in agreement with a particular academic viewpoint in determining the outcome of a case.[81]

There remains one refuge for the simple distinction between academic and judicial roles. Even if it is conceded that there is a dynamic interplay

[79] See above n 8.
[80] These sorts of concerns seem to have been behind Lord Hoffmann's disclaimer, 'There is, however, no warranty that the author will adopt the same point of view in any other capacity', at the head of his 'The Influence of the European Principle of Proportionality upon UK Law' in Evelyn Ellis (ed), *The Principle of Proportionality in the Laws of Europe* (Oxford, Hart Publishing, 1999). A clear indication that the statements of judges-as-authors are not regarded as binding is provided by *R v Mental Health Review Tribunal* [2003] EWHC 193 (Admin); [2003] 2 All ER 209 at [20], [48] & [52], where the High Court quoted, considered, and ultimately departed from the published extra-judicial views of Lord Woolf CJ relating to the quantification of damages under the Human Rights Act 1998.
[81] For a recent example, see *The Starsin* [2003] UKHL 12 at [17], [46], where the House of Lords endorsed the criticism made by academics of the Court of Appeal's judgment in the same case, citing among others, Charles Debattista, 'Is the end in sight for chartering demise clauses?', *Lloyd's List*, 21 February 2001, 5.

between the formulation of general ideas and the determination of particular fact-situations; and that academics as well as judges are concerned with refining ideas to the point of offering solutions to the outcome of specific disputes; it might still be argued that what is distinctive about the judicial function is the exercise of choice between competing solutions to a specific dispute. Although both academics and judges can come up with their own views of how the law deals with a particular fact-situation, judges, it might be thought, somehow have a capacity, that academics lack, to choose between competing viewpoints, and thus to decide the law.

Something more than the authority to decide the law is at issue here. Judges clearly possess an authority that academics lack, but in suggesting that judges, as lawyers, are performing an entirely different function to academics, some attribute of judging needs to be identified that is absent in the labours of academics. Instead of providing a clear analysis of the judicial role as a specialist performance of the lawyer's art, it is easy to mystify the judicial function at this point and to resort to speaking of the authority of the judge in metaphorical terms. Although the inflated image of the judge as one polarity of a bi-polar sovereign, or the guardian of a higher-order law, has been punctured as 'extra-judicial romanticism',[82] there seems to be a vestige of the sacerdotal in images of the judicial character to account for that extra attribute which turns the act of judgment into a higher form of legal reasoning. The superstitious reverence for the judgments of the early Roman aristocratic priesthood was supposedly dispelled by a plebeian revolt and accession to the demand for a written law, but something approaching the superstitious, or unreflecting feudal deference, seems present in the assumption often made that judges perform a distinctive legal function.[83]

The precise *legal* functions performed in reaching a judgment on a particular fact-situation can be clarified with the assistance of the investigation of legal principles and rules undertaken above. Before drawing on

---

[82] Lord Irvine, the subsequent Lord Chancellor, took pains to counter claims being made by judges on how Parliament might be subject to judicial review, in parliamentary debate (see *Hansard* for 5 June 1996, 572 HL Deb, 5th ser, cols 1254–55) and in print, 'Judges and Decision-makers: The Theory and Practice of Wednesbury Review' [1996] *Public Law* 59 (the phrase quoted appears at 77). The romantics comprised Lord Woolf, 'Droit Public—English Style' [1995] *Public Law* 57, Sir John Laws, 'Law and Democracy' [1995] *Public Law* 72, and Sir Stephen Sedley, 'Human Rights: a Twenty-First Century Agenda' [1995] *Public Law* 386.
[83] Consider the deference shown by Basil Markesinis, above n 9, eg at 35–36, in characterising academics as performing a supporting role in packaging material for judges to use, or, at 49, in describing a three-sided partnership between academic, practitioner, and judge, in which 'the junior can help the middleman to convince the senior.' A contrasting form of the relationship between judge and academic is illustrated by van Caenegem, above n 15, at 64–65.

the broader picture of legal materials that has been painted, it is worth noting an elementary point, that the most basic legal skill required is familiarity with legal materials. In fact, the task of selecting the legal materials relevant to a particular fact-situation may impose a strenuous burden on the lawyer, for the ability to see the possible relevance of materials beyond the conventionally obvious ones is a mark of advanced legal aptitude.[84] In most situations the selection will be from material found within established legal sources, but on rare occasions even the most assiduous search of established sources may reveal a complete blank.[85] In this situation the lawyer will be called upon to propose a potential legal provision for the court to adopt, on the grounds that it would make for the better law than any alternative. Even here familiarity with existing legal materials may play a part in that one of the available methods of persuasion in getting the court to adopt the provision proposed, is to demonstrate its fit with existing legal materials.[86]

---

[84] The significance of this ability in the world of practice, in top City law firms or at the bar, has been impressed on me by anecdotal evidence supplied, respectively, by Richard Youard and Richard Southwell QC.

[85] Acknowledgment of this phenomenon is to be found in *Airedale NHS Trust v Bland* [1993] AC 789, 879–80 *per* Lord Browne-Wilkinson. Short of a complete blank, the search may still end with the need to join the dots in the material provided by the sources. Where drawing in the lines may be done in a number of ways, this amounts to a weaker form of the phenomenon but the process of selection still requires an element of positive proposal of suitable material.

[86] The weakest form of fit is a negative finding that the proposed provision is not incompatible with existing law. Slightly stronger would be a case of what might be regarded loosely as a process of reasoning by analogy from established materials, but only in the sense that the proposed provision shares a feature with an established norm recognised as effective elsewhere in the law. A firmer sense of analogy holds where it is used to suggest a link between a fact-situation covered by established law and the fact-situation in question, by arguing that the same legal norm applied in the first case should equally apply in the second. This may, in effect, amount to identifying the norm applied in the first case as a principle (in use$_1$, or use$_4$) whose scope should also cover the second case. (On this, see further MacCormick, above n 22, at 161: 'no clear line can be drawn between arguments from principle and from analogy.') Alternatively, it may amount to arguing that the semantic imprecision of a rule that has been established as applying in one case should be resolved in favour of also applying to the second. These firmer arguments by analogy accordingly take place within the two stages of the task identified below, in arguing about the form of *existing* legal materials and how the further issues relating to that form should be resolved. Even in its firmer forms, the force of analogical reasoning should not be overstated. After extensive discussion, Scott Brewer, 'Exemplary Reasoning: Semantics, Pragmatics, and the Rational Force of Legal Argument by Analogy' (1996) 109 *Harvard Law Review* 923, concludes that reasoning by analogy from legal materials is not itself determinative of the issue.

Although reasoning by analogy is widely accepted as prevalent within the practice of law, there is little consensus on its precise nature and much disagreement about its merits. For further discussion, see Cass Sunstein, 'On Analogical Reasoning' (1993) 106 *Harvard Law Review* 741, and in revised form as ch 3 of his *Legal Reasoning and Political Conflict* (New York, NY, OUP, 1996); Emily Sherwin, 'A Defense of Analogical Reasoning in Law' (1999) 66 *University of Chicago Law Review* 1179; Gerald Postema, 'Philosophy of the Common Law' in Jules Coleman and Scott Shapiro (eds), *The Oxford Handbook of Jurisprudence and Philosophy of Law* (Oxford, OUP, 2002) 603–09. One common theme among the disparate accounts of reasoning by analogy is that the process (however characterised) involves the opportunity of

Another exceptional variation on the straightforward selection of legal materials occurs where the courts have the power to depart from their own previous decisons.[87] This opens up a possibility of not merely selecting relevant legal materials but also rejecting legal materials that would be relevant but are considered inappropriate for one reason or another, and hence ultimately irrelevant. In this case too, the lawyer will be called upon to argue for a potential legal provision, on the grounds that it would make the better law. I will use the phrase 'selection of relevant legal materials' in a loose sense below to encompass both the straightforward case, and the two variants involving the proposal of material in the case where no existing relevant material is to be found, or in the case where the existing material is rejected.

Once the relevant legal materials have been collected, the next task is to assess their significance. This task may be divided analytically into two stages. Although in practice things may be done less tidily (and less comprehensively), this analytical division serves to show the range of issues that may arise in considering the significance of legal materials. At the first stage, there may be room for disagreement as to which of the diverse forms identified in the above study actually applies to a particular piece of legal material.[88] Does the material constitute a rule or a principle? If it is a principle, is it merely a principle in use (i) expressing tentative legal consequences for an established category of conduct, or perhaps, a principle in use (ii) providing a rationale for definite legal consequences for a category of conduct covered by a rule, or rather, does it constitute a broad synthesising conception in use (iv) raising the issue of legal consequences over an open category of conduct? The practitioner concerned to advance the cause of his client is likely to impose on the legal material a form that best advances his client's case. The academic with no client to satisfy[89] must still make a choice but may do so to indulge his or her own

responding to the issue of how to treat the case in question. A common controversy is how the process of reasoning by analogy relates to the application of legal rules or principles. In the light of the approach developed here, it might be suggested that it would be more illuminating to abandon the attempt to provide a uniform representation of reasoning by analogy, and instead to recognise it as a characteristic of legal reasoning that may arise in different ways in different places, once we recognise the full complexity of the state of legal materials and the different kinds of opportunities they present.

[87] See, as the standard example, the Practice Statement (Judicial Precedent) [1966] 1 WLR 1234, which permits the House of Lords to depart from their own previous decisions when they consider that 'it is right to do so'.
[88] A 'piece of legal material' is not necessarily constituted by a single provision of a statute or the ratio of a single case. It might be constituted by a body of case law, or a number of related statutory provisions which combine to express a particular legal norm. Where the sources are particularly dense it may be plausible to find support for conflicting norms within them. In such circumstances, the process of selection takes on an additional significance.
[89] The presence or absence of a client as the basis for the difference in approach of practitioner and academic, without dividing their common function of 'seeking the right solution

view of what would make the better law, indirectly promoting a view of what would amount to the better condition of society. We should not overlook the fact that disagreement as to the appropriate form of the material may continue into the delivery of judgment.[90]

Disagreement as to which of the diverse forms of legal material applies, where there genuinely is room for disagreement due to the incomplete state of the law, should be distinguished from a different type of disagreement. In this other case what is being argued is that the law has reached a sufficient stage of development to be able to show that the legal material has been recognised as possessing a particular form. It is important to note that the first type of argument is essentially an argument as to what the law should best be regarded as, according to criteria from outside the law, a view of society that best fits the client's interests or is considered appealing for some other reason.[91] By contrast, the second type of argument is fought by charges and counter-accusations of ignorance as to the state of the law. It is essentially a doctrinal argument from within the law. So, to argue that the principle of negligence in Scots or English law was a broad synthesising conception in use (iv), *before* the decision in *Donoghue v Stevenson* would be an argument of the first type, but to argue it *after* that decision would be an argument of the second type.[92]

The recognition of this fundamental distinction between arguing for a law and arguing about the law, between taking the role of partisan lobbyist or social critic on the one hand, and legal expositor on the other hand, is crucial to any attempt to obtain a clear understanding of legal materials. Even if it is suggested that the state of legal materials is such as to offer so much opportunity for engaging in the former role that the chance of making an effective argument purely as a legal expositor is extremely limited, we should be able to demonstrate this from an accurate grasp of legal materials, and a clear acknowledgment of their different uses. Even if it is suggested that it is desirable for legal materials to be in such a state as to provide more opportunity for the social critic than the legal expositor, we should be able to point out what kind of legal materials we need in order to bring this about. And even if it is suggested that there should be more opportunity for the social critic than the legal expositor whatever the state of legal materials, we should be able to honestly admit the extent to which we are prepared to discard established legal materials

---

to difficult legal problems', is suggested by Richard Southwell in correspondence with the author, quoted in Halpin, above n 28, at 22 n63.

[90] The identification of the principle of negligence as a broad synthesising conception in use (iv) was only accepted by three out of the five Law Lords in *Donoghue v Stevenson*.
[91] For discussion of Lord Atkin's view of 'the needs of civilised society', see Halpin, above n 23, at 141.
[92] For other illustrations, see Klippert, above n 71.

(and the view of society established with them) for the social vision that finds favour with the judge of the moment.

All of this is threatened by a wilful refusal to admit the possibility of undertaking clear doctrinal argument from within the law, irrespective of the evidence that exists for the distinction between the different uses of legal materials that I have set out above. The greatest notoriety attached to this refusal has been earned by members of the Critical Legal Studies Movement. Their disparagement of the overstated claims of formalism and objectivism on the law has extended to embrace a nihilistic scepticism[93] towards the possibility of deriving any clear guidelines from legal materials.[94]

Scepticism towards doctrine has also permeated the world of practice. In considering trends over the previous twenty years within judicial practice in New Zealand, Jim Evans analysed a sceptical attitude culminating in 'the growth of a certain disdain for traditional legal doctrine: the sentiment being that when it stands in the way of progress the judges should overturn it.'[95] A fellow New Zealand academic, Bruce Harris, has sought to provide support for the judicial overturning of doctrine by final courts of appeal.[96] The extent to which this is desirable is a vexed question,[97] but one of the arguments Harris provides relates directly to the present issue of whether room is left to recognise doctrine at all. Harris writes:[98]

> The fact that a subsequent appellate court has the potential to be of a different doctrinal disposition to that which decided the precedent implies that the legal issue in contention is capable of being approached from more than one doctrinal point of view.

The loose phrase, 'the legal issue in contention', is used to cover the issue on which the law is required to pass judgment, but the transferred epithet effectively suggests that because the *issue* can be described as legal then any response to it has a legal quality. This mild suggestion is reinforced

---

[93] Roberto Unger, 'The Critical Legal Studies Movement' (1983) 96 *Harvard Law Review* 561, republished as *The Critical Legal Studies Movement* (Cambridge, MA, Harvard University Press, 1986). A strong reaction against 'the embrace of nihilism and its lesson that who decides is everything' is to be found in Paul Carrington, 'Of Law and the River' (1984) 34 *Journal of Legal Education* 222, 227.

[94] The enthusiasm for uncertainty is illustrated by Mark Kelman's discussion of a paradigm clear rule, a rule setting a speed limit, in which he argues that the rule lacks clarity because it will not be universally enforced, in his *A Guide to Critical Legal Studies* (Cambridge, MA, Harvard University Press, 1987) 49–50.

[95] Evans, above n 31, at 147.

[96] BV Harris, 'Final Appellate Courts Overruling Their Own "Wrong" Precedents: The Ongoing Search for Principle' (2002) 118 *Law Quarterly Review* 408.

[97] See n 111 below.

[98] Harris, above n 96, at 418.

by an explicit assertion that any one of two conflicting approaches to the issue can be described as doctrinal, and reduces legal doctrine to the personal taste of the judge, exercising an individual 'doctrinal disposition'.[99] The demolition of legal doctrine is completed by carelessly switching the subject of legal doctrine from what has been established within the law to what might be established. If Harris were seriously set upon achieving this, then his chosen subject would be a redundant topic for discussion: there could be no principles of overruling where what had previously been established enjoyed no greater status than what was proposed in its place, and hence needed no overruling.

The second stage of the task of assessing the significance of the legal materials requires us to pay closer attention to the details of the different forms that have been identified at the first stage. For whichever form has been adopted there may be the opportunity for crafting further argument. It would be helpful to summarise the particular opportunities that may arise in relation to the varied and complex usage of rules and principles that we have identified. To take principles first, where we have a principle as a weak formula in use (i), it is necessary to give consideration to other factors in arguing whether a specific instantiation of that principle should be allowed. Where we have a principle as a general rationale in use (ii), it is necessary to select a sub-rationale that can be argued to be appropriate for the legal provision. Where we have a principle as a broad synthesising conception in use (iv), it is necessary to respond to the general question raised in arguing for the extension or limitation of legal liability. And in each of the above uses, we may also have a principle in use (iii) expressing a value whose contestability needs to be resolved in arguing for the acceptance of a value which promotes a particular form of life or view of society.

When it comes to rules, some of the issues related to the uses of principle may reappear. We noted three features of the way rules operate in the law which prevent us following a simplistic model for the application of rules: (1) semantic imprecision (where content is (a) particularly complex, (b) vaguely understated, or (c) requires application of contestable

[99] The phrase is openly lifted by Harris from the judgment of O'Connor, Kennedy and Souter JJ in the American case of *Planned Parenthood v Casey* 505 US 833 (1992), at 864, but in that context it clearly refers to a judicial preference for what the law should be, or a school of thought on how the Constitution should be interpreted. It is otherwise impossible to make sense of the comment the paragraph above about 'the victories of one doctrinal school over another by dint of numbers'. If each school of thought could equally create doctrine, there would be no need for one school to gain a greater number of supporters on the bench. The phrase 'doctrinal school' used by O'Connor J is strictly inappropriate and potentially misleading. It carries a connotation from Islamic Law of being an authoritative source of doctrine (see M Cherif Bassiouni and Gamal M Badr, 'The Shari'ah: Sources, Interpretation, and Rule-Making' (2002) 1 *UCLA Journal of Islamic and Near Eastern Law* 135), but obviously fails to convey so much in the US context.

standards); (2) structural positioning; and (3) allowance for exceptions. In each of these we noticed that discussion of the rule's rationale, and hence principle in use (ii), was a possible element of the argument over the meaning or scope of the rule. In one of the cases of semantic imprecision, involving contestable standards, it is possible for a principle in use (iii) expressing a value to be directly involved. In all cases of the three features, it is possible for principle in use (iii) to be involved alongside principle in use (ii). In addition, where structural positioning is a relevant feature, we have seen that the process of determining priority between two competing rules (or between a rule and a principle) involves weighing up the relevant importance of each contender and amounts to the same process on a larger scale, that applies in deciding whether the instantiation of a principle in use (i) should be accepted in the light of other factors.

As a general point in relation to both rules and principles at this second stage, it may seem that the opportunities for further argument we have just summarised take us to criteria from outside the law. The weighing of the norm with other factors, the selection of an appropriate rationale, responding to general questions, and resolving contestable values, are all processes that require us to give consideration to matters that are not available on the face of the legal rule or principle itself. However, to stop at this point would be misleading for two reasons.

First of all, in some cases the matters extrinsic to the legal rule or principle may be so much a part of the legal or wider social culture in which the rule of principle is found that the legal norm comes with them attached.[100] The occurrence of this phenomenon may be exaggerated,[101] but that is not to say that it does not play an important part in our understanding of legal materials.[102] Secondly, there is the possibility of recognising two kinds of argument across the range of issues that have just been surveyed, in the same way that we recognised at the first stage two kinds of argument in relation to asserting the form of a particular legal norm, depending on whether the argument was made before or after the issue had been settled by the courts.

Similarly here, it is possible that the issue in question, although it has had to be resolved by reference to matters which are extrinsic to the legal

[100] See text at n 64 above for a suggestion of norms carrying with them a kind of cultural luggage when operating within a group sharing a common culture.
[101] Most notoriously in the image of 'the reasonable man', on which see Caroline Forell and Donna Matthews, *A Law of Her Own: The Reasonable Woman as a Measure of Man* (New York, NY, New York University Press, 2000). A more particular illustration is the assumption made by Lord Lane in *Ghosh* that society subscribes to uniform standards of (dis)honesty, on which see Andrew Halpin, 'The Test for Dishonesty' [1996] *Criminal Law Review* 283—now incorporated in ch 4 below.
[102] See Halpin, above n 28, *passim* and particularly at 45–46.

rule or principle *and cannot be simply 'understood'* from the background legal or social culture, has so been resolved by an authoritative determination of the court. After this event, argument over the state of the law including the resolution of this issue becomes essentially a doctrinal argument from within the law, whereas before the event it is essentially an argument as to what the law should best be regarded as depending on criteria adopted from outside the law.

So, for example, there is a conflict, and issue of relative priority, between the principle[103] that a party is bound by all the terms of a contractual document he has signed, and the rule contained in Article 23 of the Uniform Customs and Practices for Documentary Credits 1993[104] requiring the bill of lading to identify the carrier on the face of the bill, in circumstances where the front of a bill of lading is signed by the charterer as carrier but the reverse of the bill contains among its standard conditions a demise clause making the owner of the ship the carrier. Prior to this issue being resolved by the House of Lords in *The Starsin*,[105] it is possible to argue that the latter norm should take priority on criteria of 'robust market sense'.[106] After the decision of the House of Lords, the priority of the latter norm can be asserted as a matter of legal doctrine.

We come then to the point of judgment. We have identified as different legal functions in reaching this point: (A_1) the selection of relevant legal materials from established legal sources; (A_{2a}) the proposal of material as relevant in the case where no existing material is to be found, or (A_{2b}) in the case where the existing material is rejected, according to a view of what would make the better law; (B_1) identifying the form of the legal material as established within legal doctrine; (B_2) identifying the form of the legal material as a means of promoting a view of what would make the better law; (C_1) resolving further issues raised by the form and condition of the legal material as established within legal doctrine; (C_2) resolving further issues raised by the form and condition of the legal material as a means of promoting a view of what would make the better law.

All these functions may be performed by an academic lawyer, or a practitioner, concerned to propose how a particular fact-situation awaiting judgment should be decided. The only difference lies in the concern of the practitioner to promote the interests of his or her client.[107] The judge

---

[103] This might have once been regarded as a rule of the construction of contracts, but a rule that has been defeated by so many exceptions is better regarded as a general principle, which gives rise to a number of rules in those situations where the law has settled that it can be confidently relied upon. The status of a particular norm as a rule or principle may not only be a matter of controversy (see n 44 above) but may change as the law develops.

[104] *Uniform Customs and Practices for Documentary Credits* (UCP 500) (Paris, International Chamber of Commerce, 1993).

[105] Above n 81.

[106] Debattista, above n 81.

[107] See n 89 above, and accompanying text.

may, of course, take the initiative to perform these functions as well, but it will assist us in our attempt to isolate what may be distinctive in the art of judging to imagine a situation where the judge is responding to a number of proposals on how the fact-situation should be decided. The proposals may be thought of as coming from opposing counsel, or from academic commentary. One of the proposals may even be regarded as the tentative view reached by the judge on the basis of performing the above functions himself or herself.

There are a number of paths open to the judge in dealing with one of these proposals, corresponding to the different functions we have identified. It will bring things into sharper focus to take the case of a judge rejecting a proposal throughout. At (A_1) the judge may decide that the case falls to be decided on material that the proposal has failed to select as relevant. At (A_2) the judge may disagree with the proposed legal material, considering that alternative material would make for the better law. At (B_1) the judge may disagree that the form proposed for the legal material has been established within legal doctrine, on grounds either (i) that an alternative form has been established within legal doctrine, or (ii) that no form has so far been established—and he or she considers that taking the material to have a different form would make for the better law. At (B_2) the judge may disagree with the form proposed for the legal material, considering that taking the material to have a different form would make for the better law. At (C_1) the judge may disagree that the manner proposed for resolving the further issue has been established within legal doctrine, on grounds either (i) that an alternative manner of resolving it has been established within legal doctrine, or (ii) that no manner has so far been established—and he or she considers that an alternative way of resolving it would make for the better law. At (C_2) the judge may disagree with the proposal for resolving the further issue, considering that an alternative way of resolving it would make for the better law.

What is there to reaching a judgment apart from the process of responding to these different aspects of a proposal on how the fact-situation in question should be decided? Even where the judge has formed his or her own tentative proposal, the same process applies until a point of reflective equilibrium has been reached in the judge's thinking.[108] Having fully responded in this way, a decision is made. Judgment is given.

In actual fact, what may exist apart from the process we have described stems from the position of authority the judge holds to deliver judgment. This means that the judgment delivered will be regarded as authoritative

---

[108] A judge not prepared to question a preliminary view of the case in this way would be failing to properly exercise judgment (with either spelling), and be pandering to prejudice. That judges may be in a position to act out of prejudice in this way relates to an exercise of their authority (see below) rather than to a proper performance of their function.

(allowing for the exhaustion of the appeal process), even if part of the process described above has been conducted mistakenly; even if part of the process has been wholly neglected; even if part of the process has been flagrantly distorted. I do not wish to ignore this trio of judicial failings, mistake, neglect, and distortion of the law. However, their significance is diminished by the fact that the development of the law permits so much scope for creativity that it is usually possible to criticise judicial taste without imputing judicial error. Moreover, to the extent to which they do exist,[109] they constitute a separate subject of judicial pathology, and are not helpful in exploring the difference between the healthy functioning of judge and academic.

Of more interest in exploring this distinction is the aspect of judicial authority that subsists within the process we have described. For it is this alone that permits the decision to be made which elevates the preferred proposal for disposing of the fact-situation (whether that proposal emanates from counsel, academic comment, or the judge's personal musings on the case) into a judgment of the court.

We are now in a position to consider what we have learned of the difference in legal skills between judge and academic, and more particularly to revisit the conjoined suggestions that judges possess a particular skill in dealing with fact-situations, to which the 'preconceptions' of academics may serve as obstructions. We have seen that the process of reaching a proposal for dealing with a particular fact-situation involves three basic stages: (A) the selection of relevant legal materials; (B) identifying the form of the legal material selected; (C) resolving further issues raised by the form and condition of the legal material. We have also noted that both stages (B) and (C) may bifurcate, depending on the state of development of the law. Whereas (B_1) and (C_1) assume that the law is sufficiently developed for these stages to be conducted within a knowledge of established legal doctrine, the alternative (B_2) and (C_2) recognise that these stages must be conducted by promoting a view of what would make the better law. To the extent that there exists a possibility for a court to depart from its own previous decisions,[110] we must recognise here also that the

---

[109] As an example of mistake, I would suggest in *Elliott v C* Goff LJ's misreading of Lord Diplock in *Caldwell* (see Andrew Halpin, 'Definitions and directions: recklessness unheeded' (1998) 18 *Legal Studies* 294, 301—now incorporated in ch 3 below); as an example of neglect, the failure of the House of Lords to apply s 3(1) to the Human Rights Act 1998 itself in *Lambert* [2001] UKHL 37; [2001] 3 WLR 206 (see Deryck Beyleveld, Richard Kirkham and David Townend, 'Which presumption? A critique of the House of Lords' reasoning on retrospectivity and the Human Rights Act' (2002) 22 *Legal Studies* 185; and, as an example of distortion, the subversion by the House of Lords of statutory material in *Anderton v Ryan* (see Glanville Williams, 'The Lords and Impossible Attempts, or *Quis Custodiet Ipsos Custodes?*' (1986) 45 *Cambridge Law Journal* 33).

[110] See n 87 above. This power should be distinguished from the capacity for a court to make an authoritative but erroneous judgment—see further, Halpin, above n 28, at 51 (text accompanying nn 53 & 54).

alternative$_2$ state may gain access to some of the territory otherwise covered by the alternative$_1$ state,[111] as we recognised above with (A$_{2b}$).

In all of this, the legal functions performed are of two kinds. First, there are those that require expert legal knowledge: knowledge of legal materials, understanding the different forms of legal materials, recognising the further issues raised by the forms of legal materials. These are found in the alternative$_1$ state of each of the three stages we have identified. Secondly, there are those functions that require a response to be made to the negative condition of the law as revealed by the first set of functions: the absence of established legal materials has been revealed, so new legal materials are proposed; the absence of a clear form for the legal material has been revealed, so an appropriate form is proposed; the lack of a resolution of the further issue has been revealed, so a suitable resolution is proposed. These are found in the alternative$_2$ state of each of the three stages we have identified.

The second set of functions which require a creative response to be made are still in an important sense *legal* functions, for two reasons. They are dependent on the exercise of the first set of functions, requiring expert legal knowledge. The opportunity for the creative function to be performed is effectively premised on a negative result arising from the exercise of the first functions. Moreover, in being exercised the second set of functions create (or, at the very least, shape) legal material, so that the ability to draft legal material that can be made to fit in with the existing body of law will be called for here. The difference is that the second set of functions require something more than mere legal skills, for the creative response that is opened up by an expert understanding of the law, and is expertly engineered to fit into the law, is a response whose creative impulse must come from outside of the law[112]—serving the interests of a client, or, more broadly, promoting a particular view of society.

All of these functions, we have seen, can be performed equally by practitioner, academic, and judge. What ground can there then be for the

---

[111] There are limits to this encroachment although the precise boundaries may be contestable. For further discussion, see Halpin, above n 28, at 36–37 & 52; Harris, above n 96; and the different views on using the 1966 Practice Statement expressed by their Lordships in *Kansal (no 2)* [2001] UKHL 64; [2001] 3 WLR 1562. Further to the discussion of Harris's views (text following n 97 above), it is worth adding two points. His own view on this matter is coloured by a standard assumption that the law preferred by the later court is always more just, or based on 'superior reasoning' (at 416–17, 419, 421). Harris's aim to produce 'a systematic and principled approach' (at 411) to overruling falters at the sixth consideration which (at 425) admits the relevance of the possibility of differently composed courts causing fluctuations in the law, without being able to tie down when and how far this will be relevant. (There is an echo of Goff (text at n 21 above) in Harris's description of his approach.)

[112] Cp Sir Stephen Sedley, *Freedom, Law and Justice* (London, Sweet & Maxwell, 1999), in discussing issues of the individual and society, at 13: 'They are not legal questions, but they inexorably affect the law…'.

suggestions that judges possess a particular skill for dealing with fact-situations, to which the 'preconceptions' of academics may serve as obstructions? If the viewpoint of the academic as to how a particular fact-situation should be disposed of involves performance of any of the first set of functions, and the judge disagrees, then the judge is simply finding that the academic got the law wrong. This casts an aspersion on the *legal* skills of the academic, but is not an indictment of *academic* ideas. I overlook for now[113] the possibility that the judge has made an error in his or her understanding of the law, but even in this case the academic viewpoint (although a potential obstruction to judicial error) cannot be described as a preconception.

If, on the other hand, the viewpoint of the academic as to how a particular fact-situation should be disposed of involves performance of any of the second set of functions, and the judge disagrees, then the judge is simply expressing a different viewpoint as to how a creative response to the existing condition of the law should be made, as he or she is perfectly entitled to do. The fact that the judge then determines which viewpoint shall prevail, in exercising judicial authority to determine the law, obviously elevates the judicially preferred response in this matter but not on the basis of any exercise of legal skill. Imputations of *legal* error are out of place here, though criticisms of another kind may be made.[114] For although the exercise of one of the second set of functions is, as I have explained, assisted by the possession of legal skills, the point of decision in favour of one proposed response rather than another takes the person deciding beyond the skills of a lawyer.[115] In conclusion, we have found nothing to suggest that as a lawyer the judge employs different skills to the academic (or the practitioner). The only advantage we have found for the judge is the possession of legal authority to rule on how the law will dispose of a particular fact-situation.

As to our more general concerns with the nature of legal materials, I do not pretend that a clearer appreciation of the nature of legal materials will eradicate all scepticism as to their use. I do think that a grasp of the varied forms of legal materials, and the different functions that they require to be performed, is essential for the effective use of those materials, as well as for the intelligent criticism of that use. If there is one key point that emerges from this diversity to affect the different parties who make use of legal materials, it is perhaps that which emphasises both the importance and the complexity of legal doctrine. The importance of recognising legal

[113] See above n 109.
[114] For example, a judgment may be criticised for failing to make commercial sense, as was the Court of Appeal's judgment in *The Starsin*, n 81 above.
[115] Cp the concluding remarks to chs 3 & 4 of Halpin, above n 28; Sedley, as quoted in n 112 above; and Ashworth's recognition of the choice between liberal and social values, cited in n 15 above.

doctrine in relation to legal materials lies in its power to illuminate the extent to which those materials establish a legal solution as against the extent to which those materials fail to provide a solution. Recognising the complexity of legal doctrine sheds more light on how those legal materials may fall short of providing a solution and yet still determine the issues that any solution must respond to.[116]

This impacts on the roles of all who make use of legal materials. In particular, it denies to judges any justification for a preoccupation with particular fact-situations which goes so far as to inhibit them from acknowledging an idea that is adopted in a particular case, for fear that it should restrict them in dealing with the facts of a subsequent case.[117] For this is to cling on to either or both of a misconception of legal materials and a primitive notion of the role of a judge. The misconception arises from a failure to discern the different kinds of ideas, and, indeed, the different stages of the development of ideas, that can be found in legal materials, and hence to distinguish between those fact-situations whose disposal is governed through the recognition of an established idea in the law, and those fact-situations whose disposal is called for by responding in the subsequent process of judgment to an idea posed by legal materials. The primitive notion is founded on a restrictive judicial role of delivering judgment on fact-situations, which ignores altogether the development of legal materials.[118]

A richer notion of legal doctrine also impacts on the efforts of the orthodox academic commentator, for it forces the commentator to confront the insufficiency of mere rational principles (whatever is understood by them) to expound the contemporary state of the law. And when the commentator turns to reformer, it sets a more intricate agenda both for identifying present legal controversies and for providing their remedies. Even the heterodox academic commentator is not left untouched. It is no longer possible to reject legal doctrine posing as a comprehensive set

---

[116] This point is missed by Duncan Kennedy, *A Critique of Adjudication* (Cambridge, MA, Harvard University Press, 1997) 176–77: 'These ideologized modes of policy argument recur at every level of abstraction. ... Policy argument is interminably ideological, and like ideological debate, just plain interminable.' To take one of Kennedy's examples (at 175), suppose the law has established a defence of mistake where a killing has taken place in the mistaken belief that it was required for self-defence, and then the further issue arises at to whether the mistake has to be reasonable. Kennedy suggests that the same policy considerations will arise at this later stage, but this is to ignore the work already done by legal doctrine in posing the question as to which mistakes will count as a defence. Whichever way the further issue is decided (any actual mistake or only reasonable mistakes) it cannot affect that there will be some defence of mistake, for the policy of this wider issue has already been settled and is now a matter of legal doctrine.

[117] See n 11 above.

[118] This is to return to the *themistes* of the Homeric kings, relying wholly on the inspired sense of justice possessed by the regal judge, which predate the establishment of written laws. See further, Maine, above n 29, ch I.

of rules for exerting a numbing influence on the mind,[119] for the richer notion of doctrine offers far more intellectual stimulation and has a far greater chance of alerting the mind to the actual condition of the law. Nor is it possible to proclaim as a radical insight the political function of adjudication,[120] for the richer notion of doctrine insists that judge and academic alike may perform the roles of doctrinal lawyer and social critic. Nothing less is required by the condition that legal materials are in.

[119] Kelman, above n 94, at 63, denounces it as 'the opiate of the masses'.
[120] Kennedy, above n 116.

2

Criminal Law Going Critical

INTRODUCTION

THE CONDITION OF the criminal law has broadly attracted two types of academic response, which I have characterised in the previous chapter as, on the one hand, orthodox and optimistic about the possibilities of improving its condition, and, on the other hand, heterodox and displaying a pessimism reaching towards the very premises on which the criminal law is based. The challenge posed by heterodox scholars is significant for any enterprise that seeks to assess the current state of the criminal law and its potential development. If the standard assumptions about what the criminal law is seeking to do, or even what the criminal law is capable of doing, are wholly misplaced, then any efforts to improve its performance are going to be, at best, naively misguided, and doomed to failure.

Of course, it cannot be assumed that the heterodox perspective has itself got hold of a clear and accurate picture of the criminal law. In the previous chapter I suggested that one of the standard features of the heterodox position, its attack on legal formalism, had misrepresented the nature of legal doctrine.[1] That is not to say that even if the more complex notion of legal doctrine I have proposed is accepted, this plays into the hands of the orthodox commentators. The more complex notion, at the very least, creates a heavier workload for those seeking to discover the modifications to the existing body of law that will provide it with rational coherence, and identifies practical obstacles which bring into question the extent to which this is feasible.[2] The value of examining a fiercely fought intellectual debate often lies more in working through the nature of the subject matter that is capable of sustaining the disagreement, than it does in seeking grounds for aligning oneself with one or other of the parties.

Certainly there are a number of aspects of the current criminal law of England and Wales that provoke emotive and sustained argument. I hope within this chapter to examine more closely the scepticism expressed by

[1] See, in particular, text accompanying n 93; text accompanying nn 116–120.
[2] See, in particular, n 64; text following n 118.

heterodox legal scholars towards the criminal law together with some of the orthodox responses which that scepticism has provoked, as a means of considering further the scope the criminal law presents for improvement or the grounds that might exist for abandoning it. Heterodox legal scholars do not form a homogenous group, and the particular manifestations of heterodox scepticism I select for discussion below represent individual viewpoints within the grouping rather than being representative of a collective viewpoint. However, it is possible to identify some of the influences that have been dominant in nurturing the heterodox perspective, and it would be helpful to examine these as a backdrop to the strains of scepticism that we shall be considering.

INFLUENCES

Critical Legal Studies

A decade or two ago the fashionable term for the heterodox camp was Critical Legal Studies,[3] and although this movement is now widely regarded as having disappointed the expectations with which it commenced,[4] some of its core tenets or attitudes remain within the more fragmented forms of radical legal scholarship that have survived it,[5] often

---

[3] The movement is often described metaphorically in religious terms, in which case the closest thing it has to a sacred text is Roberto Unger, 'The Critical Legal Studies Movement' (1983) 96 *Harvard Law Review* 561, republished as Roberto Unger, *The Critical Legal Studies Movement* (Cambridge, MA, Harvard University Press, 1986.) For an insider account of the movement, see Mark Kelman, *A Guide to Critical Legal Studies* (Cambridge, MA, Harvard University Press, 1987.) A sympathetic account is also found in Albert Cardarelli and Stephen Hicks, 'Radicalism in Law and Criminology: a Retrospective View of Critical Legal Studies and Radical Criminology' (1993) 84 *Journal of Criminal Law and Criminology* 502. An illuminating though critical account is provided by Louis Schwartz, 'With Gun and Camera Through Darkest CLS-Land' (1984) 36 *Stanford Law Review* 413. The stirrings of a British Critical Legal Studies Movement are recorded in Peter Fitzpatrick and Alan Hunt (eds), *Critical Legal Studies* (Oxford, Basil Blackwell, 1987), a reprint of (1987) 14(1) *Journal of Law and Society*. For a selection of general orthodox responses to the movement (critical of its theoretical positions though not necessarily unsympathetic to its social aims), see John Finnis, 'On "The Critical Legal Studies Movement"' (1985) 30 *American Journal of Jurisprudence* 21, also in John Eekelaar and John Bell (eds), *Oxford Essays in Jurisprudence, Third Series* (Oxford, Clarendon Press, 1987); Owen Fiss, 'The Death of the Law' (1986) 72 *Cornell Law Review* 1; Lawrence Solum, 'On the Indeterminacy Thesis: Critiquing Critical Dogma' (1987) 54 *University of Chicago Law Review* 54; Neil MacCormick, 'Reconstruction after Deconstruction: A Response to CLS' (1990) 10 *Oxford Journal of Legal Studies* 539.
[4] Cardarelli and Hicks, above n 3; Dana Neascu, 'CLS Stands for Critical Legal Studies, If Anyone Remembers' (2000) 8 *Journal of Law and Policy* 415; Robin West, 'Re-Imagining Justice' (2002) 14 *Yale Journal of Law and Feminism* 333, 341, 344.
[5] That is not to suggest that CLS was ever uniform in its approach. Emphasising this point, Mark Tushnet, 'Critical Legal Studies: A Political History' (1991) 100 *Yale Law Journal* 1515, 1518, stresses the primary role of CLS in functioning as 'a political location'.

combined with influences of a postmodernist flavour.[6] As a movement within legal theory, CLS is an acknowledged descendant of American Legal Realism, inheriting the latter's distrust of legal formalism.[7] However, it can also be related to the broader philosophical movement of Critical Theory. The inheritance from this progenitor is a positive inclination towards a form of critical thinking that seeks to emancipate the individual from the oppressive forms of thought that have dominated society. And given the danger that a new form of thought, which succeeds in usurping the old, may prove to be equally oppressive once it becomes dominant, such critical thinking is prepared to embrace a continuous realignment with the position of the individual, so as to oppose any objective, external assessment of the individual's condition and needs.

Critical Theory

Raymond Geuss, in his helpful introduction to Critical Theory, suggests that the distinctive nature of this critical thinking, exemplified in the works of Marx, Freud, and Habermas and the Frankfurt School, can be captured by three key features. These are, first, the capacity to provide enlightenment and emancipation for those engaging in the thinking; secondly, the possession of cognitive content, the possibility of acquiring knowledge through some sort of empirical process; but thirdly, the use of a reflective epistemology, making the thinking distinct from that found in the natural sciences which relies on the observation of external phenomena.[8]

These features are commonly emphasised in portraying the process of criticism engaged in within Critical Theory as 'critique' rather than mere 'criticism'. As Seyla Benhabib has explained in her exposition of the distinction as found in the work of Marx, the specialist connotation attached to the former term serves to privilege the object of enquiry, insisting on

---

[6] Cardarelli and Hicks, above n 3, at 539, consider that as long ago as 1984 'it was apparent to many that the future would belong to feminism, postmodernism and race theory'. Postmodernism within the context of heterodox legal scholarship is associated with the work of continental philosophers, of whom Lyotard, Derrida and Foucault are preeminent. Dennis Patterson has argued on a number of occasions (eg, 'Introduction' in Dennis Patterson (ed), *Postmodernism and Law* (Aldershot, Dartmouth, 1994); 'From Postmodernism to Law and Truth' (2003) 26 *Harvard Journal of Law and Public Policy* 49) that a more fruitful understanding of postmodernism can be associated with advances in analytical philosophy. Patterson has even provocatively suggested an alternative top three list of influences on the move from modernism to postmodernism, Kuhn, Quine and Wittgenstein, in his Quinlan Lecture delivered in February 2002 at the Oklahoma City University School of Law, 'What is at Stake in Jurisprudence?' (2003) 28 *Oklahoma City University Law Review* 173.
[7] For discussion of the relationship, see Neil Duxbury, *Patterns of American Jurisprudence* (Oxford, Clarendon Press, 1995) 424–28, 459–60, 470–71.
[8] Raymond Geuss, *The Idea of a Critical Theory: Habermas and the Frankfurt School* (Cambridge, Cambridge University Press, 1981) 1–2, 26, 76, 91.

the possibility of a self-reflective form of criticism arising out of the object's consciousness of its own position. The contrast is with an external form of criticism which privileges an Archimedean standpoint, which effectively subjugates the object of enquiry to a form of dogmatism.[9]

One obvious difficulty facing those attracted to critical thinking of this sort as a means of both confronting the inadequacies of the substantive law *and* providing an emancipatory alternative, is to work out where the position of self-reflection is to be found that is capable of providing enlightenment and emancipation. It is easier to duck this issue than to confront it. Geuss is content to conclude with the observation that the process of reflective critical thinking is a recognisable and legitimate aspect of human endeavours.[10] But in these general terms reflective critical thinking is difficult to distinguish from Aristotelian practical reasoning.[11] Another strategy for displacing the burden is to celebrate the purely negative aspect of critical thinking, as George Pavlich has done in denying the possibility that critique can provide a ticket to a state of emancipation whilst arguing that it provides a permanent exit visa from problematic governmental forms.[12] This is to take the reflective character of critical thinking to such a heightened form of reflexivity that it is possible to spin away from the resolution of any substantive problem.

This kind of exit reflexivity,[13] which permits the theorist to avoid dealing with any substantive problem on the grounds that any solution offered could itself be subject to reflective evaluation, and subsequent rejection, does more than simply prioritise the internal perspective as against the imposition of an external requirement. It elevates the *process* of reflection as against the *capacity* to reflect. In a mundane situation we can readily recognise that the capacity to reflect on what is desirable is dependent on certain innate abilities plus a sufficient range of experience to permit those abilities to be adequately exercised. If we allow our children to choose what kind of ice cream to eat, we are assuming they possess the sense of taste, the ability to express preferences across different tastes, and that they have experienced the range of ice creams on offer, so as to be able to reflect on what they want. To force our children to choose between two previously untasted ice creams would not be to offer them a

---

[9] Seyla Benhabib, *Critique, Norm, and Utopia: A Study of the Foundations of Critical Theory* (New York, NY, Columbia University Press, 1986) 32–34.

[10] Geuss, above n 8, at 93–95.

[11] For further discussion, see Andrew Halpin, *Reasoning with Law* (Oxford, Hart Publishing, 2001) 166–67.

[12] George Pavlich, 'The Art of Critique or How Not to be Governed Thus' in Gary Wickham and George Pavlich, *Rethinking Law, Society and Governance: Foucault's Bequest* (Oxford, Hart Publishing, 2001) 154.

[13] For a sophisticated form of exit reflexivity, see Emilios Christodoulidis, *Law and Reflexive Politics* (Dordrecht, Kluwer Academic Publishers, 1998); and for comment on it, see the review in (2000) 4 *Edinburgh Law Review* 107.

reflective choice. If, however, we offered them the opportunity of tasting each of the new flavours prior to exercising their choice, this would amount to expanding their capacity to reflect on what they wanted.

Treating a reflective choice as revisable amounts to questioning the capacity to reflect, either for want of ability or for lack of experience. To recognise a lack of capacity in some circumstances does not nullify a reflective choice in other circumstances. So, a reflective choice may be made across a range of five previously tasted kinds of ice cream, whilst acknowledging the lack of capacity to choose when two new untasted flavours are added to the range. However, to treat *any* reflective choice as revisable denies the capacity to reflect at all, in which case it is difficult to see what point remains in engaging in the reflective process. We might as well revert to an imposed solution. A strategy adopted by exasperated parents when their children on occasion lose their capacity to make up their own minds.

The problem of finding a position for self-reflection capable of providing enlightenment and emancipation is not avoided by Benhabib. She resolutely pursues a solution through her study of the development of Critical Theory. Ultimately, through recognising the failings of a historicist basis as posited by Marx, in the light of the experiences of the Holocaust and Stalinism, she resorts to a version of Habermas's communicative interaction as the basis for the required position, though insisting on a plurality of communities of interaction capable of satisfying a variety of individual needs.[14] There are two features of Benhabib's solution that are significant for considering the application of Critical Theory to the criminal law, which I shall return to below. First, the emancipatory potential of critical thinking is realised through its being grounded within a community. Secondly, the community capable of providing this position for critical thinking is utopian.

Postmodernism

Before drawing out the significance of these points, I want to briefly refer to another constituent part of the backdrop to heterodox scholarship, the influence of postmodernism. There is in practice no clear division between Critical Theory and postmodernist approaches within the influences prevailing among heterodox scholars. The process of 'critique' and the designation 'Critical' have become appropriated for a range of heterodox works, whose authors seem linked only by an ability to mix their own intellectual cocktails from a great variety of available ingredients.[15]

---

[14] Benhabib, above n 9, at 345–53.
[15] See, as a prominent illustration, the avowed eclecticism of Duncan Kennedy, *A Critique of Adjudication* (Cambridge, MA, Harvard University Press, 1997) 15–16. And as evidence of

Nevertheless, I want to draw attention to the commonality of the problems facing Critical Theory and postmodernist approaches, by demonstrating that the difficulty of establishing a position for self-reflection capable of providing enlightenment and emancipation, together with the possible resort to exit reflexivity, resurface within postmodernist approaches—and provoke a similar solution to that offered by Benhabib for Critical Theory. I shall not attempt to provide an exhaustive demonstration that this is so across the diverse forms of postmodernist thinking, but instead shall offer a suggestive indication of this state of affairs by considering the most prominent technique of postmodernist approaches, the process of deconstruction.

Deconstruction is, not surprisingly, a misunderstood word. Jacques Derrida refused to define it on the eminently sensible grounds that any definition could itself be deconstructed.[16] In simple terms, deconstruction involves a process of confronting a privileged understanding of a text (or, by extension, a social arrangement) and upsetting it through revealing its inherent instability. This is typically done by subverting conceptual oppositions, under which one side has been traditionally privileged over the other, so as to displace the dominant with the subordinate. Whatever technicalities might or might not be involved in the process of deconstruction, it is apparent that it affords the opportunity for the exit reflexivity phenomenon. Or, more accurately, the process of endless reflection on and rejection of proposed solutions can be matched by an unending process of deconstruction of established solutions followed by deconstruction of the deconstructed solution, and so on. What is common to these processes can be brought out by reiterating the point made above that what is missing from the case of exit reflexivity is not just a solution to the problem that requires reflection. What is missing is the capacity to reflect.

the prevalence of 'the Critical', consider the fashion for book titles proclaiming that 'A Critical Approach' is being taken, or 'A Critical Introduction' is being offered.

[16] For references to Derrida's evasiveness, see Raimo Siltala, *A Theory of Precedent* (Oxford, Hart Publishing, 2000) 25 n100; Timothy Endicott, *Vagueness in Law* (Oxford, Oxford University Press, 2000) 15 n34. A concise statement on the nature of deconstruction is made in Jacques Derrida, 'Letter to a Japanese Friend' in David Wood and Robert Bernasconi (eds), *Derrida and Différance* (Coventry, Parousia Press, 1985; republished, Evanston, IL, Northwestern University Press, 1988.) Within his letter Derrida denies that deconstruction is an analysis, critique, method, act or operation; and affirms that it is 'nothing of course!'. The admission that any conception of deconstruction would itself be open to deconstruction is made by Michel Rosenfeld, 'Deconstruction and Legal Interpretation: Conflict, Indeterminacy and the Temptations of the New Legal Formalism' in Drucilla Cornell, Michel Rosenfeld and David Carlson (eds), *Deconstruction and the Possibility of Justice* (London, Routledge, 1992) 199 n22. Nevertheless, a helpful discussion of deconstruction, indicating some of the common misunderstandings of it, is provided by JM Balkin, 'Deconstruction' in Dennis Patterson (ed), *A Companion to Philosophy of Law and Legal Theory* (Oxford, Blackwell Publishers, 1996.)

Once we grasp this point, then the resort to exit reflexivity is not an exercise in practical self-reflection at all. It is undertaken by the theorist who lacking the capacity to reflect on the problem and reach an enlightened solution, *reflects theoretically* on the possibility of an endless reflection on and rejection of proposed solutions to the problem. The inability to take a practical reflective position from which the problem could be solved is indicative of some deficit in the theorist's abilities or experience, but instead of admitting his or her limitations in this matter, the pride of the theorist is salvaged by demonstrating the intellectual ability to reduce any position to a set of premises which as theoretical constructs may then be rejected and replaced by another set of premises, and so on. At bottom this is a form of intellectual self-indulgence.[17] It fails to connect with any practical position that would provide enlightenment and emancipation, and turns instead to the theoretical representation of possible solutions with which it can endlessly play.

This intellectual turn is apparent in the theoretical use of deconstruction, and is a common feature of postmodernist writing. But in origin it is not even a modern practice. Martha Nussbaum traces the practice to ancient times and identifies Sextus Empiricus as Jacques Derrida's classical counterpart.[18] However, in chiding intellectuals for their conceits, it is important not to lose sight of the practical value of the techniques that have become over-intellectualised. Enlightened self-reflection can in practice serve the purpose of emancipating the individual from an oppressive form of consciousness. So too can deconstruction be used to throw off oppressive social arrangements founded on false oppositions. Indeed, a number of authors have tried to counter the negative, nihilistic image of deconstruction, by stressing its positive, practical benefits.[19] The point is that where the process of self-reflection or deconstruction is capable of yielding practical benefits, this is possible because it is operating at a richer level than the merely intellectual.

I have made this point in relation to critical thinking by emphasising the need for a capacity to reflect. The technique of reflection is unhelpful unless accompanied by the requisite abilities and experience for responding to the practical problem to hand. A similar point can perhaps be discerned in Derrida's insistence that deconstruction cannot be reduced

---

[17] See Charles Taylor, *Sources of the Self: The Making of the Modern Identity* (Cambridge, Cambridge University Press, 1989) 489: 'what in fact comes to be celebrated is the deconstructing power itself, the prodigious power of subjectivity to undo all the potential allegiances which might bind it … the kind of unrestrained, utterly self-related freedom'. And similarly, in his *The Ethics of Authenticity* (Cambridge, MA, Harvard University Press, 1992) 60–61.

[18] Martha Nussbaum, 'Skepticism about Practical Reason in Literature and the Law' (1994) 107 *Harvard Law Review* 714.

[19] See, eg, Christopher Norris, *Deconstruction and the Interests of Theory* (London, Pinter Publishers, 1988), particularly ch 5.

to a definable method.[20] What is clear is that as soon as we theorise the technique we step outside of, and lose, the capacity to use it. If the technique of deconstruction does possess some practical value in providing emancipation from problematic situations, it must be because there is available something more than the bare technique. There must be the capacity to use it in a particular situation.

In the case of deconstruction, this additional capacity is required to transform the purely negative quality of deconstruction as an intellectual exercise into a process that can yield a positive practical outcome. That the bare technique is in itself barren is simple enough to show by applying the technique to an oppressive social arrangement, and then repeating the process to the apparently emancipated condition so as to return back to oppression.[21] More dramatically, the point can be demonstrated by taking the process of deconstruction as operating in a linear rather than circular fashion. The dilemma here is how to know when to stop. If the last point reached through the technique of deconstruction seems to offer a place of pleasant repose, that too will be rejected if subjected to deconstruction, requiring us to climb even further up an endless ladder with no place to rest. Sextus Empiricus had an answer for this. At some point we have to kick away the ladder.[22]

This assumes we have some way of identifying, outside of deconstruction as a mere technique, the place we wish to rest. This is exactly what the child offered a choice of ice cream possesses, to prevent the proffered choice turning the child into a helpless neurotic, subjected to an endless barrage of other possibilities, each time a particular flavour comes to mind as the tentative choice. More seriously, we take it for granted that

---

[20] See the discussion on this in Siltala, above n 16, at 22–29. As Siltala observes, at 25–29, there is an ambivalence within Derrida's discussion of deconstruction between considering it as a practical method and treating it as a philosophical approach to embracing the 'aporetic structures of Western metaphysics'. If only taken to be the latter, then in relation to the solution of practical problems, deconstruction only offers a form of exit reflexivity. The ambivalence found by Siltala in Derrida's texts is perhaps indicative of Derrida's own inconsistent usage of deconstruction. Quite apart from this, it is apparent that deconstruction has come to be used by others as a practical method, as 'a critique enhancing method', as Siltala acknowledges (at 25, 29.) For Derrida's own views, see in particular: his Letter, above n 16, and his statement in *Points …: Interviews, 1974–1994* (Stanford, CA: Stanford University Press, 1995) 83, denying that deconstruction is a practical method; and his essay, 'Force of Law: The "Mystical Foundation of Authority"' in Drucilla Cornell, Michel Rosenfeld and David Carlson (eds), *Deconstruction and the Possibility of Justice* (London: Routledge, 1992.) In this essay, Derrida announces, 'Deconstruction is justice' (at 15), that it 'strives to denounce not only theoretical limits but also concrete injustices' (at 20); speaks of deconstruction being 'practiced' (at 21); and refers to 'the very movement of deconstruction at work in law' (at 25).
[21] For the image of Robin Hood returning to take back the goods he had given to the poor, see Endicott, above n 16, at 17. The point is also made more generally by Balkin, above n 16.
[22] Sextus Empiricus, *Against the Professors*, VIII.481 [otherwise entitled *Against the Logicians*, II.481], as reported in Nussbaum, above n 18, at 721.

the oppressed person offered a means of enlightenment and emancipation through applying critical thinking or deconstruction to their present condition, has it within them to recognise freedom once it is on offer.

Derrida's evasiveness in defining deconstruction would be understandable if he wished to avoid it being regarded merely as a theoretical technique.[23] Yet the failure to acknowledge that what makes deconstruction more than a barren intellectual instrument, also makes it less than a self-contained process, can be criticised for being unnecessarily obscurantist. To put it another way, it is highly presumptuous to take it for granted that any person employing deconstruction, on any occasion, has the capacity to use it. That he or she knows when to step off the ladder.

The need to provide a capacity (the requisite abilities and experience) to ensure that deconstruction can yield positive practical outcomes, has been recognised by a number of authors. The capacity comes in the shape of the ability to respond to a particular social arrangement as emancipating (even if the recognition of its liberating potential harnesses imaginary experiences[24] which respond to deep needs felt within us), and as such deconstruction becomes an instrument serving the realisation of a particular vision of society. As Jack Balkin puts it:[25]

> Because all legal distinctions are potentialy deconstructible, the question when a particular conceptual opposition or legal distinction is just or appropriate turns on pragmatic considerations. Hence, deconstructive arguments and techniques often overlap with and may even be in the service of other approaches, such as pragmatism, feminism, or critical race theory.

From within feminism, the same point has been recognised by Nicola Lacey, noting the danger of a purely deconstructive technique 'effacing political action', and resorting to the emancipatory potential of a utopian vision.[26] And there is a wider acknowledgment among those drawn to deconstruction of the need to combine it with a constructionist objective.[27] The grounding of the technique of deconstruction within

---

[23] See nn 16 & 20 above.

[24] For discussion of the use of the imagination, see West, above n 4, expanded in her book, *Re-Imagining Justice: Progressive Interpretations of Formal Equality, Rights, and the Rule of Law* (Aldershot, Ashgate, 2003); also, Drucilla Cornell, *The Imaginary Domain: Abortion, Pornography & Sexual Harassment* (New York, NY, Routledge, 1995.) For wider discussion of the significance of 'imagination experiences,' see Halpin, above n 11, at 108ff.

[25] Balkin, above n 16, at 369.

[26] Nicola Lacey, 'Violence, Ethics and Law: Feminist Reflections on a Familiar Dilemma' in Susan James and Stephanie Palmer (eds), *Visible Women: Essays on Feminist Legal Theory and Political Philosophy* (Oxford, Hart Publishing, 2002) 134.

[27] Jiri Priban, 'Sharing the Paradigms? Critical Legal Studies and the Sociology of Law' in Reza Banakar and Max Travers (eds), *An Introduction to Law and Social Theory* (Oxford, Hart Publishing, 2002) 132.

a community,[28] and, since the features of a fully emancipated community remain subject to further enquiry, the utopian feel to the community that may ultimately furnish deconstruction with its practical role, provide a striking parallel to the location found for critical thinking by Benhabib so as to permit it to realise its potential for enlightenment and emancipation.

From this admittedly limited portrayal of the influences on heterodox scholarship, or the 'critical approach', I want to offer some general observations. I hope that these observations will assist us in providing a basis for working through the apparent conflicts between heterodox and orthodox approaches to the criminal law, so ultimately offering illumination on the current condition and potential development of the criminal law.

THE CRITICAL AND CRIMINAL PREMISES

A central axiom apparently shared by both the critical approach and the criminal law is the fallen condition of society. On closer inspection, however, it is not clear that this rather vague phrase refers to the same thing in each case. The criminal law assumes that certain members of society have fallen below the standards of social behaviour that can be expected of them (the criminal premise). The critical approach assumes that social relations have failed to a point where the liberating potential of social coexistence has been supplanted by oppressive forms of social life (the critical premise). The relationship between the two premises can be cast in a number of ways:

(1)   It might be thought that they are entirely complementary in one way. We may take the conduct found in the criminal premise to be the direct result of the social conditions found in the critical premise. This provides us with a critical perspective commencing with a view of society and expanding to include the criminal law.[29]

(2)   It might be thought that they are entirely complementary in another way. We may take the conduct found in the criminal premise to be wholly uncaused by social conditions, to be

[28] Nussbaum, above n 18, similarly sees the remedy for an excess of scepticism in an Aristotelian account of immersed ethical reasoning.
[29] For example, Alan Norrie, *Law, Ideology and Punishment: Retrieval and Critique of the Liberal Idea of Criminal Justice* (Dordrecht, Kluwer Academic Publishers, 1991) 202: 'It is the nature of crime as a product of social conflict and malaise ... which makes any ultimate justification of punishment in Kantian terms impossible'. For Norrie's subsequent attempt to salvage a non-Kantian account of individual moral agency, see ch 9 of his *Punishment, Responsibility, and Justice: A Relational Critique* (Oxford, OUP, 2000.)

indicative of the individual failings of the criminal rather than the failings of society; and, in addition, regard the social conditions found in the critical premise to be the direct result of the conduct found in the criminal premise. This nullifies a critical perspective on the criminal law and produces an entirely uncritical perspective on the ills of society.[30]

(3) It might be thought that they are completely disconnected. We may take the conduct found in the criminal premise to be wholly uncaused by social conditions, to be indicative of the individual failings of the criminal rather than the failings of society, but equally maintain that the social conditions found in the critical premise are wholly uncaused by criminal conduct. This would still nullify a critical perspective on the criminal law but would notionally leave room for a critical perspective on the ills of society.

Viewpoints (1) and (2) are extreme but there have been instances of them being held. I shall not have anything further to say here on (2), since it takes us outside the subject under discussion. The case of (1), however, does represent one form of a critical perspective on the criminal law and I shall comment on it below. As for (3), it would be extremely unlikely to find this held as a serious viewpoint.[31] I raise it here only to serve as an inducement to seek an alternative basis for a critical perspective in a more balanced way. How might this be achieved?

Instead of isolating the criminal and critical premises, or pitting them against each other, we might seek to explore a deeper connection between them. It is common to both that there is a human failing, whether it is manifested in criminal acts or in abuses of social relations. The institutionalisation of these abuses within an oppressive social structure does not thereby cancel out the human failing of the abuser. It is also common to both that the current condition of society has fallen below what can be expected of human society due to these human failings in the form of criminal or oppressive acts; and moreover, that it is incumbent upon us to ameliorate the condition of society by taking steps to prevent crime or overturn oppression. Finally, it is common to both that past efforts to

[30] One manifestation of this viewpoint is the implementation within criminal policy of the eliminative ideal, which, as Andrew Rutherford puts it, 'strives to solve present and emerging problems by getting rid of troublesome and disagreeable people'. See his 'Criminal Policy and the Eliminative Ideal' (1997) 31 *Social Policy and Administration* 116, 117; also in Catherine Jones Finer and Mike Nellis (eds), *Crime and Social Exclusion* (Oxford, Blackwell Publishing, 1998.)
[31] On the strength of the adage that power corrupts, in an oppressive society we would at least expect the oppressors to be given to criminal conduct in the belief that they are powerful enough to get away with it, even if we fail to recognise any crimogenic factors arising from that social oppression to affect the oppressed.

utilise the criminal law or to effect social reform have not yet succeeded in eradicating these forms of human failing; and even, that nobody yet possesses the vision for future action that will deliver complete success, in either case. Even if a utopian glance provides the motivation for improvement, there is a pragmatic realisation that limited steps falling short of utopia may be what is called for at the present time.[32]

It would seem strange then to acknowledge the phenomenon of human conduct falling short of what is required in interactions with fellow humans, however one accounts for this phenomenon, and then recognise its occurrence exclusively in either criminal conduct (viewpoint (2) above), or in social oppression (viewpoint (1) above). This seems particularly arbitrary given that human conduct regarded as criminal in one society may amount to lawful oppression in another.[33] More particularly in the case of viewpoint (1), which I have taken to be an extreme critical viewpoint, it misreads the plentiful historical and contemporary evidence of where criminal conduct is found. Not only is crime rife among the socially deprived, it occurs among the socially privileged. It is motivated by greed, jealousy, and self-obsessed sexual desire, where it cannot be motivated by need. To mount a campaign to eradicate crime by focusing exclusively on social reform runs the risk of creating a well ordered society where its members are thought to need no protection from all the vices of their fellow citizens, which, due to their material prosperity, they now enjoy ample opportunity to indulge. Of greater practical significance, in the circumstances where we have not yet attained utopia according to any vision of it, we have to acknowledge that criminal conduct among the socially deprived is not limited to offences which seek to redress the imbalance in the distribution of resources, but includes offences which threaten the bodily integrity and personal autonomy of others among the socially deprived. Any protection that the criminal law can provide to these victims, or potential victims, should not be lightly discarded.

Synthesising the criminal and the socially oppressive in this way offers scope for a more sophisticated critical approach, and I would argue, a more realistic one. At heart, the critical approach is driven by the recognition that the failing of one person can operate to deprive others of their entitlements and that this failing can be concealed as legitimate by various devices which serve to mask either, or both, of the failing of the oppressor and the entitlement of the victim. The critical approach seeks to overturn such blindness, complacency, or even wilful exploitation, by challenging the current assumptions which undergird existing social interaction. This aspect of critical thinking is boldly proclaimed in Derrida's insistence on 'the unlimited right to ask any question, to suspect all dogmatism, to

---

[32] See Lacey, above n 25, at 134.
[33] Child labour and female genital mutilation are obvious examples.

analyse every presupposition'.[34] However, as we have seen, if this is not to become an arid intellectual instrument, it needs to be complemented by a positive awareness of social conditions that are emancipating. If we further recognise that the critical approach is currently operating in order to deal with social conditions that are less than optimal (or utopian) even after a critical adjustment has been made to them, then this affords us the following opportunities.

First, and possibly most startling, the criminal law itself can be regarded as a critical resource. This follows from the recognition of oppressive conduct continuing in a less than utopian society, of the need to unmask it, and the use that can be made of the criminal law in publicly proscribing it so as to reveal its oppressive and unacceptable character. A clear illustration of this is provided by the unmasking of marital rape in the reform to the criminal law undertaken by the House of Lords in *R v R*.[35]

Secondly, the wider recognition of human failing without artificially containing it in a particular location, leaves open the possibility, even after we have recognised the criminal law as an appropriate critical resource, of that resource itself being contaminated by human failing. The criminal law may become an instrument of oppression, and so be regarded not as the resource of critical theory but as its object of scrutiny. The standard historical illustration of this is the enactment of the Black Act.[36] However, taking the criminalisation of poaching to be an example of the privileged of society using the criminal law as an instrument of oppression to preserve (or extend) their privileges, should be seen for no more than what it is. It is an instance of the criminal law being used as an instrument of oppression. It is not evidence to support the contention that the criminal law as an institution is only capable of an oppressive function. Similarly, with any evidence that the criminal law might be employed to protect private wealth so as to deprive the needy of their fair distribution of society's assets.[37] The critical approach found in viewpoint (1) above dogmatically turns this second opportunity from being one avenue of critical enquiry into a one-way street.

---

[34] Jacques Derrida, *On the Name* (Stanford, CA, Stanford University Press, 1995) 28. This is emblazoned as the motto for Siltala's book, above n 16.

[35] [1992] 1 AC 599.

[36] See Leon Radzinowicz, 'The Waltham Black Act: A Study of the Legislative Attitude towards Crime in the Eighteenth Century' (1945) 9 *Cambridge Law Journal* 56, which is a version of his *A History of English Criminal Law and its Administration from 1750*, 1: *The Movement for Reform* (London, Stevens & Sons, 1948) 49–79; EP Thompson, *Whigs and Hunters: The Origin of the Black Act* (London, Allen Lane, 1975.)

[37] Robert Sullivan in his review essay on Norrie, *Punishment, Responsibility, and Justice*, above n 29, astutely raises the question whether the case of *Hinks* should be regarded as a case about protecting the assets of the affluent, or as a case about protecting the vulnerable from the unscrupulous. See, GR Sullivan, 'Is Criminal Law Possible?' (2002) 22 *Oxford Journal of Legal Studies* 747, 757.

Thirdly, the traditional object of critical enquiry, the broader structure of society, may be examined from a wider perspective that is not tied down to a dogmatic view of the criminal law. We have rejected both placing the criminal law beyond critical enquiry and closing it off from any enquiry by a wholesale assumption of its oppressive character. We may, accordingly, respond flexibly with whatever resource is appropriate for effecting an emancipatory adjustment to the present condition of society. Bearing in mind the recognition that any such movement is still going to leave us some way from complete utopia, this flexibility may be just what is required to deal with one form of oppresssion without clumsily providing encourage-ment to another. It may in reality be more appropriate to effect redistribu-tion of resources by taxation than by abolishing the law of theft.

These three opportunities represent what I claim to be a more balanced critical approach: critically considering how to enlist the criminal law as a positive resource; critically rejecting oppressive uses to which the crimi-nal law has been put; and being critically open to a flexible use of meth-ods to alter the structure of society in a manner that reduces oppression. Placing the positive potential of the criminal law before its negative potential may seem to reverse the conventional critical agenda, but I would argue that it is analytically more illuminating and historically more accurate. If we search for the origins of the criminal law in ancient tales and myths, it comes about not to secure the position of the privileged. In ancient societies the position of the privileged was already secure enough. It arises to redress wrongs committed between peers.[38] However history or myth might be reconstructed, it is evident that the criminal law still has that role to play in today's society.

VISIONS OF SOCIETY

It remains now to consider just how a critical or heterodox approach dif-fers from the approach taken by orthodox scholars to the criminal law. I think the clue to this stage of the investigation lies in recalling how our understanding of the critical approach has stressed the centrality of pro-viding a positive vision of society alongside the deployment of critical techniques. In practice, the three opportunities for engaging a critical approach mentioned above are each grounded in a sense of community, which is hostile to the conduct to be proscribed by the criminal law, or is hostile to the conduct which the criminal law upholds, or is dependent upon an alteration to existing social arrangements. Supporting and

---

[38] For example, the establishment of a court of justice on the Areopagus by Athene was to hear a case where the victim and alleged perpetrator were both of royal blood (see, eg, Aeschylus' *Eumenides*.)

expressed through the particular critical techniques, lies the conviction, 'This is (is not) the sort of society we should be living in'.

A big part of the perceived motivation for going critical is that such a voice is stifled by existing social arrangements, prevailing ideologies, and, in particular, an entrenched legal viewpoint on how things are to be done. So the instruments of the critical approach are taken up to create a possibility for this other voice to be heard. Yet when orthodox scholars clash with heterodox scholars on particular points of the substantive criminal law, their argument is not simply put in terms of it being axiomatic that existing social arrangements are fine, the unintelligibility of the proposal (due to their ideological preconceptions keeping them from understanding it), and the impossibility of changing the existing law. When orthodox scholars do reject the heterodox proposal they do so with the same sort of conviction, 'This is not the sort of society we should be living in'.

Consider as an example of such an exchange, a proposal made in the heady days of CLS by Catherine MacKinnon that consent given at the time of intercourse should not prevent rape being committed if the woman on subsequent reflection felt herself to have been violated.[39] Responding to this proposal, Louis Schwartz pointed out that it turns sexual intercourse into rape at the discretion of the woman,[40] clearly an argument about the sort of society we should be living in.

Of course, there may exist complacency over the existing state of the law, and the instruments of the critical approach can be extremely effective as sharp prods to arouse the complacent from their slumbers. However, once the discussion is started it is conducted in the same way on both sides. Moreover, igniting controversy to arouse the complacent may just as well be undertaken by orthodox scholars. It is not the sole preserve of the heterodox. Despite no reference to deconstruction, and without proclaiming a specifically critical position from which to do it, one of the most accomplished and effective examples of this genre within the English and Welsh criminal law was undertaken by a paragon of orthodox scholarship, Glanville Williams.[41]

In fact, measuring the effectiveness of critical or heterodox approaches, as against orthodox approaches, in bringing about changes to the criminal law, puts the former in rather a poor light. Complaints about their accomplishments in relation to the criminal law have been expressed both internally and externally. David Nelken, writing in 1987, complained that 'criminal law seems to have been strangely neglected by critical scholars',

---

[39] Catherine MacKinnon, 'Towards Feminist Jurisprudence' (1982) 34 *Stanford Law Review* 703, 705.
[40] Schwartz, above n 3, at 458.
[41] Glanville Williams, 'The Lords and Impossible Attempts, or *Quis Custodiet Ipsos Custodes?*' (1986) 45 *Cambridge Law Journal* 33. For the aftermath, see *Shivpuri* [1987] AC 1.

expressing a particular concern over the absence of 'critical discussion of substantive legal doctrine'.[42] The classical piece of CLS work on the criminal law by Mark Kelman[43] was attacked by Schwartz for 'its focus on "theory" and its lack of concern with practical application',[44] and for a failure to think through the practical implications of such substantive proposals that were made.[45] Some thirteen years after Kelman's article, an insider assessment by Katheryn Russell complained that 'it is surprising that critical legal scholars have focused so little of their attention upon criminal law'.[46] She complained further that '[t]he few CLS writings in this area have critiqued abstract criminal law doctrine rather than case law analysis'.[47]

Despite Russell appearing to follow the basic critical methodology of 'deconstructing' legal reasoning advanced by Mark Tushnet and Jennifer Jaff,[48] she found it inadequate to deal with the case she was concerned with, which involved the issue of racial discrimination in capital sentencing.[49] Significantly, she concluded that, in general, something more than an abstract technique of deconstruction is required in order to achieve radical reform,[50] and, in particular, a view of society informed by race consciousness was required in order to produce an appropriate result in the case in question.[51]

The importance of providing a positive vision of society alongside the deployment of critical techniques is reinforced by the observation made by Elizabeth Iglesias in her survey of different critical legal discourses:[52]

> each subjects law and legal institutions to critical analysis for the express purpose of producing a more just and egalitarian society; and each articulates a … perspective on what justice and equality ought to mean.

---

[42] David Nelken, 'Critical Criminal Law' (1987) 14 *Journal of Law and Society* 105, 105— republished in Fitzpatrick and Hunt, above n 3, with the same pagination.
[43] Mark Kelman, 'Interpretive Construction in the Substantive Criminal Law' (1981) 33 *Stanford Law Review* 591.
[44] Schwartz, above n 3, at 456.
[45] *Ibid* at 451.
[46] Katheryn Russell, 'A Critical View from the Inside: An Application of Critical Legal Studies to Criminal Law' (1994) 85 *Journal of Criminal Law and Criminology* 222, 223.
[47] *Ibid* at 226.
[48] Mark Tushnet and Jennifer Jaff, 'Critical Legal Studies and Criminal Procedure' (1986) 35 *Catholic University Law Review* 361. Their methodology amounts to offering a more advanced set of legal formalisms to replace the outworn rule-formalism, which may then be subjected to critical attack.
[49] *McCleskey v Kemp* 481 US 279 (1987).
[50] Russell, above n 46, at 240 n139 and accompanying text; cp Nelken, above n 42, at 112–15.
[51] *Ibid* 237–39. Russell endorses Kimberlé Crenshaw, 'Race, Reform, and Retrenchment: Transformation and Legitimation in Antidiscrimination Law' (1988) 101 *Harvard Law Review* 1331, in her attack on mainstream CLS for failing to incorporate race consciousness in its critique.
[52] Elizabeth Iglesias, 'Latcrit Theory: Some Preliminary Notes towards a Transatlantic Dialogue' (2000) 9 *University of Miami International and Comparative Law Review* 1, 7.

An illustration of what can be achieved within the field of criminal law, by matching critical techniques to a specific vision of society, is provided by the achievements that Iglesias records for Feminist Critical Legal Theory.[53]

Even where critical techniques are held onto as the distinctive and unifying feature of radical scholarship it is still possible to discern the need for an independent source of social concern, to which the techniques can be harnessed. This is apparent in the discussion by Wendy Brown and Janet Halley of the importance of 'critique' in resuscitating left communities and energising left political projects.[54] At times they appear to embrace self-indulgence in celebrating the 'enormous pleasure' of critique,[55] and come close to a form of exit reflexivity in affirming that 'the work of critique is potentially without boundary or end'.[56] Nevertheless, this exhuberance is balanced by other statements which indicate they envisage a location for critique in pursuing specific social aims.

For example, they caution, 'Not knowing what a critique will yield is not the same as suspending all political values while engaging in critique'.[57] And in the particular case they then discuss, it is clear that the authors are passionately committed to educational opportunities for those historically deprived of them, *prior to* unleashing the force of critique against any obstacle to the realisation of the political value they have committed themselves to. Brown and Halley acknowledge that the force of critique may be such that the form of their commitment may not be able to contain it. Nevertheless, in acknowledging that their political commitments may be changed by critique, in, for example, being faced with the realisation that a particular case of unjust deprivation of educational opportunities was not based on race, it is the 'shape' of their commitment that is being refined by critique.[58] Their prior commitment

---

[53] *Ibid* 20. As successes, Iglesias cites, at n 46: Susan Estrich, 'Rape' (1986) 95 *Yale Law Journal* 1087; Frances Olsen, 'Statutory Rape: A Feminist Critique of Rights Analysis' (1984) 63 *Texas Law Review* 387; and, Elizabeth Schneider, 'Equal Rights to Trial for Women: Sex Bias in the Law of Self-Defense' (1980) 15 *Harvard Civil Rights-Civil Liberties Law Review* 623. George Fletcher, 'The Fall and Rise of Criminal Theory' (1998) 1 *Buffalo Criminal Law Review* 275, 278–79, similarly contrasts the dearth of impact made by CLS in general on the criminal law with that made by feminism. For further examples of feminist approaches to the criminal law, see Christine Boyle, Marie-Andrée Bertrand, Céline Lacerte-Lamontagne and Rebecca Shamai, *A Feminist Review of Criminal Law* (Ottawa, Ministry of Supply and Services, 1985); Caroline Forell and Donna Matthews, *A Law of Her Own: The Reasonable Woman as a Measure of Man* (New York, NY, New York University Press, 2000) chs 7–12; Donald Nicolson and Lois Bibbings (eds), *Feminist Perspectives on Criminal Law* (London, Cavendish Publishing, 2000).
[54] Wendy Brown and Janet Halley, 'Introduction' in Wendy Brown and Janet Halley (eds), *Left Legalism / Left Critique* (Durham, NC, Duke University Press, 2002) 31, 33.
[55] *Ibid* at 28–29, 31–33.
[56] *Ibid* at 26–28.
[57] *Ibid* at 27.
[58] *Ibid* at 28.

to the political value of fair educational opportunity remains unscathed. Indeed, its retention is essential in order to allow the sharp instrument of critique to fashion a positive outcome in which that political commitment can be 'advanced'.[59] This is made explicit in a further statement made by the authors to express the liberating potential of critique. What is illuminating here is not the state that critique liberates from, but that 'it can free us ... *to our mostly deeply held values* and rekindle the animating spirit of those values'.[60]

The values the theorist holds inform the view of society the theorist would like to live in (or thinks suitable for others to live in). I suggest that this much is common to theorists of a heterodox or orthodox persuasion. Moreover, inasmuch as it is a difference in the values embraced that divides theorists, this factor operates within these persuasions as much as it divides those representing different persuasions.[61] If it is only a matter of a difference of values that separates the heterodox and orthodox scholar, then the position of the heterodox scholar need not be regarded (as it often seems to be) as expressing a scepticism towards the criminal law itself but as expressing dissatisfaction with the particular values (or some of those values) that the criminal law has been used to uphold. This possibility becomes more pronounced when we take into account the broader critical approach suggested above, with its three opportunities for engaging with the law in order to promote a critical agenda; when we recall that the capacity to provoke complacency exists on both sides of the heterodox-orthodox divide; when we recognise that effective employment of critical techniques requires a positive vision of society capable of arousing the social concerns of the theorist.

THREE ASPECTS OF DISAGREEMENT

Before settling on a difference in values as being the basis for the heterodox-orthodox divide, we need to unravel more fully the differences between heterodox and orthodox approaches. In order to do this, we need to be conscious of three different aspects of disagreement, and also of the extent to which one aspect may be connected with or concealed within another. The first aspect is a straightforward disagreement over the values the

---

[59] *Ibid.* At this point, the process of critique differs little from a process of reaching reflective equilibrium, that is more associated with orthodox scholarly work on the pursuit of political values.
[60] *Ibid* at 30 (emphasis added).
[61] Clear examples are provided by Iglesias, above n 52, of a rupture between one critical legal discourse and another being provoked by a clash in values. For example, the rejection of Feminist Critical Legal Theory by Critical Race Feminism (discussed at 23–25) amounted to a rejection of the values prioritised by the predominantly white, affluent, First-World membership of the former movement.

criminal law should uphold; the second is disagreement over the wider legitimacy of the criminal law; the third is disagreement over the technical capability of the criminal law. I have deliberately avoided the suggestion that there exists a further aspect of disagreement in the kind of technique employed by either side, in advancing their own positions or in seeking to discredit the positions of the opposition. Since this may be regarded as controversial, I shall take some time to defend this omission below. I shall also consider how critical techniques are related to the three aspects of disagreement that have been recognised, as a way of exploring further the relationship between the aspects themselves. First of all, I want to illustrate the three aspects of disagreement by referring to some of the leading British critical works on the criminal law. This will serve to introduce some of the ways in which the three aspects are interrelated.

In passing, it can be noted that the works we shall be examining confirm the waning influence of CLS discussed at the beginning of this chapter.[62] Although they acknowledge it sympathetically, contemporary British critical criminal scholars have sought to move beyond CLS.[63] If we look for one dominant characteristic of their scholarship which sets it apart from orthodox academic work, it is most easily found in an insistence that criminal law must be studied in its social and historical context.[64] This emphasis relates to the wider legitimacy of the criminal law, for the insistence on context is meant to challenge any assumption that legal doctrine could possess its own, acontextual, ahistorical, legitimacy.[65] It does not

---

[62] See text at n 4 above.

[63] On occasion explicitly, as Alan Norrie, *Crime, Reason and History: A Critical Introduction to Criminal Law* (2nd edn, London, Butterworths, 2001) ix.; sometimes implicitly, as Peter Alldridge, *Relocating Criminal Law* (Aldershot, Ashgate, 2000), treating CLS (at 15–18) as one of 'a range of pespectives' (at 1).

[64] Nicola Lacey and Celia Wells, *Reconstructing Criminal Law: Critical Perspectives on Crime and the Criminal Process* (2nd edn, London, Butterworths, 1998) vii: 'concerned to develop an external, socio-legal analysis which reaches beyond legal doctrine and which sets criminal laws in their social, historical and procedural context'. Developments in the social context are surveyed in the Preface to the third edition (with Oliver Quick, 2003.) Norrie, above n 63, at 8: 'seen as the product of a particular kind of society generating particular historical forms of social control peculiar to itself'. Alldridge, above n 63, at 1: 'an attempt to understand a range of interlocking problems in various areas in criminal law within their societal and historical contexts ... '. This emphasis is also evident in Lindsay Farmer's study of the criminal law within the Scottish legal tradition, *Criminal law, tradition and legal order: Crime and the genius of Scots law, 1747 to the present* (Cambridge, Cambridge University Press, 1997.) See also, Antony Duff, Introduction to *Philosophy and the Criminal Law: Principle and Critique* (Cambridge, Cambridge University Press, 1998) 2–4, representing the critical perspective (at 3) as 'understand[ing] the law not (even in its aspirations) as a system of rational principles but rather as the site of various political and social conflicts'. Duff gives as one of the aims of this anthology the attempt to bring about a fruitful dialogue between critical and more orthodox scholars, which is conducted in particular through the contributions of Lacey, Norrie and Duff himself.

[65] Taking works cited in the previous note—Lacey and Wells (at vii) challenge 'criminal law's claims to be susceptible of rationalisation in terms of an apolitical, coherent body of doctrine'; Norrie (at 8) challenges the view that 'the principles upon which the criminal law is founded are natural and ahistoric'; Alldridge (at 24) challenges criminal law 'as a timeless set of examples on which to work out the implications of positions in moral philosophy'.

matter whether the assumption of doctrinal legitimacy challenged is a purely positivist one,[66] or whether the doctrinal legitimacy is related to an external position of some degree of philosophical sophistication.[67] The important point that the challenge carries is that the legitimacy of the criminal law as a whole cannot be established so as to render particular points as being beyond debate simply because they are to be found within established criminal law doctrine; or even (if we accept that existing doctrine is still subject to some imperfections) a perfected form of that doctrine.

The attack on the wider legitimacy of criminal law doctrine is heavily involved with the use of critical techniques, which we shall discuss in greater detail below. For the moment, I want to concentrate on how this disagreement over wider legitimacy relates to another aspect of disagreement, disagreement over values. An obvious connection to make, which is already apparent in the principal motivation I have attributed to this attack, is that rejection of wider legitimacy opens up to debate the values which have historically been responsible for promoting specific points of the substantive criminal law. Hence disagreement over wider legitimacy permits direct disagreement over values. This is the case even in more sophisticated versions of the attack on wider legitimacy, where the doctrinal legitimacy is attacked for posing on false philosophical foundations. Reducing the foundations to rubble allows for constructive debate on which values ought to be put in place within the criminal law.[68] Indeed, there would seem to be little point in challenging the wider legitimacy of a scheme which delivered values at the substantive level with which one completely concurred, even allowing for the possibility of a spurious legitimacy delivering substantive value.[69]

There are then grounds for connecting disgreement over wider legitimacy with disagreement over the substantive values of the criminal law. However, some issues of wider legitimacy may seem too remote to have any connection with the substantive criminal law at all. For example, concern that the legitimacy of the criminal law is founded on an assumption

---

[66] Lindsay Farmer, 'The Obsession with Definition: The Nature of Crime and Critical Legal Theory' (1996) 5 *Social and Legal Studies* 57, 57; Lacey and Wells, above n 64, at 2–3, 6, 12 (3rd edn: 3, 8.)

[67] This is the approach taken by Alan Norrie, who over the course of three books—*Law, Ideology and Punishment*, above n 29; *Crime, Reason and History*, above n 63, 1st edn (1993); culminating in *Punishment, Responsibility and Justice*, above n 29—has argued that the doctrinal legitimacy of the criminal law has been founded on contradictory Kantian premises.

[68] This is seen in the work of Norrie, cited in n 67 above, and in his 'From Criminal Law to Legal Theory: The Mysterious Case of the Reasonable Glue Sniffer' (2002) 65 *Modern Law Review* 538, where he proposes a more particularistic form of social justice.

[69] Personally, I doubt that this is feasible: schematic illegitimacy will, I think, be found out in lack of substantive value. The classical, fictional, portrayal of schematic illegitimacy being in harmony with substantive value is to be found in Plato's *Republic*, where a false founding myth is deliberately propagated to ensure that the values of social coexistence are maintained. But in this case it is crucial *not* to challenge wider legitimacy.

of free will which cannot be sustained, does not challenge particular points of the substantive criminal law. It challenges the whole enterprise of the criminal law, when viewed as a response to human wrongdoing, premised on an understanding of individual responsibility, turning on acceptance of free will. Such an extreme disagreement with the legitimacy of the criminal law cannot sensibly be regarded as relating to disagreement over the substantive values of the criminal law, since it denies any room to such values. One can simply abandon any efforts to grapple with the criminal law, its doctrines, or its values. In short, we no longer require any scholarship on the criminal law, and have taken ourselves outside the discussion of the different forms of criminal law scholarship.[70]

Another common feature of the work of contemporary British critical criminal scholars is to express disagreement with the orthodox understanding of the technical capability of the criminal law. There is a readiness to show up the technical failings of the criminal law, which is often linked to professing a disagreement with the values which the criminal law is conventionally taken to uphold.[71] Again, this aspect of the heterodox campaign is linked with the deployment of critical techniques, which will be picked up below. However, it would be helpful to make a preliminary point here about the ways in which disagreement over technical capability may relate to disagreement over values.

To question the technical capability of the criminal law is to consider the extent to which the legal materials constituting the criminal law can produce determinate answers to questions of criminal liability in particular fact-situations. If we bring in the issue of values, then the question becomes to what extent the criminal law has the capability to produce determinate answers reflecting given values in particular fact-situations. The answer provided in the previous chapter to the first, more general, question was that the possibility of determinate answers will vary depending on the actual condition of the legal materials. The second, expanded, question is more complex. Our answer to this does not just

---

[70] Schwartz, above n 3, at 457: '[Kelman] seems to envision converting ... every law school classroom discussion into a debate over determinism and free will'. There is the possibility that what masquerades as a discussion of free will, conceals a specific debate over the appropriate values to be used in deciding what behaviour could reasonably be expected of the defendant. On this, see Jeremy Horder, 'Criminal Law: Between Determinism, Liberalism, and Criminal Justice' (1996) *Current Legal Problems* 159, 160–72. As Horder observes (at 164), 'Questions about whether she "really" had a choice are irrelevant, or subordinated to this ethical evaluation of the conduct in which she engaged'. For wider discussion of the irrelevance of the free will question to issues of legal responsibility, see Peter Cane, *Responsibility in Law and Morality* (Oxford: Hart Publishing, 2002) 4, 22–24, 66–67.

[71] Lacey and Wells, above n 64 (3rd edn), at 39–41, disputing (41) that 'the scheme [of principles] is a rational, coherent and even-handed one which is both generally realised in criminal law and justified in terms of political morality'. Norrie, above n 63, at 13: 'There are principles of rationality and justice in operation within the law but they must be seen as elements in tension with other contradictory elements'.

depend on our understanding of the use of legal materials. It relies also on our understanding of the use of values.

One possible characteristic of values which entered the discussion of the previous chapter is their contestability. Professed agreement over the adoption of a value (say, dishonesty for the definition of theft) may break down when it comes to applying that value to a particular fact-situation because the detailed meaning or content of dishonesty is contestable among different users of the term. Another possible characteristic of values, mentioned in passing in the previous chapter, is their competivity. By this I refer primarily not to competing values which are strictly mutually exclusive, as are found supporting opposing positions, for example in a debate over abortion law, the value of respect for the life of the foetus opposed to the value of autonomy of the pregnant woman. This may be taken to be a case of exclusive competivity. I mean to refer rather to values which may be held together in one position, and, indeed, may be regarded as collectively necessary for maintaining that position, although they compete among themselves for implementation on particular occasions (such as the values of freedom of expression and security, in a modern democracy). This may be taken to be a case of inclusive competivity.

For example, at the most general level, we might consider that any fair system of criminal law must subscribe to both the value of protecting the legitimate interests of citizens to bodily autonomy and the secure enjoyment of their property by providing general prohibitions against conduct that interferes with those interests; and also, the value of respecting the individual circumstances of anyone accused of criminal conduct when assessing their culpability. It would be difficult to think of any system of criminal law, even in primitive times, which did not subscribe to both of these values in some way or another. However, it remains debatable just where the one value should be implemented and where the other.[72] This debate affects specific matters of criminal law doctrine, such as whether a particular offence should be one of strict liability, or whether the defence of mistake should be available for a particular offence, and, if so, whether it should be limited to mistakes that are reasonable. Such tension between values that are both implemented by the criminal law does not reveal a contradiction within the criminal law, as would be evidenced by the criminal law in one provision prohibiting theft in order to uphold the value of protecting secure enjoyment of personal property, and in another prohibiting arrest of a person alleged to have taken property from another in order to endorse the value that all things are to be regarded as held in common.

Of course, given the development of the criminal law over a considerable period of time, by different persons and different bodies embracing

---

[72] For discussion, see Kelman, above n 43, at, eg, 596 ('Broad and narrow views of the defendant'); Schwartz, above n 3, at 457.

different values, we would expect not just the phenomenon of the inclusive competivity of values but also the possibility of exclusive competing values within criminal law materials. The appearance of these characteristics of values (contestablity, inclusive competity, and exclusive competivity) within the criminal law may hamper the technical capability of the criminal law to deliver determinate answers in particular fact-situations. Yet merely to point this out does not in itself discredit the values that may be present in the criminal law. What it does is to draw attention to the possibility of disagreement over values; to the possibility of that disagreement continuing at a number of levels of refinement, as values which have been adopted are contested or compete with each other; and to the relevance of disagreement over values to resolving certain problems to do with the technical capability of the law.

Critical Techniques

The omission of techniques as an aspect of disagreement may seem bewildering in the light of the earlier discussion of the distinctive techniques of critique and deconstruction associated with heterodox scholarship. However, our discussion has led us to a more careful appraisal of the apparently stark characteristics of these techniques. In the light of this appraisal we should be wary of accommodating a claim that the mere utilisation of these techniques produces a distinct approach to resolving disputes over social relations. The use of either technique in dealing with substantive issues involves both a negative feature, in rejecting what is regarded as a falsely legitimised form of oppression, as well as a positive feature, in promoting a state of emancipation. What we have learned is that for these techniques to operate effectively they must be harnessed to a positive vision of society, ie the acceptance of certain values as appropriate for determining social relations. The significance of the values adopted affects both the negative and positive features, since the recognition of both oppression and emancipation is governed by the values we subscribe to. Nobody even considers using critique or deconstruction against a social arrangement which, according to their own values, they feel wholly comfortable with. Accordingly, the extent of the disagreement between the heterodox scholar employing critical techniques and the opponent whose position is being subjected to critique or deconstruction can be captured by the first aspect of disagreement I have mentioned, disagreement over values.

This point requires some amplification to make it convincing. For it appears to overlook two important features of the use of critical techniques. First, there is the richness to be found in the practice of these techniques, which seems to be downgraded by making the importance of the techniques secondary to the substantive positions they are supporting. This is a reasonable objection, and I shall deal with it when I come to discuss more fully the relationship between the three aspects of disagreement. Nevertheless, I shall maintain that the techniques do not of themselves contribute to a difference between heterodox and orthodox approaches. Secondly, there is to be found among those practising these techniques a view that the techniques are proof against any assertion of value; and for those practising the techniques in this way the suggestion that they can be regarded as secondary to positions taken up on the basis of the values adopted would seem particularly galling. This objection requires us to recall some of our earlier discussion on the nature of these techniques.

In considering the nature of both critique and deconstruction, I made the point that a fundamental distinction lies between the purely theoretical deployment of these techniques and the use of them to effect practical solutions to problems of social interaction. As a purely theoretical device, critique or deconstruction can be an instrument of scepticism in treating the position to be rejected as an intellectual construct, a premise which may then, as part of the same intellectual exercise, be rejected. I used the phrase 'exit reflexivity' to capture the sustained use of either technique in this manner, in order to avoid the burden of providing a solution to substantive problems.[73] I dismissed such practice of these techniques as a form of intellectual posturing concealing the inadequacy of the theorist, the lack of a capacity to provide a solution to the practical problem to hand. However, what of the theorist who retains the sceptical (theoretical) use of the device in dismissing solutions to problems of social interaction which are considered unfavourable, but then takes up an activist (not theoretical) stance in proferring a favoured solution to the problem?

This combination of hardline scepticism and radical activism adopts a position between the theorist who is content to indulge in exit reflexivity,[74] on the one hand, and the activist who is prepared to soften the tones of critical techniques by subordinating them to an adopted set of values,[75] on the other hand. It is perhaps best exemplified in the work of Duncan Kennedy.[76] In declining to subordinate critical techniques to adopted values, in accepting that any preferred value is itself susceptible to these critical techniques,[77] and in still taking an activist role, this position

---

[73] See text accompanying nn 12–13, and n 17, above.
[74] For example, Pavlich, above n 12.
[75] For example, Brown and Halley, text accompanying nn 57–60 above.
[76] See, in particular, Kennedy, *Critique of Adjudication*, above n 15. A version of part of this book appears as 'The Critique of Rights in Critical Legal Studies' in Brown and Halley, above n 54.
[77] Kennedy, *Critique of Adjudication*, above n 15, at 11, 19–20, 345–46; and 361: 'caught up for better or worse in the "viral" progress of critique'. Similarly, in 'The Critique of Rights', above n 76, at 221.

resorts to engaging in activist projects on the basis of what the theorist-activist feels like getting involved in.[78] In the context of problems of social interaction, to which there exists a number of conflicting solutions on offer, this amounts to expressing a preference not so much in terms of, 'This is the sort of society we should be living in', but rather in terms of, 'I want all the problems of society to be resolved by people who feel the same way as I do'. People 'I much prefer to hang with'.[79] No matter how cultivated or erudite its presentation, such a position displays the level of intellectual development, and political inclusiveness, found in the school playground.

What is clear is that the actual position advanced, the activism engaged in, is not at all dependent on the use of critical techniques. It has been insulated from those techniques by representing it as political sentiment rather than moral value, which would be subject to sceptical attack on the theoretical level. However, in rejecting values as its basis, neither can the position be defended by subordinating critical techniques to values. This leaves the position ultimately impotent in dealing with a contrary position which adopts the same strategy: representing its own favoured outlook as a matter of political sentiment. At least, intellectually impotent. One can still resort to the playground battle cry, 'My gang's bigger than your gang'. More ironically, the device of using political sentiment to lift the favoured position above the reach of critical techniques, places it in just that state of assumed legitimacy associated with established values, which gave rise to critical techniques in the first place.

One might doubt whether the notion of political sentiment is really that much different from the notion of 'deeply held values' other than that the avoidance of value serves to excuse it from the need for any sort of justification. Appealing to values elevates a cause above the mere profession of sentiment but carries with it the burden of justifying the higher status. It is altogether less troublesome to find a group of friends

[78] Kennedy, *Critique of Adjudication*, above n 15, at 362; also in 'The Critique of Rights', above n 76, at 222: 'Those of us who are not moral realists (believers in the objective truth of moral propositions) are used to committing ourselves to projects and deciding on strategies on the basis of a balancing of conflicting ethical and practical considerations. In the end, we make the leap into commitment or action.'

[79] Kennedy, *Critique of Adjudication*, above n 15, at 364; also in 'The Critique of Rights', above n 76, at 224. The importance of the shared outlook as the basis for political activism is also found in *Critique of Adjudication*, at 9; and 346: 'Ecstasy came when ... one found oneself passionately planning ... something to do with others of like mind'. That this is problematic has been recognised in both a generally favourable assessment of Kennedy's book, Joanne Conaghan, 'Wishful Thinking or Bad Faith: A Feminist Encounter with Duncan Kennedy's *Critique of Adjudication*' (2001) 22 *Cardozo Law Review* 721, 745 ('This leads me to suspect that Kennedy's critique merely shifts the site of denial away from adjudication towards his own perception of the social world'.); as well as in a less favourable one, Donald Galloway, 'Nothing If Not Critical' (1997) 36 *Alberta Law Review* 273, 284 ('he seems to end the book by calling on those who share his alienation to do the right thing. This is neither insightful as strategic analysis nor powerful as rhetoric.').

who feel the same way and just get on with things. Whether we do or do not suspect that Kennedy's political sentiments are nothing more than the opportunity to promote values on the sly, it is indisputable that they afford the same opportunity to protect a preferred vision of society from critical techniques. In precisely the same way as Brown and Halley give priority to political values, or the 'most deeply held' of those values, over critical techniques,[80] Kennedy allows a priority to political sentiment, or, at least, the most deeply held sentiments. Critique may change 'a particular sentiment of rightness'. But, 'It leaves us whatever we had before critique, in the way of tools for working out our commitments'. And for Kennedy 'resources of this kind' are beyond the reach of even 'a veritable Hercules of critical destruction'.[81] Clearly the primary resource for working out a political commitment is possession of the sentiment providing attachment to the cause.[82]

If, notwithstanding this doubt, some real difference remains between political sentiment, as used by Kennedy, and political values, then there needs to be a corresponding amendment to the first aspect of disagreement. We should talk of disagreement over the values or sentiments that the criminal law should uphold; or, speak in general about disagreement over the vision of society that should be implemented, taking that phrase to encompass both value and sentiment based approaches. This adjustment does not, however, alter the basic point that the disagreement between the heterodox scholar employing critical techniques and the opponent whose position is being subjected to critique or deconstruction can be captured by the first aspect of disagreement rather than the kind of technique that each side is using. As for the other feature of the use of critical techniques that I mentioned above, the richness of their practice, I shall turn to this now in considering more fully the relationship between the three aspects of disagreement I have enumerated.

The Well-Formed Notion of Law

The three aspects of disagreement I introduced related to values, wider legitimacy, and technical capability. Although critical techniques are readily

---

[80] See text accompanying nn 57–60 above.
[81] Kennedy, *Critique of Adjudication*, above n 15, at 362. Kennedy alters the wording of this passage in 'The Critique of Rights', above n 76, at 222, to soften the blunt admission that there exists something 'we had before critique'. Nevertheless, the import remains the same.
[82] Kennedy's change from a 'sentiment of rightness' while retaining the deeper political sentiment, can be compared with Brown and Halley's change in the 'shape' of their commitment while retaining their most deeply held values (text accompanying nn 58–60 above.)

employed by heterodox scholars in the course of disagreements which evidently reject the values of orthodox scholars, they are also found used in denunciations of spurious assertions of the legitimacy of the criminal law, and of false assumptions about its technical capability. I have made some introductory remarks above on how disagreement over legitimacy and disagreement over technical capability may relate to disagreement over values. I have not, as yet, tied in the connections between the three different aspects of disagreement with the use of critical techniques. This is the main aim of the present section.

Perhaps the most obvious relationship is not between critical techniques and disagreement over values, but between critical techniques and disagreement over technical capability. Disagreement over technical capability is concentrated in the heterodox rejection of legal formalism. I shall not repeat here what I have said in the previous chapter on the nature of legal doctrine, which calls into question the way this controversy has been conducted.[83] What is more interesting for our present concerns is the way that the use of critical techniques to make allegations of technical defects (demonstrations of the failings of formalism) have been connected to disagreements over values or legitimacy. Running through the heterodox assault on technical capability and its connection to the broader range of issues encompassing values and legitimacy, there exists a constant assumption, namely that the target for critical attack is a well-formed notion of law.

The well-formed notion of law is presupposed to be based on a coherent set, of authoritative values, capable of generating a comprehensive body of legal materials, which in turn are capable of providing determinate answers to any problem arising before the courts.[84] Once the contest has been staged as an attack on this target, then the tendency is to regard a fatal blow to any one of its features as an effective disposal of the well-formed notion of law in its entirety. In particular, demonstrations of the technical incapability of the law to provide determinate answers to particular problems are taken to question the coherence of the values behind the law, and to call into question the existence of a set of authoritative values.[85] The richness of the practice of critical techniques is largely accounted for by the willingness of practitioners to use them upon the target in a manner which mixes the direct (external) critique of the target's values with an

---

[83] See n 1 above.

[84] A notable example of the well-formed notion of law as target is found in Unger, above n 3, at, eg, 11: 'the coincidence of the greater part of substantive law and doctrine with a coherent theory, capable of systematic articulation and relentless application'. It is produced by his closely connecting (2–12) the elements of formalism and objectivism within the conventional idea of law.

[85] Unger, *ibid*, and authors as cited in n 71 above.

indirect (internal) critique, which attacks its values through questioning the stability of its constituent parts.[86]

To describe the target of the well-formed notion of law as a straw man would be inadequate to capture the subtlety and strength of the discourses that have engaged with it. It might be more apt to describe it as having a straw genealogy. Its origins are not so easily traced, but it still turns out to be made of chaff. The truth of the matter is that none of the joints between the different parts of the well-formed notion of law has been discovered. More than that, the parts themselves have not been found in the simplistic form in which they are presented.

As to the joints, we could, for example, recognise authoritative values, without accepting that they have been arranged in a coherent manner. Coherence depends on factors such as the commensurability of the values,[87] and the uniformity of their practice. One may take it as authoritative that a healthy body requires food and drink and exercise, without having a coherent regime for putting these values into practice. And it hardly needs to be said, that it may be indeterminate on a particular occasion whether one should go to the gym or go to the pub, notwithstanding that one accepts these values as authoritative.

As for the simplistic form of its parts, each of them may be scrutinised. In much the same way as, in the previous chapter, the crude representation of formalism was rejected in favour of a richer notion of legal doctrine, so too we can recognise that treating the law as either being constructed out of a coherent set of authoritative values or as being incapable of establishing any values as authoritative, simply misconstrues the debate. We need to look far more carefully at a range of issues. How are values established as legal values? How do established values relate to each other? How do they relate to the disposal of particular fact situations? To what extent are they contestable? To what extent are they sufficient? To what extent are they stable over time? By what lights are these values regarded as legitimate?

Without attempting to provide detailed answers to all these questions here,[88] I suggest that the picture emerging would replicate the duality found in the previous chapter in our investigation of legal materials. As legal materials both provide answers and pose questions, so too we can

---

[86] Lacey and Wells, above n 64 (3rd edn), at 39, 69. Norrie, above n 63, at 13: 'Criminal law is relatively unpredictable in its development and this stems from the fundamental ambiguity of its central organising principles'.

[87] Horder, above n 70, at 183, refers to 'the mistake, commonly made in much contemporary criminal law scholarship, of treating all values and principles in the criminal law as commensurable'.

[88] Some sense of the details is given in my discussion of the way that rights and the different visions of society they relate to can be found in a settled or unsettled form within legal materials, in chs V & VI of Andrew Halpin, *Rights and Law – Analysis and Theory* (Oxford, Hart Publishing, 1997).

expect the values of the law to be at times coherent and at times setting the problem of finding a coherent path; at times clearly established and at times hotly contested. And given the changes made to this picture over a period of time, we would also expect the question of the wider legitimacy of the criminal law to be similarly complicated by the condition the criminal law is in: different perspectives on legitimacy might take favourable or hostile views to different parts of the criminal law. However these questions are answered, it should be clear that the picture of the criminal law that we are left with comes nowhere close to the well-formed notion of law.

This dismantling of the well-formed notion of law is brought about by observation of the criminal law as it is practised. It is not the product of taking a peculiarly critical approach to the criminal law. When heterodox scholars write as if employing critical techniques is essential in order to reveal the limitations of the criminal law, which would otherwise remain obscured in a false notion of the law, the astonished response of orthodox scholars is to point out that they too are capable of appreciating those limitations. As Schwartz has commented, the CLS preoccupation (with the well-formed notion of law) betrays 'its inability to accept, tolerate, or understand a social world in which a variety of discordant ideals and conflicting human wants must be reconciled, in part, through law'.[89] That these efforts at reconciliation do not produce a well-formed notion of law is emphasised by Jeremy Horder: 'there is no coherent set of justifying values in terms of which the variegated and sprawling city of the criminal law could plausibly be explained'.[90]

Worse still, where heterodox scholars associate these limitations with a *false notion* of the criminal law (the well-formed notion), they are prone to two tendencies. One is to enter debate with a view merely to take the false notion apart and leave it in pieces. The danger here is that they are 'left with a normative void in the face of the real social events of which, they urge, account must be taken'.[91] This brings us again to the point made above, that the negative use of critical techniques needs to be supplemented by a positive vision of society, drawing on the values upheld by the theorist, if there is to be any practical impact upon the law. The other tendency is to enter debate with the more ambitious objective of providing a *correct notion* of the criminal law, capable of furnishing society with the criminal law that it needs. Yet even this may be undertaken

---

[89] Schwartz, above n 3, at 457; and similarly, at 428–29. See, more widely, ch 1 above, text at n 28.

[90] Horder, above n 70, at 184.

[91] Andrew von Hirsch and Andrew Ashworth (eds), *Principled Sentencing: Readings on Theory and Policy* (2nd edn, Oxford, Hart Publishing, 1998) 365 (discussing the approach of critical writers to sentencing theory).

as an alternative to proposing practical improvements to the law.[92] Apart
from the search for a correct notion of the criminal law serving as an
unhelpful distraction from more practical endeavours,[93] there is little to
indicate that it has met with any measure of success.[94]

CONCLUSION

Opposed to the strategies of unmasking false notions and constructing correct notions, lies an approach which seeks to present an accurate picture of
the criminal law as practised. The value of an accurate picture would be to
reveal where the criminal law reflects dominant views of what society
needs, and where the criminal law allows room for competing viewpoints;
where the criminal law is determinate, and where it is indeterminate. It
should also reveal the extent to which it is possible to make it more or less
determinate; and to make it more or less subordinate to one view of social
needs or another. A study with these aims would not purport to identify
which vision of social needs is to be preferred. It would allow for disagreement over which values the criminal law should uphold, and over the
wider legitimacy of the criminal law; while permitting assessment of the
technical capability of the criminal law effectively to serve an adopted set
of values, and to honour an endorsement of its legitimacy. It should, moreover, permit these disagreements to be conducted in a way which makes it

---

[92] Sullivan, above n 37, at 757, sees the 'more modest query' raised by the state the criminal
law is in to be: 'Can we, in a polity such as ours, do any better in terms of the clarity and
coherence of the criminal law?' Cp Schwartz, above n 3, at 427.

[93] For wider concerns about the distractions of abstract theory, see Paddy Hillyard, 'Invoking
Indignation: Reflections on Future Directions of Socio-legal Studies' (2002) 29 *Journal of Law
and Society* 645.

[94] Lacey and Wells, above n 64, at vii–viii, indicate that they are more concerned with
methodology and providing a more illuminating approach to the criminal law. They consistently doubt the point of seeking a general idea of criminal law (3, 9, 10, 12, 56; 3rd edn: 3, 11,
12, 14, 69.) Alldridge, above n 63, hints that it is possible to draw the range of perspectives
on the criminal law into an eclectic (23) but holistic (xxv) approach. In a generally sympathetic review of Alldridge's book, (2002) 65 *Modern Law Review* 151, Andrew Sanders complains (152) nevertheless, that the book lacks coherence. (In the same place, Sanders offers
the same complaint against Lacey and Wells—less justifiably given their professed position
that a coherent view of the criminal law does not seem plausible.) Norrie attempts to move
from a Kantian approach (see n 67 above) to propounding 'a relational view, in which matters of social structure are inherently connected to the possibility of individual agency' in
Punishment, Responsibility and Justice, above n 29, at 230. Despite Norrie's assertion that his
notion of the criminal law does provide 'a potential practical outcome' (235), in the view of
Sullivan, above n 37, at 751: 'the individual and individual agency are part of Norrie's ontol-
ogy and yet the mechanics of individual agency are unexplored'. In stressing the dialectical
character of his notion of the criminal law (*op cit*, 226–27), there is a real possibility that
Norrie has provided us with another instance of exit reflexivity, leaving us endlessly 'to
consider ways in which such relations might be transformed' (235).

clear just what is the nature of the disagreement, and what are the limits to any agreement reached.

Central to such a study is an examination of the workings of definition in the criminal law, for it is in a detailed observation of the formation and use of definitions that an accurate picture of the practice of the criminal law will be formed. Any general pronouncements on the nature or capabilities of the criminal law are only as convincing as their specific implications turn out to be, when tested out in practice. The following studies present the opportunity to seek a clearer understanding of the role and practice of definition in the criminal law, and through that to gain a clearer picture of the criminal law itself.

3

The Unlearned Lessons of Recklessness

INTRODUCTION

I T IS DIFFICULT to capture even metaphorically the state of the criminal law, when considering the approach of the appellate courts over recent years to the definition of recklessness. If law is treated metaphorically as a science, allowing, as Lord Denning suggested,[1] its principles to be revised by the demands of justice, in the way that scientific principles are revised by the demands of experimental data, then there should at least be a coherent development of the subject where identifiable principles of law are matched to a more sophisticated grasp of the requirements of justice. Of course, such a formal image is less fashionable today than it once was, but even if we take a more 'critical' perspective of legal materials, we lack a suitable image. As we saw in the previous chapter, critical scholars of the criminal law need the appearance of formal coherence to provide significance to their efforts to reveal the incoherence beneath. There is no point in trashing a rubbish tip.[2]

Before sinking to wholly derisory images of the criminal law, it is worth comparing in a fairly modest manner the criminal law with a body of knowledge. A body of knowledge may be dynamic, changing as the available understanding increases, is corrected, or reconsidered. A body of knowledge may have room for ignorance over matters that remain as

---

[1] Lord Denning, *The Discipline of Law* (London, Butterworths, 1979) 292.
[2] The term 'trashing' has been applied to the more exuberant activities of the critical legal studies movement in destroying the cherished tenets of the conventional formal representation of legal materials so as to disclose the lack of any coherent underpinning to legal doctrine. In his article taking a critical perspective on recklessness, Alan Norrie shows some sensitivity to the issue of overt incoherence in the law, but claims that this can be attributed (by orthodox legal scholars) to 'false judicial reasoning' whilst maintaining an 'implicit logic of the legal categories behind the necessary flux of judicial practice'. —'Subjectivism, Objectivism and the Limits of Criminal Recklessness' (1992) 12 *Oxford Journal of Legal Studies* 45, 45. This is a rather generous allowance for inverted logic to supply from incoherent conclusions coherent premises, and effectively transfers the target of purported coherence from the law to the efforts of orthodox legal scholarship.

yet located in obscurity on the boundaries of current understanding. There may be dispute among the learned as to the proper perspective to take on some matters where the existing state of knowledge does not furnish unequivocal answers. Such an image is not out of place elsewhere. We would not, for example, brand all medical practitioners quacks, because medical understanding is still developing and has undergone significant changes in recent decades, or because there exists great ignorance over the working of the brain, or because two eminent surgeons can disagree on when exactly a ceasarian section is appropriate.

However, for a body of knowledge to exist, if only at an elementary level, certain strictures apply. There must be some way of distinguishing present understanding from the existence of ignorance. The ignorance of a first year medical student differs from the ignorance of a brain surgeon. There must be some basis, or a number of criteria, for determining that current understanding is inadequate and needs changing. Significantly higher mortality rates from a particular procedure will inform us that we have misunderstood its benefits. There must be some way of tying in learned disagreement to accepted understanding, so that the charlatan does not join the company of the learned. Drug trials should be distinguishable from peddling patent medicines.

How then would law in general, or the criminal law in particular, stand as a body of knowledge? The greatest burden for establishing this status falls on the appellate courts. For it is they who determine what is accepted knowledge of the law and what is false, when it is appropriate for acceptable understanding of the law to develop or even change, and in their reaction to arguments presented before them may also determine whether a view of the law is learned or not.

It is not simply engaging in these practices but the manner in which the practices are conducted that signifies that the courts are dealing with a body of knowledge. A temperamental despot could conduct the business of the courts—determining what is acceptable as law, when it should change, and whose views should be highly regarded—without professing a body of knowledge. Early Roman law was practised in the courts as an esoteric practice by aristocratic priests before the plebeians revolted and demanded that they should have knowledge of the law.

Even when the body of knowledge has grown in complexity beyond a number of statements chiselled on stone tablets in the market-place,[3] and has fallen into the hands of lawyers, two basic characteristics remain to indicate that we are still in fact dealing with a body of knowledge: there must be a uniform way of recognising what is known amongst the

---

[3] The XII Tables were placed in the Roman forum c450 BC.

knowledgeable, and what is known must be capable of application to the subject matter over which knowledge is professed. If these two requirements are not met, we shall either be dealing with a mutual adulation society where obscurity is presumed to signify great learning, or with some sort of fantasy game whose members communicate coherently with each other but whose activities have no bearing on reality.

In the case of the criminal law, I would suggest that these two basic characteristics of a body of knowledge should each be evident in a particular place. We should expect to be able to tell what is known amongst the knowledgeable from the *definitions* to be found in the criminal law—of offences, defences, and of other elements of the subject that may apply generally or specifically to different areas of the criminal law. And we should expect that what is found within the definitions of the criminal law is capable of application to the conduct of people which the criminal law professes to deal with, that it enables the determination of particular fact-situations.

It may be that legal definitions found in the complex formulations of legal materials do not obviously satisfy this second characteristic, at least without further application of the requisite knowledge in order to render these materials into a form more readily applicable to the conduct of ordinary people. But the one place in which this should be evident is in the *directions* given by trial judges to juries, for this is where the criminal law has to be applied to concrete situations of human conduct in an intelligible manner.

I want to apply these two tests of a body of knowledge to one fundamental area of the criminal law, recklessness. Before commencing the study, we should remind ourselves that mere change in the law will not of itself count against recognising a body of knowledge, which is capable of accommodating change—even an expansion of knowledge to shed light on what was previously misunderstood. But the tests suggested will indicate whether we have such a body of knowledge either side of the change.

It is also worth pointing out that the two tests although clearly related are yet distinct. It may well be that the definitions of the criminal law as commonly employed by the learned are too rarefied, or simply too general in form, so as to directly translate into jury directions.[4] We accordingly need to be conscious of the uses of *both* definitions and directions in order to get a clearer picture of the changes brought about by the appellate courts to recklessness in the criminal law.

---

[4] Cp the observation of Diplock LJ, in *Mowatt* [1968] 1 QB 421, 426: 'The function of a summing-up is not to give the jury a general dissertation upon some aspect of the criminal law, but to tell them what are the issues of fact on which they must make up their minds ...'.

THE *CALDWELL-CUNNINGHAM* DIVIDE

The *Caldwell* and *Cunningham* cases are now firmly identified with two distinct types of recklessness in the English criminal law. The starting point for the divide precedes either of them in Professor Kenny's *Outlines of Criminal Law*, in which, within a single sentence definition of malice as encompassing intention and recklessness, is added parenthetically a definition of recklessness itself: 'the accused has foreseen that the particular kind of harm might be done, and yet has gone on to take the risk of it'.[5]

Lord Diplock in *Caldwell*, in discussing Kenny's definition which had by then been approved in *Cunningham*, points out that the effect of the definition was to narrow the scope of the term in legal usage from the breadth of meanings it conveyed in ordinary usage:[6]

> recklessness covers a whole range of states of mind from failing to give any thought at all to whether or not there is any risk of those harmful consequences, to recognising the existence of the risk and nevertheless deciding to ignore it. Conscious of this imprecision in the popular meaning of recklessness as descriptive of a state of mind, Professor Kenny ... was, as it seems to me, at pains to indicate ... the particular species within the genus, reckless states of mind, that constituted 'malice' in criminal law.

It is particularly important to note that Lord Diplock here recognises a number of states of mind which can be conveyed by the term recklessness, but attempts neither a comprehensive list—he indicates only two within an indefinite range, nor a general synthesising definition which would be capable of spreading over the complete range of states of mind with their individual characteristics.[7]

---

[5] JWC Turner (ed), *Kenny's Outlines of Criminal Law* [1st edn, 1902] (16th edn, Cambridge, Cambridge University Press, 1952) 186. Although Jeremy Horder has provided forceful arguments against the historical basis for the correspondence principle as an aspect of 'ideal subjectivism' in 'Two Histories and Four Hidden Principles of Mens Rea' (1997) 113 *Law Quarterly Review* 95, these arguments do not encompass the crucial aspect of a subjective approach to recklessness at issue here: taking into account the individual circumstances of the defendant in determining whether he had actual awareness of the risk. Horder's preoccupation with the correspondence principle as a target distracts his attention from this key point—in his perception of differing viewpoints between Turner and Kenny (at 114–15, 117); of a conflict between *Mowatt* and *Cunningham* (at 114); and even of the impact of *Cunningham* itself (at 117–18). On this key requirement of actual awareness of the risk by the defendant all these authorities are at one. This does not detract from the possibility of disagreement as to the issue of what is the subject matter of the appreciated risk required for each offence, nor denigrate Horder's suggestion that the correspondence principle is not the appropriate answer.

[6] [1981] 1 All ER 961, 964.

[7] It is possible to define words at both of these levels, such that there is consistency at the general level whilst conflict between meanings at the level of particular instances. Take, for

In short, at this point, Lord Diplock does not provide us with a definition of recklessness. In fact, from all that is stated in this passage it is strictly unwarranted to speak, as Lord Diplock does, of 'the popular *meaning* of recklessness'. From all that Lord Diplock has to say here, it would appear that the term in ordinary usage bears a *number of meanings*, whose disparate nature leads to 'imprecision', and his scientific taxonomical metaphor of genus and species is accordingly inappropriate, in the absence of an available definition for the genus.[8]

This is not merely a matter of inelegant phraseology. The practical implications for Diplock's subsequent exposition of recklessness in *Caldwell* will be considered shortly. But we should first observe that by adopting the Kenny definition in *Cunningham* the Court of Criminal Appeal, apart from anything else, avoided the need to explore any further the ramifications of current usage through adopting a technical legal definition for the term.

There is a further advantage of simplicity in the *Cunningham* approach, which has a direct bearing on our present interest. The definition adopted is readily translatable into jury directions. In Kenny's definition, given above—substitute for 'the accused' the defendant in the particular case, and substitute for 'the particular kind of harm' that harm which is the subject matter of the particular charge, and relate to the facts of the case what amounts to 'tak[ing] the risk of it'—and a direction to the jury is readily produced.[9]

The contrast with the approach favoured in *Caldwell* in these respects is great. In that case there is no correlation between definition and direction for the simple reason that no definition is given. Although, as we have

example, 'a cry', which at the general level can be defined as a loud utterance, but within particular instances can be variously, an expression of pain, a call for help, etc. I consider this in greater detail in relation to 'claim' in 'More Comments on Rights and Claims' (1991) 10 *Law and Philosophy* 271 (also found as ch IV of *Rights and Law – Analysis and Theory* (Oxford, Hart Publishing, 1997)). The mere identification of a general synthesising definition does not close our enquiry unless it is at that level that our concerns are expressed.

[8] The same error is perpetrated by Lord Hailsham in *Lawrence* [1981] 1 All ER 974, 978. In following Lord Diplock in taking the ordinary language, or dictionary meaning, Lord Hailsham asserts that the word, though varying in pronunciation over the centuries, has borne 'the same *meaning*' (emphasis added). But in the words immediately following which amount to an attempt to amplify that meaning, Lord Hailsham simply informs us that it is 'applied to a person or conduct evincing a state of mind stopping short of deliberate intention, and going beyond mere ... carelessness'. Again, the device of a range is used which might cover a number of disparate instances without any attempt at identifying a synthesising feature. More remarkably, Lord Hailsham's range ends before 'mere carelessness', but carelessness is to be found *within* the range of dictionary meanings given for recklessness, as Lord Diplock points out in the same case, at 981.

[9] The exercise was performed by the Court of Criminal Appeal in *Cunningham* in suggesting how the jury should have been directed in that case: 'he foresaw that the removal of the gas meter might cause injury to someone but nevertheless removed it'—[1957] 2 All ER 413, 415.

noted, Lord Diplock chose to embrace the wider dictionary, or ordinary 'meaning', no specific definition of recklessness is approved, no singular meaning given, but rather the possibility of a range of meanings is indicated. This is true in Diplock's discussion of Kenny's definition quoted above, and also in the sentences immediately preceding it where 'the popular or dictionary meaning' is introduced in the spurious singular but given in disjunctive forms:[10]

> the popular or dictionary meaning is 'careless, regardless, or heedless of the possible harmful consequences of one's acts'. It presupposes that, if thought were given to the matter by the doer before the act was done, it would have been apparent to him that there was a real risk of its having the relevant harmful consequences ...

In neither of these sentences are we given a specific definition, in the form of a chosen instance from the available range (as Kenny provided), or in the form of a general synthesising definition. The first sentence gives us at least three separate possibilities (each of the three may be capable of opening up to further possibilities), and the second sentence shirks from providing a general definition covering all of the instances by its awkward introductory locution, 'It presupposes'. The singular pronoun must be in apposition to the singular subject of the preceding clause, ie, 'the popular or dictionary meaning of recklessness'.[11] This is a simple grammatical point whose neglect by Goff LJ in *Elliott v C* had far reaching repercussions, as we shall see. The semantics are not so clear. As the singular form of the popular or dictionary meaning remains an apparition, we are left in the second sentence with a stated inference to be drawn from something insubstantial, in an ungiven manner. Even if one were to be charitable about correcting the error of portraying a plurality of meanings by the singular term, it certainly is not evident how this presupposition fixes generally on the different instances of the popular or dictionary 'meaning' that Diplock provides. Notably, the requirement that it would have been apparent to the defendant himself simply does not fit the objective strain of 'carelessness', where no such requirement is made. It is not surprising that there is more to be made of this particular sentence in the subsequent exegesis of *Caldwell* recklessness.[12] Suffice it to note for the present that we are still lacking a definition of recklessness.

---

[10] [1981] 1 All ER 961, 964.

[11] More rigorously, it could also be taken back to the main subject of the preceding sentence, ie the word 'recklessness', but as this is found qualified in the relative clause with its popular or dictionary meaning, this amounts to the same thing.

[12] A key clause in the sentence underwent a remakable transformation on the very same day in the House of Lords when the speeches in *Lawrence* were given, which unanimously purported to follow *Caldwell*, yet provided in the corresponding clause a presupposition that

Nor subsequently, as he approaches his famous direction, does Lord Diplock provide further illumination, but rather reiterates the 'ordinary' range of meanings, from which he takes two favoured instances:[13]

> 'Reckless' as used in the new statutory definition of the mens rea of these offences is an ordinary English word. It had not by 1971 become a term of legal art with some more limited esoteric meaning than that which it bore in ordinary speech, *a meaning which surely includes not only deciding to ignore a risk of harmful consequences resulting from one's acts that one has recognised as existing, but also failing to give any thought to whether or not there is any such risk in circumstances where, if any thought were given to the matter, it would be obvious that there was.* (emphasis added)

It is true that the latter italicised part of this passage, indicating the two favoured instances of recklessness, is capable of translating directly to a direction for a jury, and Lord Diplock demonstrates just that in formulating three paragraphs later the appropriate direction for an offence under s 1(1) of the Criminal Damage Act 1971,[14] and again in *Lawrence* in formulating an appropriate direction for the offences of reckless driving under ss 1 and 2 of the amended Road Traffic Act 1972.[15] However, the crucial difference from the approach taken in *Cunningham* remains: the approved *directions* do not relate to an approved *definition* of recklessness.

That two favoured instances of recklessness have been approved is a less happy condition to be in, because the door has been left open to others found in the range covered by 'the popular or dictionary meaning' without authoritatively determining the application or extent of approval for other instances. The situation is worsened by concealing real conflicts that may arise between different instances to be found in the popular or dictionary range by erroneously representing this range as a singular meaning for recklessness. Moreover, since the two approved instances are not themselves anchored in an approved definition of recklessness, but approved for particular directions for the offences under consideration, this leaves even their precise status vulnerable.

---

the risk would have been apparent to 'an ordinary prudent individual', making a switch from subjective to objective—[1981] 1 All ER 974, 982. The subjective form of the original clause in *Caldwell* was ammunition for academic commentators who sought to put a qualified subjectivity on the *Caldwell* direction. For a more recent survey of the discussion, see DW Elliott, 'Endangering Life by Destroying or Damaging Property' [1997] *Criminal Law Review* 382, 383–87; and for persistence in the qualified subjectivity reading, see LH Leigh, 'Liability for Inadvertence: A Lordly Legacy?' (1995) 58 *Modern Law Review* 457, 462–63. I consider below the further mischievous impact of the sentence in *Elliott v C*.

[13] [1981] 1 All ER 961, 966.
[14] *ibid* at 967.
[15] [1981] 1 All ER 974, 982, 983.

The basic instability of a direction centred approach which lacks a firm definitional basis, as found in *Caldwell*, has become only too apparent in subsequent cases. In tracing later developments, we can discern how the instability gives rise to both a hardening and a loosening of the approach taken in *Caldwell* itself.

HARDENING A DEFINITION IN *ELLIOTT v C*

The decision of the Divisional Court in *Elliott v C*,[16] perhaps bolstered by the refusal of the House of Lords to grant leave for a further appeal, came to be regarded as the authoritative interpretation of *Caldwell* recklessness.[17] Of the two judges sitting, Glidewell J used *Lawrence* as the principal foundation for the interpretation taken, effectively relying on the switch in the presupposition clause, noted above,[18] to the perspective of 'an ordinary prudent individual' as a basis for grounding a wholly objective interpretation of *Caldwell*. Since this strand of *Lawrence* diverged from the corresponding part of *Caldwell* which it purported to follow,[19] this in itself would have been a particularly shaky foundation for the interpretation offered in *Elliott v C*. However, Goff LJ reached the same conclusion through a direct consideration of the reasoning of Lord Diplock in *Caldwell* itself.

The judgment of Goff LJ is noteworthy for its candour: he acknowledged that the conclusion reached was one that he would have preferred to have avoided but felt 'constrained to do so by authority.'[20] It is also remarkable for two steps he takes in reaching his conclusion. The first is Goff's consideration of the ordinary meaning of reckless:[21]

> Yet, if I next pause ... and ask myself the question: would I, having regard only to the ordinary meaning of the word, consider this girl to have been, on the facts found, *reckless* whether the shed and contents would be destroyed, my answer would, I confess, be in the negative.

Goff, like Diplock, slips casually into the convention of speaking of a singular 'meaning' of recklessness without establishing that such a meaning exists, and in his following amplification of this observation provides a number of different instances of recklessness, none of which is satisfied by the facts of the case he is considering: 'deliberate disregard', 'mindless

---

[16] [1983] 2 All ER 1005.
[17] It was soon followed by the Court of Appeal in *Malcolm R* (1984) 77 Cr App R 334 and in *Bell* [1984] 3 All ER 842.
[18] See n 12 above.
[19] *ibid*.
[20] [1983] 2 All ER 1005, 1010.
[21] *ibid* at 1011.

indifference', and 'where failure to give thought to the possibility of the risk was due to some blameworthy cause, such as intoxication'. Leaving to one side for the moment the absence of a clear meaning for recklessness in either Diplock's or Goff's reasoning, what is remarkable is that the ordinary, popular, or dictionary meaning which Lord Diplock professed to use in *Caldwell* is found by Goff LJ to be inapplicable to the facts of the present case, and yet he feels constrained to apply Diplock's meaning of recklessness. If it were not for the fact that neither judge was dealing with a clear definition of recklessness taken from the dictionary, this might have been enough to decide *Elliott v C* the other way.

The second remarkable point in Goff's reasoning is the one that is decisive in his concluding that he was bound to hold that the *Caldwell* test was 'purely objective',[22] as opposed to the alternative possibility of a reading that would make it a requirement in Lord Diplock's second favoured instance of recklessness that the risk which the defendant had failed to consider 'would have been obvious to *him* if he had given any thought to the matter'.[23]

This is the crucial point in *Elliott v C*, for on the Magistrates' finding that C, given her age, lack of understanding, and state of tiredness and exhaustion, would have been incapable of appreciating the risk even if she had given any thought to the matter, this reading would necessarily have led to an acquittal.[24]

Goff's determination of the point the other way is preceded by an observation that this reading does not appear in the simple words found in Lord Diplock's direction, but this was not in itself conclusive. What was decisive was Goff's finding that Lord Diplock in *Caldwell* had clearly rejected this alternative to the purely objective test:[25]

> when considering earlier in his speech Professor Kenny's definition of recklessness (which he rejected as being too narrow), Lord Diplock expressly adverted to the fact that *that definition presupposed* that 'if thought were given to the matter by the doer before the act was done, *it would have been apparent to him* that there was a real risk of its having the relevant harmful consequences ... '. It seems to me that, having expressly considered that element in Professor Kenny's test, and having (as I think) plainly decided to omit it from his own formulation of the concept of recklessness, it would not now be legitimate for an inferior court, in a case under this particular subsection, to impose a qualification which had so been rejected by Lord Diplock himself. (bold italic indicates emphasis added by Goff, other emphasis added by author)

[22] *ibid.*
[23] *ibid.*
[24] As in fact occurred before the Magistrates who were persuaded that it was the proper reading of the *Caldwell* test.
[25] [1983] 2 All ER 1005, 1011–12.

But this completely misreads Lord Diplock's speech. The first italicised section, 'that definition presupposed', occurs in Goff's paraphrase preceding the actual quote he gives from Diplock. In the original, which has been reproduced above, it occurs in the form 'It presupposes', and as we have already remarked,[26] the pronoun is not in apposition to Professor Kenny's definition but to 'the popular or dictionary meaning' which Kenny rejected. This is apparent not only from a grammatical reading of Lord Diplock's speech, but also by reflection on what Kenny's definition involved. Since it made a mandatory requirement of actual awareness of the risk by the defendant it could not possibly be satisfied by the lesser requirement of a hypothetical consideration of what the defendant might have been aware of if he had stopped to consider the risk.

So Goff rejects what he would have preferred as a reading of Diplock's test on the basis that he is compelled to do so, because Diplock had himself rejected the crucial element of the favoured reading, in rejecting Kenny's definition; whereas Diplock had in fact located the crucial element not in Kenny's definition but in the popular or dictionary meaning, which Kenny had rejected and Diplock had himself approved.[27]

One may conclude that there was no proper basis for the decision in *Elliott v C*. A proper reading by Goff LJ of the critical passage from Lord Diplock would have led him to the opposite conclusion. But what is of more general interest is the way in which this confusion springs from the lack of a sound legal definition of recklessness in *Caldwell*. Had both Diplock and Goff had a clear statement of such a definition, on which Diplock's direction was founded and by which it could be clarified, then there would not have ensued the muddle of confusing the 'meaning' Diplock had adopted with a definition that he had rejected.[28] This very muddle was facilitated by the apparitional nature of the ordinary, popular, or dictionary meaning, which serves as a poor substitute for a clear legal definition.

Ironically the cause of the muddle is remedied as its consequence: the absence of a legal definition of recklessness in *Caldwell* gives way to a wholly objective test being established in *Elliott v C*, which implicitly links Diplock's direction to a legal definition of recklessness. For if the direction no longer simply comprises Diplock's two favoured instances of a wider approach to recklessness (which has not been properly defined),

---

[26] See text at n 11 above.

[27] The correct reading is provided by Lord Ackner in *Reid* [1992] 1 WLR 793, 805, but remarkably their Lordships in that case fail to discuss *Elliott v C* (despite its having been cited in argument).

[28] It would also have been impossible for Lord Diplock himself to make the subjective-objective switch in the presupposition clause in *Lawrence*. See n 13 above.

but involves an *exclusively* objective test, then by implication the test found in the direction provides us with all that we need to know to arrive at a definition of '*Caldwell* recklessness'.[29]

We now appear to have a direct correlation between definition and direction for *Caldwell* recklessness as enjoyed by *Cunningham* recklessness, but the shaky foundations on which the former is built become apparent in the subsequent case law.

LOOSENING THE DIRECTION IN REID

Whereas the Divisional Court in *Elliott v C* narrowed down the *Caldwell* approach to recklessness by positing a purely objective test in the direction, and by implication providing a specific definition for *Caldwell* recklessness, the House of Lords in *Reid*[30] opened it up by leaving Lord Diplock's spurious ordinary or dictionary meaning in place and then exploiting it to provide a variety of possible directions for recklessness. The key practical change in *Reid* is that Lord Diplock's *model direction*[31] becomes a *specimen direction*.[32]

This quiet revolution in recklessness is astutely performed by the House of Lords. For by leaving the Diplock direction its status as an approved specimen direction, it retains its authority and does not require overruling, but by changing the emphasis to *a specimen* direction it becomes possible to displace it when thought desirable, in any particular set of circumstances save the narrow limit of those circumstances prevailing in

---

[29] It should not be overlooked that the first of Lord Diplock's favoured instances unequivocally adopts the Kenny/*Cunningham* approach to recklessness, but not *as a definition* for this would knock out the other instance. The ability of this strong subjective type of recklessness to trail alongside whatever is made of Lord Diplock's second instance is uncontroversial, and it is common practice to focus on the second instance as distinctively bearing the *Caldwell* brand.

[30] [1992] 1 WLR 793.

[31] The *Caldwell* direction had been regarded as a model one, in the sense of governing how juries should be directed, for criminal damage in *Elliott v C* [1983] 2 All ER 1005, particularly by Goff LJ at 1010–11. The *Lawrence* direction had been held by the Court of Appeal to be a model one for reckless driving in *Madigan* (1982) 75 Cr App R 145, 148. Both these positions are overruled by *Reid*. Given the switch in Lord Goff's own attitude from *Elliott v C* to *Reid*, it is again surprising that no mention is made by their Lordships in the latter case of the former.

[32] [1992] 1 WLR 793, 796 (Lord Keith), 805 (Lord Ackner), 813–14 (Lord Goff), 819 (Lord Browne-Wilkinson, also concurring with Lord Goff); Lord Roskill concurring with all the other speeches. Much is made in these speeches of Lord Diplock referring to his direction as '*an* appropriate instruction' (emphasis supplied by Lord Goff at 813). That this did not bear the indefinite connotation that their Lordships seek to place upon it is evident from the full description that Lord Diplock gives: 'an appropriate instruction to the jury *on what is meant by driving recklessly*' (emphasis added), rather than an appropriate instruction for the circumstances of this particular case—see [1981] 1 All ER 974, 982.

the case in which it was formulated. It is clear that this applies to both the *Lawrence* and *Caldwell* directions.[33]

The loosening of the Diplock directions by the House of Lords leaves open the possibilities of different directions for (a) different offences,[34] and (b) different circumstances,[35] where recklessness is involved. The definition of recklessness which supports this liberality is the 'ordinary', 'everyday', 'popular', or 'dictionary' meaning of recklessness.[36]

I have already stressed that to assert a singular ordinary meaning for recklessness is misconceived, and the correction is in fact provided by Lord Goff in *Reid*, who after referring to the 'ordinary or popular sense' more accurately states:[37]

> I first bear in mind that recklessness is an ordinary English word, but that, as used in ordinary speech, and likewise as used in our law, it has more than one meaning.

And given that the contexts clearly demonstrate their Lordships employing different meanings for recklessness,[38] we can dismiss the references to a singular ordinary meaning as a solecism. But this leads on to a deeper problem.

Accepting that there are a number of different ordinary meanings for recklessness, and also that the legal meanings for recklessness may vary for different offences and even for different circumstances relating to the same offence, the unanswered question is how do we tell which meaning to use on any given occasion?

The two available solutions to the problem have been discounted:

(1)   All ordinary meanings apply in all legal contexts—No, because different meanings apply in different legal contexts.
(2)   The different ordinary meanings self-evidently fit different appropriate legal contexts—No, because courts have in the past applied different meanings of recklessness to the same legal context,[39] and it is precisely this problem which calls for authoritative directions to be given.

---

[33] Lord Browne-Wilkinson does state that he does not propose to address *Caldwell* in his own comments ([1992] 1 WLR 793, 817) but does concur with Lord Goff (at 816), who, in common with Lord Ackner, does embrace *Caldwell* (at 807, 804). Both Lords Keith and Roskill concur with Lords Ackner and Goff.

[34] *ibid* at 805, 807, 814, 817.

[35] *ibid* at 796, 799, 806, 813, 814–15, 816, 819.

[36] *ibid* at 796, 804, 807, 815, 819.

[37] *ibid* at 807, 815.

[38] See nn 35 & 36 above.

[39] To give only one prominent example, the conflict between *Stephenson* and *Caldwell*.

And the approach which would remove the problem has been rejected:

(3)   We avoid the confusion in the ordinary meanings of reckless-ness by stipulating a legal definition[40]—This is the approach overtly taken by Kenny and *Cunningham*, and effectively taken in a different form in *Elliott v C*,[41] but not taken in *Caldwell* and not favoured in *Reid*.[42]

The resultant dislocation of a multiplicity of possible directions on reck-lessness from any stable definition of recklessness can only beget confu-sion. Before considering how this has promoted confusion elsewhere, it is worth briefly examining some of the practical confusion already evident in their Lordships speeches in *Reid*.

Each of the four substantial speeches in *Reid* addressess what we might loosely call exceptional cases in a consideration of reckless driving:

(a_1)   Driver acting under a mistaken view that no risk exists, which is reasonable, understandable, or excusable—eg relies on pas-senger's assurance that the part of the road he cannot see him-self is clear.

(a_2)   Driver acting under an unreasonable and hence culpably mis-taken view that no risk exists—eg where he is performing stunts with a high powered car and is so consumed with con-fidence in his own driving skills that he concludes that there is no risk to pedestrians who are endangered by his driving.

(b)   Driver's capacity to appreciate risks affected by some condi-tion for which he is not at fault—eg the onset of illness or shock.

(c)   Driver's action justified in circumstances not of his own making—eg avoiding hitting a child who runs into the road.

(d)   Driver's action brought about due to circumstances beyond his control—eg a sudden mechanical failure whilst in the process of overtaking.

Lord Keith states that each of the cases he considers ((a_1), (b) and (c)) requires dealing with by a modified direction other than a straightforward

---

[40] This may involve stipulating one or a number of legal meanings. So long as it is clear which meaning(s) apply to which offence, this still effectively removes the problem.

[41] *Elliott v C* differs from *Cunningham* in stipulating two legal meanings for recklessness: leaving the *Cunningham* meaning for offences involving malice, and adding a hard objective meaning for criminal damage (and other offences?).

[42] The correct inference to draw from this is, I think, that *Reid* overruled *Elliott v C*. This con-clusion is supported more specifically by dicta of Lord Keith at 796 and Lord Ackner at 805 (see n 50 and text at n 51 below). For comment see Leigh, above n 13, at 465. But the picture was not left as clear as it might have been due to the remarkable omission of their Lordships in *Reid* to make an explicit reference to *Elliott v C* (see nn 27 & 31 above).

Diplock direction.[43] Lord Ackner discusses cases (a_1), (d) and (c) as examples where the normal inference that dangerous driving amounts to recklessness on the part of the driver can be rebutted, but does not call for any modification to the Diplock direction.[44] Lord Goff, whilst upholding the general evidential presumption with its exceptions,[45] in discussing cases (a_1), (b) and (c), indicates that there may need to be some modification to the directions in dealing with such cases.[46] Lord Browne-Wilkinson treats all of cases (a_1), (b) and (c) as examples of the 'so called "loophole" or "lacuna" in Lord Diplock's direction' and immediately follows this with the observation that the Diplock direction is not applicable to all cases,[47] so seems to be adding his voice to the requirement for modified directions in such cases.

Apart from the fact that there is not a uniform indication from their Lordships' speeches as to when directions need to be modified, there is certainly no provision of a single modified direction for any of the cases discussed. The mere possibility of multiple directions seems to be used as a convenient blanket to throw over all awkward cases, which can then be left to be dealt with in their own way and at their own time. But this only covers up the confusion, which is evident if we pause to consider the nature of the cases discussed.

Case (d) requires no modification to the Diplock direction in *Lawrence* because the risk does not arise from the manner of the defendant's driving.[48] Case (c) is a case of justified risk taking, and as such requires no modification to the law and direction found in *Lawrence*, since the justification of the risk must be taken to be an issue which preempts any need for the *Lawrence* direction.[49]

Case (b) is more interesting in that at its widest point[50] it could amount to a reinterpretation of the whole *Caldwell-Lawrence* approach to recklessness, in acknowledging that blameless inadvertence is not to count as recklessness, which would be diametrically opposed to the interpretation adopted in *Elliott v C*.[51] If this is the view of their Lordships then what they are proposing will not find fulfilment in multiple directions but in

---

43 [1992] 1 WLR 793, 796.
44 *ibid* at 806.
45 *ibid* at 811, 813.
46 *ibid* at 813, 816.
47 *ibid* at 819.
48 *Lawrence* [1981] 1 All ER 974, 982: ' ... the defendant was in fact driving the vehicle in such a manner as to create an obvious and serious risk ... '. Note also the preceding paragraph for further amplification of these words.
49 See Sir John Smith, Smith and Hogan's *Criminal Law* (10th edn, London, Butterworths, 2002) 77–78; Andrew Ashworth, *Principles of Criminal Law* (4th edn, Oxford, OUP, 2003) 181.
50 Lord Keith proposes a wide formula: 'where his capacity to appreciate risks was adversely affected by some condition not involving fault on his part'—[1992] 1 WLR 793, 796.
51 See further, n 89 below.

a statement of what amounts to recklessness which should enter the direction used in every case. A narrower interpretation would lock this into the limited scope of an automatism defence, which would not in any case require modification to the *Lawrence* approach, which again must be assumed to be operating with the backdrop of the general defences.

Cases (a$_1$) and (a$_2$) would *both* fall into the lacuna between the two limbs in Lord Diplock's test of recklessness.[52] This is so because the driver has neither failed to appreciate the existence of a possible risk, but by concluding that the perceived risk is not active nor has he decided to run it.[53] The problem of the lacuna in adopting recklessness as a test for culpable risk taking in relation to driving was recognised by Lord Atkin in *DPP v Andrews*.[54] Lord Atkin concluded that the culpable case that fell into the lacuna, (a$_2$), would have to be dealt with by recognising *a form of gross negligence that did not amount to recklessness*.[55] If the House of Lords in *Reid* is deciding to keep the culpable form of the lacuna case, (a$_2$), within recklessness, but not the excusable form, (a$_1$), then this amounts to a change for recklessness which will be of general effect, including cases falling under the Diplock directions. It cannot be accommodated by multiple directions but in a statement of what amounts to recklessness which again should enter the direction used in every case.

The approach of multiple directions with no foundational definition favoured in *Reid* causes confusion not only as to what the House of Lords has decided the law to be but also confusion as to how the law should give effect to their determinations.[56]

WIDE OPEN RECKLESSNESS IN *ADOMAKO*

Three of the key points accepted in *Reid* are reiterated by the House of Lords in *Adomako*:[57] the treatment of Lord Diplock's directions as 'specimen';[58] the enthusaism for an ordinary or dictionary meaning for recklessness;[59] and the endorsement of multiple directions.[60] But in

---

[52] Though not the other cases that Lord Browne-Wilkinson mistakenly runs together.
[53] For further discussion, see Smith and Hogan, above n 50, at 82–83.
[54] [1937] AC 576.
[55] *ibid* at 583. For further discussion, see n 68 below and accompanying text.
[56] Clear evidence of this state of confusion can be found in the observation by Lord Taylor CJ in *Prentice* (considered in the following section): 'the effect ... has been to create conflicting approaches and uncertainty .... The diversity of views is illustrated by the stances adopted in these three appeals which have not been consistent even among counsel for the Crown on the one hand and those for the defence on the other.'—[1993] 3 WLR 927, 936.
[57] [1994] 3 WLR 288.
[58] *ibid* at 296.
[59] *ibid* at 296, 297.
[60] *ibid* at 296, 297–98.

Adomako the House of Lords go even further than they did in *Reid*—even further than the Court of Appeal decision which is upheld in *Adomako*.[61]

The further widening of recklessness in *Adomako* is due to the House of Lords recognising a departure taken by the Court of Appeal from *Caldwell-Lawrence* recklessness for cases of gross negligence manslaughter, and then contrary to the caution expressed by the Court of Appeal embracing the different states of mind in that approach into the multiple direction, definition free, territory of recklessness.

It is true that both the Court of Appeal and the House of Lords follow an older House of Lords authority, *Andrews*,[62] but even in this respect the House in *Adomako* goes further. To appreciate the details of these moves, we need to commence with the Court of Appeal's approach to handling the convictions of gross negligence manslaughter of three doctors (of whom Adomako was one) and an electrician.

In *Prentice* the Court of Appeal decides to abandon as far as it can a *Caldwell* approach to recklessness for manslaughter in favour of the approach taken by the House of Lords in *Andrews* to gross negligence manslaughter. This it is able to do because the cases of three doctors and an electrician all involve 'expert fields where duty is undertaken' and can be regarded as distinct from cases of motor manslaughter where the prevailing House of Lords authority, *Seymour*[63] had held that the *Lawrence* test applied.[64] There are two significant implications of this move, both clearly recognised in the judgment of Lord Taylor CJ.

The first is that the emphasis in *Andrews*[65] on finding a level of culpability for gross negligence that is sufficiently grave as to amount to criminal conduct means that factors can be taken into account for this test that would be redundant to a straight application of the Diplock test:[66]

> In effect, therefore, once the jury found 'that the defendant gave no thought to the possibility of there being any such risk,' on the judge's directions [applying the Diplock test] they had no option but to convict. Mr Arlidge's point is that if the jury had been given the gross negligence test, they could properly have taken into account 'excuses' or mitigating circumstances in deciding whether the necessary high degree of gross negligence had been established. The question for the jury should have been whether, in the case

---

[61] The Court of Appeal's decision in *Prentice* [1993] 3 WLR 927, in which *Adomako* joined three other appeals involving cases of gross negligence manslaughter.
[62] [1937] AC 576.
[63] [1983] 2 AC 493—subsequently overruled in *Adomako* so as to remove the motor manslaughter exception.
[64] [1993] 3 WLR 927, 936–37.
[65] In Lord Atkin's famous passage: 'Simple lack of care such as will constitute civil liability is not enough: for purposes of the criminal law there are degrees of negligence: and a very high degree of negligence is required to be proved ... '—[1937] AC 576, 583.
[66] [1993] 3 WLR 927, 942—cp 950–51.

of each doctor ... [it] was grossly negligent to the point of criminality having regard to all the excuses and mitigating circumstances in the case.

It was precisely because the trial judge's directions in the case of two of the doctors and the electrician were considered to be tainted by the too restrictive approach of the Diplock test, in not allowing consideration of factors that might displace gross negligence,[67] that the appeals were allowed by the Court of Appeal.

The second implication recognised by Lord Taylor was that in a different respect the gross negligence test could be tighter than the Diplock test, in a way that had been recognised in *Andrews* by Lord Atkin, which we have already mentioned. It would allow for a grossly negligent assessment that no risk remained after having considered the risk, to ground liability despite the absence of recklessness.[68] This amounts to closing the *Caldwell* lacuna for culpable cases.

A third difference pointed out by Lord Taylor is less significant. This arises from the fact that Lord Diplock's 'obvious risk' relates to what is obvious to the ordinary prudent individual rather than to the prudent expert (electrician or doctor),[69] but this is less important because it can be dealt with by simply making explicit in Lord Diplock's formulation that the prudence expected is of the person possessing the expertise that the defendant purports to possess.[70]

---

[67] Significantly, at 936, Lord Taylor suggests that the 'modifying effects' of Reid have 'brought the *Lawrence/Caldwell* approach closer to the *Andrews* gross negligence test.'
[68] Lord Atkin in *Andrews* [1937] AC 576, 583 (see above, text at n 55); Lord Taylor CJ in *Prentice* [1993] 3 WLR 927, 933, 936, 947. There may be more to analyse here than simply closing the culpable sector of the lacuna, though that is certainly included. Part of the complexity relates to which risk we make the subject of the test. As Lord Taylor points out at 936, the initial risk to the patient in an emergency department is not created by the doctor's conduct but rather causes the doctor to respond. Nothing the doctor does can amount to taking that recognised risk. However, if the doctor's response is incompetent then that creates a further risk to the patient. If the doctor is ignorant of his incompetence and so fails to consider this second risk, or if (less likely) the doctor is aware of it but goes ahead anyway, then either way he can be caught by the Diplock test. But there may be cases where the doctor is aware of the risk to the patient of adopting the wrong procedure, seeks to avoid it but, with gross negligence, still gets it wrong. This is the standard lacuna case that would still be caught by the gross negligence test.
There is a further nice point to raise about the lacuna analysis itself. Can one not always proceed to a further level of risk, which the defendant has failed to consider? In the example considered, the doctor is aware of (1) the risk to the patient's health which brought him into the hospital, and (2) the further general risk of his choosing the wrong treatment, but fails to consider (3) the risk obvious to a competent doctor of choosing that particular wrong treatment which he erroneously believes to be correct. Leigh, above n 13, at 463 & 466–67, also concludes that the lacuna does not exist on the grounds: (a) Lord Diplock's lack of a comprehensive test for recklessness; (b) recklessness in the assessment of there being no risk (rather than in the subsequent course of conduct)—differing in perspective though not in impact from the view suggested here.
[69] [1993] 3 WLR 927, 936.
[70] As must be implicit in *Lawrence* in dealing with an ordinary prudent *motorist*. Cp the Law Commission proposal in this respect, which in the proposed gross carelessness variant of

Given these two significant differences between the gross negligence test and the *Caldwell* test, and recognising the confused state of recklessness in the criminal law, Lord Taylor exercised a sensible degree of caution in suggesting that the gross negligence test should not be labelled as a test of recklessness[71] (though among the possible states that it encompassed recklessness was included[72]).

So although the Court of Appeal in *Prentice* still favoured multiple directions with the 'judge tailor[ing] his summing-up to the specific circumstances of the particular case',[73] there is at least some effort to link the range of directions to different states of mind falling under a definition of gross negligence.[74] There is, furthermore, a sensitivity to the fact that different definitions may conflict and have different practical outcomes, evidenced not only in the careful distinction drawn between gross negligence and *Caldwell* recklessness, but also in the refusal to apply 'recklessness' as a label for gross negligence.

Adomako as the only unsuccessful appellant before the Court of Appeal, his trial judge having adequately directed the jury on the basis of gross negligence rather than *Caldwell* recklessness,[75] appealed further to the House of Lords. Not surprisingly the appeal was grounded on the argument that the *Caldwell-Lawrence* test should have been applied rather than the gross negligence test.[76] This was rejected by the House of Lords, which upheld the approach favoured by the Court of Appeal.[77]

---

involuntary manslaughter makes explicit reference in cl 2(2) to the accused's actual knowledge and any skill or experience he professed to have—Law Com No 237 (HC 171, 1996), *Legislating the Criminal Code: Involuntary Manslaughter.*

[71] [1993] 3 WLR 927, 937.

[72] This repeats Lord Atkin's view in *Andrews* [1937] AC 576, 583. Of the four states of gross negligence given by Lord Taylor ([1993] 3 WLR 927, 937 & 952), (a) and (b) amount to the two limbs of *Caldwell* recklessness with the important qualification of indifference added to (a); (c) covers the lacuna subject to there being a high degree of negligence; and (d) covers gross negligence in performing a duty. The list is explicitly stated to be not exhaustive. For further comment, see Graham Virgo, 'Back to Basics—Reconstructing Manslaughter' (1994) 53 *Cambridge Law Journal* 44, 46ff.

[73] [1993] 3 WLR 927, 937.

[74] The four cases, n 72 above, are offered 'without purporting to give an exhaustive definition' but it is still an attempt at definition. The point is reinforced by the subsequent observation on the distinction between two of the cases identified (at 952).

[75] [1993] 3 WLR 927, 947.

[76] [1994] 3 WLR 288, 292. The argument mounted by counsel for *Adomako* ([1995] 1 AC 171, 175–77) suggested that the 'gross' qualification on negligence was insufficient to capture the requisite state of mind and could be satisfied by what was regarded as a particularly bad case of 'ordinary human error or thoughtlessness'. The state of mind required for recklessness comprised 'actual disregard of, or indifference to' the risk—which, given counsel's reliance on the *Seymour* adoption of the *Caldwell-Lawrence* test for manslaughter seems to be an attempted paraphrase of that test. Counsel for the Crown argued (at 180) that the *Caldwell-Lawrence* test was not appropriate. Ironically, in the three successful appeals in the Court of Appeal the allegiances of defence and prosecution towards the two conflicting tests had been the other way around.

[77] [1994] 3 WLR 288, 297.

However, the House of Lords paid no heed to the careful consideration in the Court of Appeal of the distinction between gross negligence and *Caldwell* recklessness, and overrode Lord Taylor's caution in avoiding the use of 'recklessness' to cover gross negligence. Lord Mackay indicated that 'it is perfectly open to the trial judge to use the word "reckless" in its ordinary meaning'.[78]

In addition, Lord Mackay reiterated the *Reid* position on multiple directions and avoiding definitions, so pouring cold water on what attempt there had been in the Court of Appeal[79] to move towards a definition and classify different states of mind:[80]

> the circumstances to which a charge of involuntary manslaughter may apply are so various that it is unwise to attempt to categorise or detail specimen directions. ... Personally I would not wish to state the law more elaborately than I have done. In particular I think it is difficult to take expressions used in particular cases out of the context of the cases in which they were used and enunciate them as if applying generally.[81]

The practical outcome is that in any case of involuntary manslaughter the trial judge in his direction may, but need not, refer to recklessness; he need not, but may, use the *Lawrence* test.[82] Since the cases coming before the Court of Appeal and the House of Lords in *Prentice* and *Adomako*, which Lord Mackay had been dealing with, had been disposed of precisely on the basis as to whether the trial judge had or had not used one direction or another, specifically turning on the use of a *Caldwell-Lawrence* test or not, it is difficult to see how all this can be left to 'what appears appropriate in the circumstances of a particular case' to the trial judge.[83]

BACK TO *ELLIOTT v C* WITH *COLES*?

Some illustration of how exactly the poor trial judge is supposed to cope is provided by the next turn of events I wish to consider, in the case of *Coles*.[84] The trial judge in this case had been asked by counsel to modify

---

[78] *ibid* at 297.
[79] See above, in particular nn 72 & 74 and accompanying text.
[80] [1994] 3 WLR 288, 296, 297.
[81] If this last sentiment is fully adopted it is difficult to see what remains of case law, given that it is precisely the enunciation of general principles out of particular contexts on which it is based—on which, see John Finnis, *Natural Law and Natural Rights* (Oxford, Clarendon Press, 1980) 269.
[82] [1994] 3 WLR 288, 297—in the answer to the certified question.
[83] *ibid* at 298. Further obfuscation also remains as to the status of the lacuna, entrenching that found in *Reid*, since the advance made by the Court of Appeal in *Prentice* in dealing with this depended on a recognition of the distinction between gross negligence and recklessness.
[84] [1995] 1 Cr App R 157.

the *Caldwell* direction for arson so as to allow consideration of the particular capacity of the defendant to appreciate the risk. The trial judge refused, which the Court of Appeal upheld and in so doing reinstated the *Elliott v C* interpretation of the *Caldwell* test,[85] with an extremely narrow and very vague allusion to the possibility of special treatment for 'meritorious cases'.

The Court of Appeal's ability to conclude that *Caldwell* was 'still the governing authority in the present class of case'[86] is not altogether surprising in the light of how we have seen that the subsequent 'modifications' brought about in the appellate courts have been allowed to coexist amongst multiple directions in the absence of any definition of recklessness that would exert some sort of discipline over their specific applications—or, indeed, conflicts.

Before considering what room the Court of Appeal in *Coles* was prepared to allow for recent developments in 'meritorious cases', it is illuminating to consider part of the argument used to buttress the *Elliott v C* interpretation of *Caldwell*, for this illustrates the importance of operating with clear directions *and* definitions.

Having raised the issue of how 'the second leg of the *Caldwell* direction' should be interpreted, Hobhouse LJ then points out that Lord Diplock had 'declined to narrow the *definition* of the mental element in recklessness because neither aspect of his *definition* was less blameworthy than the other.'[87]

But this switch from direction to definition begs the whole question, in a far conciser fashion than did *Elliott v C*, so as to reach the same conclusion: that the direction could be hardened into a definition, which in turn determines that the same direction must be applied in other cases.

Yet we have seen that the *definition* that Lord Diplock was relying on was the popular or dictionary definition. Set aside for the moment Diplock's spurious form of a singular meaning for this definition, the point to be made here is that inasmuch as Diplock (unlike Kenny) was not prepared to narrow down this definition in order to provide a technical legal definition, so in drawing his directions from this source he was not elevating them to the status of competing definitions of recklessness. To put it bluntly, his directions were not definitions at all.[88]

We can now see exactly what was not less blameworthy than what: the alternative states of mind covered by the directions. These were discussed

---

[85] *ibid* at 167.
[86] *ibid* at 168.
[87] *ibid* at 163 (emphasis added).
[88] See above, text at nn 7–8 & 10–11. The confusion in appellation (from which easily proceeds an error of substance) is common. Lord Mackay in *Adomako* [1994] 3 WLR 288, 297, refers to 'the definition of recklessness in *Reg v Lawrence*'.

in some detail by Lord Diplock in the passage referred to by Hobhouse LJ. The statement quoted refers specifically to the preceding mention of cases where the defendant's 'mind was affected by rage or excitement or confused by drink' and 'for any of these reasons, he did not even trouble to give his mind to the question whether there was any risk'—all cases consistent with the view that the directions are governing cases in which the defendant himself had the capacity to appreciate the risk (when he was not affected by rage, etc). But if the Diplock test is seen as a suitable direction for this sort of case (rather than as a general definition of recklessness) then it is wholly inappropriate to treat it as a direction directly applicable to a different sort of case.

More specifically, this conclusion would deny the applicability of the Diplock test to encompass two different states of mind such that one *was* less blameworthy than the other. Yet this is precisely what is involved, in Goff LJ's reported view, in applying the *Caldwell* test in *Elliott v C*.[89]

What seemed to be particularly influential on the Court of Appeal in *Coles* was that it involved an unmeritorious defendant.[90] As to meritorious cases, the Court seems to acknowledge the exceptional cases discussed in *Reid*, and suggests that they can be dealt with as proposed by Lord Ackner as matters rebutting the normal inference that can be used in applying the Diplock test.[91] This wholly ignores the point made above that these exceptions require actual changes to be made to the Diplock test.

At the end of *Coles* we are left with the determination of merit by the trial judge as the arbiter of how a particular case is to be approached. That a body of legal knowledge has by now been displaced is evident. That decisions truly based on merit may arise out of this state of legal confusion is not. One practical upshot thus far is that when it comes to endangering life the courts judge the conduct of qualified adults

---

[89] See above, text at n 20 and following n 21; and for criticism of the failure to draw on Lord Diplock's insistence on equivalent culpability, Leigh's third proposition, above n 12, at 462. The contrast in culpability is also evident in Hobhouse LJ's judgment where on the same page he cites Lord Diplock's requirement in *Miller* that the risk 'must be one that would be obvious to *anyone*' (emphasis added) followed by the justices determination in *Elliott v C* that the risk 'would not have been obvious to her'—[1995] 1 Cr App R 157, 166. One must assume that directions based on such expansive requirements are dealing with the class of people with a normal capacity to appreciate risk, and accordingly applicable only to such persons. Otherwise, the existence of a single person to whom the risk was not obvious would render them nugatory.

[90] [1995] 1 Cr App R 157, 169. Since he had set fire to hay in a barn on which his friends were sleeping and had in evidence admitted to having taken the risk that they might not have woken up in time and got up, the case is quite different from *Elliott v C* in which the justices found the defendant did not have the capacity to appreciate the risk to her own life (at 160–61 & 166).

[91] [1995] 1 Cr App R 157, 165, 169. See above n 44.

(doctors or electricians) more leniently than the actions of incapable young persons.

REINFORCEMENT IN *GEMMELL AND RICHARDS*

Further endorsement by the Court of Appeal of the *Elliott v C* interpretation of *Caldwell* recklessness occurred in *Gemmell and Richards*,[92] a case in which two boys aged 11 and 12 had left some burning newspapers under a wheelie-bin, thinking they would burn themselves out on the concrete under the bin. Instead, the bin and adjoining buildings caught fire, causing close to £1m in damage. Given the ages of the defendants, this was an ideal opportunity to revisit the issue considered in *Elliott v C*, and to work through the modification to *Caldwell* brought about in *Reid*. There was every indication that the defendants in this case fell into the meritorious defendant rather than the unmeritorious defendant category of *Coles*.[93] However, the Court of Appeal completely ignored this aspect of *Coles*, and treated it as authority for taking *Reid* to be no obstacle to returning to the narrow interpretation of recklessness upheld in *Elliott v C*.[94]

Central to the wholehearted support by the Court of Appeal for *Elliott v C* is their reliance[95] on Goff's decisive misreading of the critical passage from Diplock, which we examined above.[96] The plausibility of this is left unquestioned, on the ground that *Elliott v C* had not been mentioned (despite being cited by counsel) in any of their Lordships speeches in *Reid*: 'If the House of Lords considered that [it was] wrong, it is most surprising that they did not say so.'[97] What was truly extraordinary about *Reid* is that the Law Lords failed to say *anything* about *Elliott v C*, as to whether they approved or disapproved of it, despite its being cited in argument, and in the face of their endorsing an approach which is clearly incompatible with the purely objective approach that case had taken.

If the Law Lords in *Reid* were selective about what they did and did not say, they clearly provided a precedent for style of judgment which the Court of Appeal in *Gemmell and Richards* seemed only too willing to follow, even if they wished to ignore the substance of *Reid*. The Court of Appeal were prepared to state that they were bound by two previous Court of Appeal decisions which supported the narrow interpretation of

[92] [2002] EWCA Crim 1992; [2003] 1 Cr App R 23.
[93] See n 90 and accompanying text above. That Gemmell and Richards were 'meritorious defendants' seems to have been recognised by the trial judge and jury, and to have been significant in influencing the thinking of the House of Lords subsequently (see [2003] UKHL 50 at [7], [33]).
[94] [2002] EWCA Crim 1992 at [14], [22].
[95] *ibid* at [9], [20]–[21].
[96] See text accompanying nn 25–27 above.
[97] [2002] EWCA Crim 1992 at 22.

recklessness in *Elliott v C*,[98] but were not prepared to discuss those parts of the two House of Lords cases, *Reid* and *Adomako*, which explicitly rejected a narrow version of the *Caldwell* test as the exclusive approach to recklessness. *Adomako* was wholly overlooked,[99] and any comments made by their Lordships in *Reid* which did indicate a modification to *Caldwell* were sidelined as obiter dicta, or distinguished as only being applicable to reckless driving offences.[100]

It is unjustifiable to render the modification to *Caldwell* in *Reid* as obiter, given that it constitutes the answer to the certified question of law that the appeal turned on. The question asked whether a direction should be given in terms of Lord Diplock's test 'without modification', to which the answer was given in the negative.[101] As we have seen, the *direction* given by Diplock in *Caldwell* and *Lawrence* constituted the ratio of each case, rather than a *definition* of recklessness which was lacking. There simply is no place to fall back on a definition approved in *Caldwell* or *Lawrence*, from which to contemplate modified directions in different circumstances. Modification to Lord Diplock's model direction accordingly amounts to an alteration to the *Caldwell* test itself. This point is wholly obfuscated by the Court of Appeal in *Gemmell and Richards*. First, it is spuriously claimed that the House of Lords in *Reid* had refused to depart from a *definition* of recklessness in *Lawrence*.[102] Then, the half-truth is offered, that the House of Lords in *Reid* 'endorsed the reasoning in *Caldwell* and *Lawrence*' to the effect that recklessness should extend beyond cases where there is an awareness of risk,[103] without providing the other half of the picture, that the extension to culpable indifference in *Caldwell* and *Lawrence* had itself been modified in *Reid*.

As to the tactic of distinguishing *Reid* as applying to driving offences but not to criminal damage, this goes against the House of Lords in *Lawrence* and *Reid* as taking the approach in *Caldwell* to apply inseparably to both. Moreover, the Court of Appeal in *Gemmell and Richards* refer at two points to the clear indication by Lord Diplock himself that in *Caldwell*, which is taken to be the source of the appropriate authority flowing through *Elliott v C*, the approach to recklessness is not peculiar to the offence of criminal damage.[104] The selectivity of the Court of Appeal is

[98] *ibid* at [21], the two cases of *Stephen Malcolm R* (1984) 79 Crim App R 334 and *Coles*.
[99] It was cited in argument, though not discusssed in the judgments, when the case reached the House of Lords.
[100] *ibid* at [13], [22].
[101] [1992] 1 WLR 793, 795, 797.
[102] [2002] EWCA Crim 1992 at 11. A refusal was made to depart from the *decision* in *Lawrence*— see, eg, [1992] 1 WLR 793, 812.
[103] *ibid*.
[104] [2002] EWCA Crim 1992 at [8], quoting Diplock in *Lawrence*, describing *Caldwell* as clarifying 'the concept of recklessness in criminal law'; and at [19], acknowledging the high level of generalisation of Diplock's test in *Caldwell*.

again illustrated by the fact that even where mention is made of this point, no discussion of its significance ensues.

AND ABANDONMENT IN *R v G*

The condition the law had reached after the Court of Appeal's decision in *Gemmell and Richards* was impossible to justify. Instead of the development of a coherent body of knowledge, we had witnessed the delivery of judgments in both appellate courts which had displayed a selective disregard for the law that had preceded them, and a diminished sense of responsibility for the course that the law was to follow. Cases had been disposed of, sometimes in open defiance of their merits, shorn up by arguments lacking in rigour, persisting in error, and distracted by confusion. The instability of the law over this period of time testified to its defects. The same approach to recklessness was taken by the House of Lords in *Caldwell* and *Lawrence* for criminal damage and reckless driving offences; a uniform approach recognised by the House of Lords in *Seymour*[105] (and the Privy Council in *Kong Cheuk Kwan*[106]) encompassing manslaughter;[107] multiple approaches were preferred by the House of Lords in *Reid* and *Adomako*.

At different stages it had been possible to find authorities linking five different approaches to recklessness to different groupings of offences within the criminal law: (1) *Cunningham* recklessness maintained for assaults;[108] (2) narrow *Caldwell* recklessness for criminal damage offences;[109] (3) modifiable *Caldwell* recklessness for reckless driving offences;[110] (4) adapted *Caldwell* recklessness for rape;[111] (5) recklessness

---

[105] [1983] 2 AC 493.

[106] (1985) 82 Cr App R 18.

[107] Though not so uniform as to include assaults, as eventually clarified by the House of Lords in *Savage, Parmenter* [1992] 1 AC 699.

[108] See n 107 above.

[109] Following the Court of Appeal in *Gemmell and Richards*.

[110] Following *Reid* as distinguished by the Court of Appeal in *Gemmell and Richards*.

[111] The recklessness required for rape has been considered by the Court of Appeal in a number of cases without achieving much clarity. In *Pigg* (1982) 74 Cr App R 352, *Caldwell* was applied with some modification for the offence; in *Satnam and Kewal S* (1984) 78 Cr App R 149, *Caldwell* was rejected as inapplicable; in *Breckenridge* (1984) 79 Cr App R 244, there was an attempt to reconcile the earlier authorities around the colloquial 'couldn't care less' test, which had also been put forward in *Satnam and Kewal*. Other formulations of a test have been provided in *Gardiner* [1994] *Criminal Law Review* 455—'carry on regardless', which was also adopted in *Taylor* (1985) 80 Cr App R 327, 332, in a combined 'couldn't care less but pressing on regardless' test; and, again in *Satnam and Kewal*—absence of a genuine belief in consent. The last mentioned formulation comes closest to the approach adopted in the Sexual Offences Act 2003, s 1(1)(c). The Act avoids the term recklessness in its definition of rape, preferring a requirement that 'A does not reasonably believe that B consents'. Nevertheless, this may be regarded as covering some of the ground that the Court of Appeal

as gross negligence for manslaughter.[112] This classification became even more refined for the period between the Court of Appeal's decision in *Prentice*[113] and the House of Lords' decision in *Adomako*. Manslaughter had to be split between 'motor manslaughter'[114] retained within the *Caldwell* class of recklessness due to the binding House of Lords' authority of *Seymour*, and the rest of manslaughter located within the gross negligence class—until the House of Lords in *Adomako* overruled *Seymour*.

Apart from the sheer inconsistency, across offences and over time, there was evident unfairness in the recognition given to the need to ameliorate the strict version of *Caldwell* recklessness in some cases (*Reid* modifying *Lawrence*, *Adomako* departing from *Seymour*), but, according to the Court of Appeal in *Gemmell and Richards* (as in *Coles*), no recognition afforded to the needs of defendants in criminal damage cases. As has already been mentioned, this meant in practice judging the criminal culpability of children whose activities endangered life, more harshly than professionally qualified adults. The particular status of the defendants as children in *Gemmell and Richards* raised broader concerns under the European Convention on Human Rights, and the Convention on the Rights of the Child. Although these concerns were not ultimately determinative of the direction the appeal took in the House of Lords, they cast further doubts on the acceptability of the *Caldwell* decision.[115] The appeal provided an ideal setting for a frontal assault on *Caldwell* itself.

---

has at one time or another labelled recklessness. For discussion, see Ashworth, above n 49, at 349, and 3rd edn (1999) at 356 (which discusses a text closer to the eventual wording of the new Act). For wider discussion of the appropriate form of recklessness for rape, see Celia Wells, 'Swatting the Subjectivist Bug' [1982] *Criminal Law Review* 209; Susan Estrich, 'Rape' (1986) 95 *Yale Law Journal* 1087, 1096–105; Caroline Forell and Donna Matthews, *A Law of Her Own: The Reasonable Woman as a Measure of Man* (New York, NY, New York University Press, 2000) ch 12; Jennifer Temkin, 'Rape and Criminal Justice at the Millenium' in Donald Nicolson and Lois Bibbings (eds), *Feminist Perspectives on Criminal Law* (London, Cavendish Publishing, 2000) 183, 189–90; Jennifer Temkin, *Rape and the Legal Process* (2nd edn, Oxford, OUP, 2002) 116–36; Mayo Moran, *Rethinking the Reasonable Person: An Egalitarian Reconstruction of the Objective Standard* (Oxford, OUP, 2003) 252–76, 291–301.

[112] Following *Adomako*.

[113] See n 61 above.

[114] Presumably including 'hydrofoil manslaughter'—see *Kong Cheuk Kwan*, n 106 above.

[115] Lord Steyn, [2003] UKHL 50 at [53], stated that Article 40.1 of the Convention on the Rights of the Child, 1989, which requires 'every child ... accused of ... infring[ing] the penal law to be treated in a manner consistent with the promotion of the child's sense of dignity and worth', was in itself sufficient to justify reconsidering *Caldwell*. Lord Steyn pointed out that the provision imposed substantive as well as procedural obligations. An attempt by counsel to invoke Article 6 of the ECHR in the Court of Appeal had foundered on the ground that it was not concerned with the fairness of substantive law, and in the House of Lords argument on the ECHR was not pursued beyond the written submissions (see [2003] UKHL 50 at [40]). (*Note continues overleaf.*)

The success of the appeal in the House of Lords produced a historic moment in the development of the criminal law of England and Wales. It was not simply a matter of the House of Lords overturning one of its previous decisions in a criminal case, which should have been rarity enough.[116] On this occasion, they did so after previously refusing to do so in an earlier case.[117] This might suggest that the appeal turned on a complex point of legal doctrine, or a convoluted issue of policy, on which it was difficult to reach a clear perspective. Yet the basis of their Lordships' decision was the recognition that in *Caldwell* their predecessors had committed a simple technical error. They had erroneously taken the Criminal Damage Act 1971 to have introduced a different concept of

An interesting line of argument on the ECHR that might have been developed is suggested by Ben Emmerson and Andrew Ashworth, *Human Rights and Criminal Justice* (London, Sweet & Maxwell, 2001) paras 11-04–11-08. This involves focusing on the age of the defendants, incorporating Article 14, and arguing that to attribute full criminal responsibility to a child aged 10 but no responsibility to a child just under 10 years of age, amounts to discrimination against the former child because he or she is treated in an arbitrary manner relative to the child in a similar position, and that treatment is disproportionate to any legitimate aim of the state. The argument based on Articles 6 and 14 was raised in *T and V v United Kingdom* (2000) 30 EHRR 121, but was not developed before the Court due to the success of an argument on Article 6 alone. As Emmerson and Ashworth record, there is also a dissenting view of five judges in that case finding that the imposition of full criminal responsibility on children aged 10 or 11 amounts to a breach of Article 3. Even if this line of argument does not directly engage with the substantive test of recklessness, at the very least it raises serious misgivings about the inability of the strict *Caldwell* test to take account of the particular abilities of young children to appreciate risks. In considering the need for procedural safeguards under Article 6, the Court in *T and V* stressed that it was 'essential that a child charged with an offence is dealt with in a manner which takes full account of his age, level of maturity and intellectual and emotional capacities' (*ibid* at para 86). The idea that these safeguards should be in place to ensure that the child is capable of participating in the proceedings, and then removed when it comes to determining the child's criminal responsibility, is inherently absurd.

[116] The statement issued by the House of Lords indicating their recognition of a power to depart from their own previous decisions, Practice Statement (Judicial Precedent) [1966] 1 WLR 1234, acknowledged 'the especial need for certainty as to the criminal law'. The particular import of this qualification, after there had been some overruling of criminal precedents, was discussed by Jim Harris, 'Towards Principles of Overruling—When Should a Final Court of Appeal Second Guess?' (1990) 10 *Oxford Journal of Legal Studies* 135, 172–77. Harris's attempted guidelines on this issue are difficult to square with the decision in the present case. There has been a growing boldness for judicial law-making in the criminal law generally. The notable example (not technically a case of overruling one of its own decisions) of establishing liability for marital rape by the House of Lords in *R v R* provoked the concerns of academic commentators—see John Smith's Comment on *R v R* [1992] *Criminal Law Review* 207, 208; Marianne Giles, 'Judicial Law-Making in the Criminal Courts: the case of marital rape' [1992] *Criminal Law Review* 407. And despite the expressed reluctance in the 1966 Statement, the Law Lords in the present case now seem more willing to correct what they perceive to be an error in the criminal law, than they are to correct an error relating to human rights—see *Kansal (No 2)* [2001] UKHL 64; [2001] 3WLR 1562 and *Benjafield* [2002] UKHL 2; [2002] 2 WLR 235, discussed in Deryck Beyleveld, Richard Kirkham and David Townend, 'Which presumption? A critique of the House of Lords' reasoning on retrospectivity and the Human Rights Act' (2002) 22 *Legal Studies* 185, 204–07.
[117] *Reid* [1992] 1 WLR 793, 800–01, 804–05, 811.

recklessness to that used for establishing malice within the previous law under the Malicious Damage Act 1861.

According to Lord Steyn, there was 'overwhelming evidence', which had been available to the House of Lords in *Caldwell*, that Parliament's intention in adopting the recommendations of the Law Commission was to modernise the language but retain the same mental element for the offence of criminal damage as had been used in the previous law. Indeed, Steyn considered that the evidence was so overwhelming as to be described as 'all one way', and on this ground he reached the 'inescapable' conclusion, that the interpretation of the 1971 Act in *Caldwell* 'was beyond the range of feasible meanings.'[118] Similarly, Lord Bingham, with whom Lord Browne-Wilkinson concurred, regarded the House of Lords in *Caldwell* as having committed a 'clearly demonstrable error.'[119] Lord Hutton concurred with both Steyn and Bingham. Lord Rodger concurred with Bingham subject to some qualifying comments.[120]

The simple error found to have been made in *Caldwell* is easy enough to grasp, and in itself invites no comment. It was raised by academic commentators immediately after the decision in *Caldwell* became known.[121] What does arouse comment is the idea that such an obvious error could have been persisted in for so long, even after an explicit invitation to correct it.[122] And this in turn raises the possibility that perhaps there is another way of regarding the wording of the 1971 Act, which would avoid the stark denunciation of the approach taken in *Caldwell*.[123] The heart of the matter is whether the words of the Act are to be taken at face value and left to the judges to clarify their meaning, or whether the judges are bound to search beyond the words for the meaning that Parliament intended to place upon them. Lord Diplock in *Caldwell* may have preferred the former option.[124] The Law Lords have now decided otherwise.

---

[118] *R v G and another* [2003] UKHL 50; [2003] 3 WLR 1060 at [50]–[51].

[119] *ibid* at [29].

[120] *ibid* at [71]. Significantly, these comments include (at [64], [68]–[70]) a rather softer approach to the range of plausible interpretations of the 1971 Act.

[121] Lord Steyn refers, *ibid* at [50], to John Smith's Comment on *Caldwell* [1981] *Criminal Law Review* 393, as an example.

[122] See n 118 above.

[123] A possibility acknowledged in the comment raised by Lord Rodger, referred to in n 120 above.

[124] As suggested by Lord Rodger, *ibid* at 64. Rodger refers to Diplock's speech in *Black-Clawson Ltd v Papierwerke Waldhof-Aschaffenburg AG* [1975] AC 591, 636–37, as evidence of the view which prevailed at the time of *Caldwell*, which strictly limited resort to extrinsic materials in order to discover the intention of Parliament. Diplock's view that, 'Parliament, under our constitution, is sovereign only in respect of what it expresses by the words used in the legislation it has passed' (at 638), commanded the respect of the majority in *Black-Clawson* but failed to prevail in *Pepper v Hart* [1993] 1 All ER 42, where the House of Lords liberalised the use of extrinsic materials. For the impact of this case on the use of reports of advisory committees, see John Bell and George Engel, Cross's *Statutory Interpretation* (3rd edn, London,

Given the awful instability, confusion, and injustice that have been the consequences of Lord Diplock's approach to recklessness in *Caldwell*, the desirability of overturning *Caldwell* may be regarded as unquestionable. The significant question to ask, now that this change in direction has been recognised, is what contribution their Lordships have made by their decision towards obtaining at last a coherent body of knowledge in the criminal law. We might reasonably have hoped that the case to overturn *Caldwell* would bring in a calmer, clearer, and fairer approach to recklessness in the criminal law. There are three aspects of the leading speeches of Bingham and Steyn which indicate serious failings with regard to this wider aspiration. The first cause for concern is Bingham's understanding of mens rea. The second is his restriction of the overruling of *Caldwell* recklessness to the case of *Caldwell* itself, so leaving *Caldwell* recklessness in *Lawrence*, and any offence other than criminal damage, untouched. The third cause for concern is Steyn's approval of the outcome of *R v G* in terms of its congruence with *DPP v Morgan*.[125] We shall explore each of these three aspects in some detail, as a way of examining the general state of the criminal law in the aftermath of this latest House of Lords decision.

THE UNDERSTANDING OF MENS REA

The decision to overrule *Caldwell* involved two stages. The first amounted to identifying the simple error held to have been committed in the interpretation of recklessness under the 1981 Act. The second stage required their Lordships to find grounds for using their power under the 1966 Practice Statement[126] to depart from an earlier decision they now considered to be wrong. Of the four reasons provided by Bingham for doing so,[127] his understanding of the basic principle of the criminal law, *actus non facit reum nisi mens sit rea*, constituted the first ground[128] and came into the fourth.[129] Moreover, it was also cited by Bingham[130] as being a

---

Butterworths, 1995) 160–61. For wider discussion of the use of extrinsic material, surveying a number of Commonwealth jurisdictions, see Jim Evans, 'Controlling the Use of Parliamentary History' (1998) 18 *New Zealand Universities Law Review* 1. The article concludes (at 45) that the cases surveyed 'display sufficient errors to give rise to considerable disquiet.'

[125] [1976] AC 182.
[126] See n 116 above.
[127] [2003] UKHL 50 at [31]–[35].
[128] *ibid* at [32].
[129] *ibid* at 35. The error of interpretation was only considered serious enough to be a reason because it offended principle—the principle being that which constituted the first reason. (Bingham's second and third reasons were the unfairness the decision had caused, and the criticism of academics, judges and practitioners, that it had attracted.)
[130] *ibid* at 38: 'it does not meet the objection of principle'.

ground for rejecting the refinement to the *Caldwell* test that had been proposed by Glanville Williams[131] and adopted by the Magistrates (prior to being overruled by the Divisional Court) in *Elliott v C*: the risk would have been obvious to the actual defendant if he or she had stopped to consider it.

Bingham's understanding of this principle may, accordingly, be regarded as a turning point in his judgment. It is built upon the strict subjectivist view of mens rea. According to this view, mens rea is limited to a subjective condition found in a cognitive state. The exclusive link of subjective conditions to cognitive states within this viewpoint makes 'cognitivist' an alternative (and perhaps more accurate) appellation to 'strict subjectivist'.[132] In practice this limits mens rea to the subjective will of the particular defendant found in intention, or the subjective awareness of risk by the particular defendant found in recklessness.[133] In general, whether for strict subjectivists or others, the role performed by mens rea in the basic principle cited by Bingham is to establish the culpability[134] of the defendant before convicting him or her of a crime. Bingham follows the strict subjectivists in restrictively associating culpability with either an intention to bring about an injurious result or an awareness of

---

[131] Glanville Williams, 'Recklessness Redefined' (1981) 40 *Cambridge Law Journal* 252, 268–72.
[132] See further, John Stannard, 'Subjectivism, Objectivism, and the Draft Criminal Code' (1985) 101 *Law Quarterly Review* 540. The most influential strict subjectivists (or cognitivists) for English law in recent times have been Glanville Williams and John Smith, but significantly for the development of recklessness, their number has included JWC Turner, the editor of the edition of *Kenny's Outlines* (above n 5) followed in *Cunningham*. Further articulation of the subjectivist position has been provided by Andrew Ashworth, notably in his 'The elasticity of mens rea' in Colin Tapper (ed), *Crime, Proof and Punishment: Essays in Memory of Sir Rupert Cross* (London, Butterworths, 1981); and 'Belief, Intent, and Criminal Liability' in John Eekelaar and John Bell (eds), *Oxford Essays in Jurisprudence, Third Series* (Oxford, Clarendon Press, 1987).
[133] For present purposes we can keep things simple. Awareness of risk reaching a high degree of probability, eg, foresight of an outcome as a virtual certainty if one follows *Nedrick* [1986] 1 WLR 1025, may be regarded as intention, but such formulations only play with the classifications within a strict subjectivist approach.
[134] George Fletcher, 'The Theory of Criminal Negligence: A Comparative Analysis' (1971) 119 *University of Pennsylvania Law Review* 401, 411–14, traces this role back to the earliest statement of the principle in Coke's *Institutes* (although Turner, above n 5, at 12, sought to trace its origins to Augustine). Fletcher suggests that this role is denied by the strict subjectivists who limit mens rea to a mental (cognitive) state. Yet even for these writers, the limitation to such a mental state is for the purpose of establishing an appropriate basis for culpability. Fletcher himself (at 416) cites Jerome Hall, 'Negligent Behaviour Should Be Excluded from Penal Liability' (1963) 63 *Columbia Law Review* 632, 635–36, to this effect. Similarly, Turner, whom Fletcher cites, at 412, as adopting 'the view that *mens rea* means nothing more than the state of mind proscribed by the statute', took the view in his edition of Kenny, above n 5, at 24, that mens rea constituted by a 'subjective element of foresight' was the historical and logical result of recognising that mens rea expressed the moral culpability of the defendant. Fletcher's confusion seems to turn on treating mens rea as synonymous with culpability in general (thus including such issues as duress or necessity, at 414), as 'equivalent to the normative concept of culpability' (*ibid*), rather than as performing the necessary though not sufficient role of establishing culpability.

the risk that such a result might occur, ie, *Cunningham* recklessness. The boundaries of *Caldwell* recklessness are then considered to offend this basic principle because they permit the conviction of those who are not culpable.[135]

Despite the impressive support for strict subjectivism,[136] Bingham is mistaken in taking this position for two reasons, which are in fact alluded to in the supporting speech of Lord Rodger. In passing, one may point out that these comments by way of qualification in Rodger's speech, if they were made in a less allusive manner, would do much to negate the explicit agreement given to Bingham's speech.[137] The two reasons for regarding the strict subjectivist position as untenable are provided respectively by the practice of the law and by academic discussion. First, the practical implications of taking up the strict subjectivist position would be to regard all major offences which could be established without the requirement of an intention to bring about an injurious result or an awareness of the risk that such a result might occur, as lacking mens rea, and hence as being capable of being committed without proof of fault on the part of the defendant. In effect, such offences would be relegated to the category of strict liability offences. It is clear from the speeches in *R v G* that these offences would include reckless driving offences in general, and causing death by reckless driving in particular, since *Caldwell* recklessness in *Lawrence* and *Reid* is specifically upheld.[138] It is also clear by implication from their Lordships' failure to discuss *Adomako* (despite its being cited in argument), that the broad approach to gross negligence established in that case is to be retained for manslaughter. Furthermore, if we include the offence of rape in our survey, it may not be clear from the authorities exactly what has been required in order to establish this offence, but it is clear that something other than the two cognitive states favoured by the strict subjectivists has sufficed, and will suffice under the Sexual Offences Act 2003.[139] If we took Bingham's support of the strict subjectivist position seriously, it would follow that liability for the serious offences of causing death by reckless driving, manslaughter and rape has been established under English law without any requirement of mens rea, and without any need to find fault on the part of the defendant. Yet it is incontrovertible that in none of the cases in which the elements of these

---

[135] [2003] UKHL 50 at [32].
[136] See n 132 above.
[137] For the explicit agreement, 'subject to these comments', see [2003] UKHL 50 at [71]; for the allusive comments, see *ibid* at [68]–[69].
[138] *ibid* at [25], [28]. The practical implications of upholding *Lawrence* are severely limited by the replacement of the reckless driving offences by offences of dangerous driving under the Road Traffic Act 1991, s 1. Dangerous driving is defined in accordance with standards of 'a competent and careful driver'.
[139] See n 111 above.

offences have been discussed, has it ever been held that no mens rea is required, or that liability may be established without fault. And this includes the case of *R v G* itself.

It is, accordingly, quite proper for Rodger to qualify Bingham's assertion that the only ways of establishing the culpability of the defendant are to establish one or other of the two cognitive states preferred by the strict subjectivists,[140] by the observation that 'it is equally clear that other views are not only possible but have actually been adopted by English judges'.[141] Rodger also refers in his comments to the other reason for finding the strict subjectivist position untenable. Its basic premises have been 'demolished' within academic discussion.

Rodger cites[142] an essay by Herbert Hart,[143] though this is only one of a number of academic sources[144] which can be relied on for undermining the twin assumptions of the strict subjectivist position: that only a cognitive state may be regarded as a subjective state; and, that only a cognitive state may be regarded as a form of mens rea (and hence establish culpability). It is worth repeating some of the more relevant points from Hart's essay here. Before doing so, it is important to note that Hart's essay discusses 'negligence' rather than 'recklessness', but the subject of his discussion is inadvertent risk taking, and the burden of his essay is to establish the basis for a form of culpable inadvertence which might be appropriately used to establish criminal liability. For present purposes it does not matter whether one prefers to label a culpable form of inadvertent risk taking as negligence or as recklessness. However, in the concluding section I shall comment more fully on the relationship between *Caldwell* recklessness and gross negligence.

Hart attacks the restrictive approach to mens rea favoured by the strict subjectivists by arguing for an extension 'beyond the "cognitive" element of knowledge or foresight, so as to include the capacities and powers of normal persons to think about and control their conduct'.[145] This extends our understanding of responsible conduct beyond the limitations imposed by the strict subjectivists, but, as Hart points out, it is a notion of responsible conduct that we are already familiar with in everyday contexts. A striking illustration of the point, used by Hart, is the case of

---

[140] [2003] UKHL 50 at [32].
[141] *ibid* at [68]. Although at [68] the times of these judicial positions are somewhat remotely considered as having occurred 'over the centuries', by [69] Rodger comes up to date with a reference to *Lawrence* and *Reid*.
[142] *ibid*.
[143] HLA Hart, 'Negligence, *Mens Rea* and Criminal Responsibility' in *Punishment and Responsibility: Essays in the Philosophy of Law* (Oxford, Clarendon Press, 1968); previously published in AG Guest (ed), *Oxford Essays in Jurisprudence* (Oxford, Clarendon Press, 1961).
[144] For other examples, see Fletcher, above n 134; Stannard, above n 132.
[145] Hart, above n 143, at 140.

a workman mending a roof who throws slates onto the street below without bothering to check whether anyone is passing at the time.[146]

As to the requirement that culpability must be linked to the individual defendant and so involve a subjective state, Hart is prepared to retain an element of subjectivity (if that is the terminology preferred[147]), but he forcefully denies the strict subjectivists' assertion that this can only be satisfied by a cognitive state. Instead, individual defendants' circumstances and characteristics are allowed for by insisting that they possessed, 'when they acted, the normal capacities, physical and mental, for doing what the law requires and abstaining from what it forbids, and a fair opportunity to exercise these capacities.'[148]

At the core of Hart's argument is the simple recognition that more than one alternative is available to the subjective awareness, or advertence to risk, required by the strict subjectivists.[149] Inadvertence may be either non-culpable 'mere inadvertence', or culpable inadvertence where the defendant has 'failed to comply with a standard of conduct' required of him.[150]

Of course, it would be possible for the law to impose a standard of conduct which made no allowance for the individual defendant's circumstances and characteristics. Standards may be objective or subjective, or, in order to avoid the confusion associated with these terms, as Hart proposes, we may distinguish between 'invariant standards' and 'individualised conditions of liability'.[151] Hart recognises that the distinction may be a matter of degree. No legal system could individualise standards to take account of *all* the possible circumstances and characteristics of each defendant.[152] Nevertheless, Hart provides us with the general form of culpable inadvertence that he considers appropriate for use in the criminal law:[153]

(i)   Did the accused fail to take those precautions which any reasonable man with normal capacities would in the circumstances have taken?

(ii) Could the accused, given his mental and physical capacities, have taken those precautions?

If, as it seems, Bingham's principal reason for rejecting *Caldwell* recklessness (and a reason for rejecting the variant suggested by Williams) is that

---

[146] *ibid* at 147, 149.
[147] Hart sees a danger of the use of this terminology obscuring the issue, *ibid* at 153.
[148] *ibid* at 152.
[149] *ibid* at 146–48.
[150] *ibid* at 147–48.
[151] *ibid* at 154.
[152] *ibid* at 155.
[153] *ibid* at 154.

it offends the principle of *actus non facit reum nisi mens sit rea*, then his judgment founders on a misunderstanding of that principle. Moreover, by adopting a strict subjectivist position at a key point in his argument in order to overturn *Caldwell*, Bingham lands himself in inconsistency, having stated[154] that he wishes to uphold *Caldwell* recklessness for reckless driving offences without suggesting that these offences should be understood as requiring no mens rea.

LINKING RECKLESSNESS TO THE OFFENCE

If the restriction of the overruling of *Caldwell* recklessness to the case of *Caldwell* itself, so leaving *Caldwell* recklessness in offences other than criminal damage untouched, was not based on the unacceptable proposition that these other offences were to be understood as requiring no mens rea, how is it to be explained? To be fair, the idea that *Caldwell* recklessness could be modified according to the offence involved did not originate in *R v G* but in *Reid*. However, their Lordships in *Reid* did not go so far as to suggest that it could be dispensed with altogether for some offences but not others. Nevertheless, it appears that the thinking present in *Reid* which supported modifying *Caldwell* recklessness in accordance with the offence, was borrowed in *R v G* to support a selective rejection of *Caldwell* recklessness depending on the offence.[155] In either case, the thinking is flawed. This can be demonstrated by a careful consideration of the approach taken in *Reid*.

It is unquestionably a legitimate exercise, having recognised that different concepts of recklessness might be employed in the criminal law, to seek to discover which concept has historically been introduced into the law for a particular offence. Hence, we might discover that the concept of recklessness introduced by the Criminal Damage Act 1971 for criminal damage differed from the concept used in the Road Traffic Acts for driving offences. This exercise, involving what we may refer to as *the historical context*, forms one aspect of the discussion of offence-sensitive recklessness in *Reid*.[156] This is not the aspect we are interested in.

The modification of *Caldwell* recklessness in an offence-sensitive manner in *Reid* turns more on an exercise undertaken *after* it has been recognised that *Caldwell* recklessness is normally the appropriate concept of recklessness for the offence in question. The attempt to justify this

---

[154] [2003] UKHL 50 at [25], [28].
[155] Significantly, Bingham cites an offence-sensitive approach in *Reid* ([2003] UKHL 50 at [25]) prior to emphasisng (*ibid* at [28]) that his own approach should not be regarded as affecting driving offences.
[156] See [1992] 1 WLR 793, 807 (*per* Lord Goff), 816–17 (*per* Lord Browne-Wilkinson).

exercise in *Reid* is made by suggesting that there is something intrinsic to the particular offence which makes it necessary to modify the requirements of *Caldwell* recklessness in order to fit the offence properly. So, we find Lord Ackner in *Reid* suggesting that damaging another's property in the offence of criminal damage is already illegal (before we find it criminal), whereas driving a car is a (lawful) ordinary everyday activity; and so, the role performed by recklessness in the two offences is intrinsically different, focusing more on the conduct in reckless driving (to turn ordinary conduct into unlawful conduct), and more on the state of mind in criminal damage (to turn unlawful conduct into criminal conduct). Ackner concludes that *the context of the offence* may modify the meaning of recklessness.[157]

This thinking is flawed because it diverts attention from the real issue, which, when considering what form of mens rea is appropriate for a particular offence, is the issue of what is the basis for establishing culpability for that offence. For this issue, it is irrelevant whether the conduct involved in the offence is ordinarily lawful or not. Driving a car may be ordinarily lawful conduct, damaging another's property may be ordinarily unlawful, but the point of establishing what is required for mens rea, in both offences, is to mark out the difference between culpable criminal conduct and conduct that is harmful and undesirable but not criminally culpable. The need to make this distinction for a driving offence indicates that we have already passed beyond the ordinary conduct that is the subject of the unhelpful distinction between ordinarily lawful and ordinarily unlawful.[158] For we are now dealing with the conduct that was ordinarily lawful (because it is harmless) in the extraordinary circumstances where it causes (or is likely to cause) harm to others. Hence the subject matter for the issue with which we are concerned in the two offences is, on the one side ordinarily harmful conduct, and on the other side extraordinarily harmful conduct. The common issue is when D should be regarded as culpable for his harmful (or potentially harmful) conduct towards others.

The issue, of course, can be resolved in different ways. And however it is resolved, reference will need to be made to the specific elements of the conduct in question. But there is nothing intrinsic about the elements of one offence as opposed to another that requires the issue to be resolved in

---

[157] *ibid* at 805. Similarly, Browne-Wilkinson, at 817C.
[158] The distinction is not only unhelpful in distracting our attention from the proper point of focus, but also at times inaccurate. Ackner fails to address the common occurrence in cases of *reckless* criminal damage, that D's conduct will not amount to ordinarily unlawful conduct (directed at harming V's property) but ordinarily lawful conduct undertaken in a manner which indirectly causes harm to another's property. Playing football near a greenhouse, lighting a bonfire next to a haystack, demonstrating martial arts next to a plate glass window, are examples that spring to mind.

a particular way. In relation to the two offences of criminal damage and reckless driving, this can be demonstrated by noting that the model directions embracing *Caldwell* recklessness for criminal damage in *Caldwell*, only needed modifying with respect to the specific elements of the proscribed conduct for reckless driving, when *Caldwell* recklessness was employed in *Lawrence* for that offence. Similarly, we could take Hart's approach to culpable inadvertence reproduced at the end of the previous section, and fit within it the elements of either offence. There is nothing intrinsic to any of these elements that requires us to modify Hart's basic approach. Furthermore, we could take a modification to *Caldwell* recklessness approved in *Reid* for reckless driving, and use the same modification for the offence of criminal damage. For example, we might take the modification to *Caldwell* recklessness considered by Lord Keith for reckless driving, 'where the driver acted under some understandable and excusable mistake or where his capacity to appreciate risks was adversely affected by some condition not involving fault on his part',[159] and decide that the same modification should be used for the offence of criminal damage—requiring us only to substitute 'defendant' for 'driver'.

Two things should be stressed at this point. First, I have not demonstrated that the issue of what is the basis for establishing culpability for an offence, must be resolved in the same way for every offence. I have simply shown that there is nothing intrinsic about the element of any offence that requires us to resolve this issue in a particular way for that offence. We may decide to resolve the issue differently for different offences, but such a decision needs to be viewed for what it is, not concealed under the pretence that the particular form of mens rea selected is somehow necessarily connected to the kind of conduct which the offence deals with. A great failing of the speeches in *R v G*,[160] in distinguishing the approach they have adopted in overruling *Caldwell* recklessness to the offence of criminal damage, is to close off a proper discussion, both of the basis for rejecting it for criminal damage and of the basis for keeping it for other offences.

The second thing to stress is that when the issue is resolved in the same way for different offences, this may still leave open important sub-issues that cannot be dealt with uniformly for different offences. One way of putting this is to say that the issue is resolved by selecting what questions (sub-issues) the court is now required to ask about the defendant, but this does not resolve which answers the court will find acceptable.[161]

---

[159] *ibid* at 796.

[160] On this point, Rodger provides no redeeming comment, referring only to 'the context of reckless driving', [2003] UKHL 50 at [69].

[161] For further discussion of the different roles of posing questions and providing answers found within legal materials, see ch 1.

For example, if we take Lord Keith's proposed modification to *Caldwell* recklessness considered two paragraphs above, and decide to use it for criminal damage as well as reckless driving, we will still have to decide what amounts to an 'understandable and excusable mistake' in the context of criminal damage. This will clearly not be answerable by referring to what we have decided to accept as an 'understandable and excusable mistake' in the context of reckless driving. There is then a residual offence-specific element of recklessness, but this should not be confused with an offence-specific requirement to select a particular form of mens rea. Just how important this offence-specific element is, and how it can be openly accommodated in a definition of recklessness within the criminal law, are matters that can be explored further in considering the third aspect of the leading speeches in *R v G* which provides cause for concern.

BRINGING IN *MORGAN*

The third cause for concern is Lord Steyn's approval[162] of the outcome of *R v G* in terms of its congruence with *DPP v Morgan*.[163] One startling feature of this remark is that it clothes *Morgan* with a respectability that it has long since lost.[164] Another is that it ignores the limited impact of *Morgan* on the Court of Appeal's attempts to clarify the mens rea for rape.[165] Yet another is that it overlooks the recent statutory reform of rape, which takes an approach diametrically opposed to *Morgan*.[166] However, in terms of failing to provide a coherent body of knowledge for the criminal law, the most troubling feature of Steyn's remark is that it compresses the issue of mens rea, or culpability, with the doctrine of mistake.[167] Since this is a failing of *Morgan* itself, we need to return to that case in order to see if it is possible to extricate ourselves from this particular mess.

---

[162] [2003] UKHL 50 at [55].
[163] [1975] 2 All ER 347.
[164] For a concise statement, see Temkin (2000), above n 111, at 189. For more detailed discussion, see Temkin (2002), above n 111, at 116–22, 127–36.
[165] See the cases discussed in n 111 above. The strongest influence of *Morgan* is found in *Satnam and Kewal S*, where the court purports to follow *Morgan* and reject *Caldwell*, (1984) 78 Cr App R 149, 154. Yet even here the finer text of the judgment moves from an acceptance of the *Morgan* doctrine that consideration of whether D's belief was genuine is sufficient, to consideration of the evidence for such a belief in terms of whether 'he had reasonable grounds for such a belief' (at 155). Weighing the evidence by this objective standard may permit the jury to conclude he had no genuine belief. This is stated by the Court of Appeal immediately before providing the 'couldn't care less' test (*ibid*).
[166] See n 111 above.
[167] Steyn, having made no reference to any of the materials dealing with the mens rea of rape, backs up *Morgan* by citing a number of cases on mistake, [2003] UKHL 50 at 55.

At the core of *Morgan* is the 'inexorable logic' of Lord Hailsham, captured in the following two extracts from his speech:[168]

> Once one has accepted ... that the guilty state of mind is an intention to commit it, it seems to me to follow as a matter of inexorable logic that there is no room either for a 'defence' of honest belief or mistake, or of a defence of honest and reasonable belief and mistake. Either the prosecution proves that the accused had the requisite intent, or it does not.
>
> ...
>
> I am content to rest my view of the instant case on the crime of rape by saying that it is my opinion that the prohibited act is and always has been intercourse without the consent of the victim and the mental element is and always has been the intention to commit that act, *or the equivalent intention* of having intercourse willy-nilly not caring whether the victim consents or no. A failure to prove this involves an acquittal *because the intent, an essential ingredient, is lacking.* (emphasis added)

The logic is inexorable if we accept Hailsham's premises. One of the premises is bland and uncontroversial: an intention to bring about an outcome of one's conduct involves a belief that the circumstances required for that outcome exist or might exist (and so, a belief that the circumstances do not exist negatives that intention[169]).

Hailsham's other premise, found in the second italicised part of the extract above, is more interesting: intention is an essential ingredient of rape. At the time of *Morgan* the statutory provision on rape, in the Sexual Offences Act 1956, s 1, made it an offence for 'a man to rape a woman' but provided no definition of rape. Nevertheless, it was accepted that at common law rape required mens rea, and the mens rea could be satisfied by intention or recklessness. This much is clear in the section of Hailsham's speech commencing with the first italicised part above, which ends in something close to the more recent 'couldn't care less' test of recklessness. So a preliminary issue (arguably, the issue) in *Morgan* was what was the precise form of recklessness appropriate for the mens rea of rape, or, in other words, what was the basis for establishing culpability for that offence.

This issue was suppressed by Hailsham (in the first italicised part of the extract above) treating the recklessness for rape as intention, which allowed him to reach his premise that intention is an essential ingredient of rape. Accepting the premise sets up the inexorable logic, by which we reach, through a general principle of the doctrine of mistake that an actual[170] mistake (however unreasonable) negates intention, the conclusion

---

[168] [1975] 2 All ER 347, 361–62.
[169] *ibid* at 361: 'honest belief clearly negatives intent'.
[170] The adjective preferred by Hailsham, 'honest', is purely rhetorical.

that any mistaken belief that the victim consented will acquit a defendant of rape. The real issue of what is the basis for establishing culpability for rape has not even been raised.

There are two features of Hailsham's transformation of recklessness into intention which need to be considered. First, the object of the italicised intention in the extract above is the reckless conduct (having intercourse not caring whether the victim consents). For the purposes of specifying the mens rea of an offence this is superfluous to the recklessness already attributed to the conduct. By this device any mens rea constituted by a form of recklessness could be represented as requiring an intention, by simply interpolating the intention before the conduct that is being engaged in recklessly. It is as significant for the purposes of determining the mens rea of an offence, as would be an intention to engage in intentional conduct. What this supernumerary intention relates to is not the form of mens rea but a background assumption that the defendant's conduct is voluntary. It is only inviting confusion to bring this further intention into a discussion of mens rea.[171] Quite clearly, in the particular problem that Hailsham is dealing with, a mistaken belief that the victim is consenting does not negate the defendant's *intention to engage in the conduct*. It does negate, as we have accepted above, an *intention to have intercourse without consent*. Whether it negates recklessness as to having intercourse without consent, remains for the moment an open question whose answer depends on what we understand by recklessness.

The second feature of Hailsham's transformation is his assertion of equivalence between the intention to commit the act of having intercourse without the victim's consent, and the intention of having intercourse not caring whether the victim consents. If these two intentions are both taken to be the supernumerary intentions to engage in the conduct that is intentional/reckless as regards the victim's consent, then they are equivalent in that they both indicate the defendant's conduct is voluntary, but they are irrelevant to the issue of mens rea.

The more interesting possibility to consider is to take the first intention as being the mens rea intention covering having intercourse without consent,[172] to ignore the supernumerary intention in the second case as an unhelpful distraction, and then to make the comparison with the recklessness in the second case. Is it possible to consider a mens rea requirement of recklessness as being in some sense equivalent to a mens rea requirement of intention? The answer to this question will depend on the

---

[171] For general observations, see Hart, above n 143, at 140–45.
[172] Hailsham's wording, in the passage excerpted at n 168, is ambiguous. The words 'the intention to commit that act' could refer to the supernumerary intention to engage in the conduct, or to the mens rea intention to have intercourse without the consent of the victim. This ambiguity assists the confusion, and promotes the suggestion that what is being found comparable are two mens rea states.

criterion of equivalence *and* on what form of recklessness we take to be appropriate. One way of establishing equivalence would be to take the criterion to be whether the defendant is prepared by his conduct to expose the victim to an unreasonable risk of harm, and then to stipulate that the appropriate form of recklessness is *Cunningham* recklessness, requiring the defendant's awareness that his conduct exposes the victim to an unreasonable risk of harm. Since this criterion is also met where the defendant engages in the same conduct[173] with the intention of bringing about that harm to the victim, we have established an equivalence between the two forms of mens rea. This way of establishing an equivalence in culpability between two different forms of mens rea will be considered more fully in the concluding section. For the moment I want to pursue what is a more pertinent point in considering how Hailsham in *Morgan* closed off discussion of the mens rea issue: how different forms of recklessness might or might not be susceptible to the ineluctable logic of his argument. In other words, I want to consider what forms of recklessness satisfy a *logical equivalence* with intention within the argument he uses.

For this requirement to be satisfied we must be able to substitute a form of recklessness for intention in the first of Hailsham's premises, considered above.[174] This will create the proposition: recklessness in bringing about an outcome of one's conduct involves a belief that the circumstances required for that outcome exist or might exist (and so, a belief that the circumstances do not exist negatives that recklessness).

This proposition is sound if we select *Cunningham* recklessness as our form of recklessness, because this requires an awareness of risk of the outcome which involves a belief that the circumstances required for the outcome might exist, and so is negated by the belief that the circumstances do not exist.

The proposition is unsound if we select strict *Caldwell* recklessness, because this can be satisfied by a failure to consider the risk which obviously need involve no belief that the circumstances required for the outcome might exist, and is accordingly not affected at all by the belief

---

[173] This formulation avoids the extreme case where the equivalence is not met. Technically, though rarely in practice, it is possible to come up with a case where the conduct is changed to be less risky than conduct involving an unreasonable risk—and so not reckless—but still done with the intention of causing the victim a prohibited harm and hence culpable for this reason. This suggests another criterion for intentional wrongdoing alongside being prepared to expose the victim to an unreasonable risk of harm: being prepared to bring about a prohibited harm to the victim. The fact that intentional wrongdoing embraces, within the range of culpable conduct, instances of each of these criteria being satisfied might suggest that either criteria suffices, and hence that a form of reckless wrongdoing that satisfies one of these criteria is equivalent to intentional wrongdoing. This does not follow. The equivalence is only made out if the appropriate criterion is selected.

[174] See text at n 169 above.

that the circumstances do not exist. A practical illustration of this scenario is provided by the approach taken by the Divisional Court in *Elliott v C*: even if Miss C had been regarded as believing that there was no danger in lighting a fire on the wooden floor of the shed, this would not prevent her from being found to be reckless for failing to consider the risk of burning down the shed. Far from negating an element of this form of recklessness, the mistaken belief that the circumstances required for the outcome do not exist contributes to the failure to consider the risk, and so helps to establish a finding of recklessness.

The proposition is also unsound if we take Williams' softer form of *Caldwell* recklessness preferred by the Magistrates in *Elliott v C*, or the form of culpable inadvertence proposed by Hart we considered above, both of which require that the particular defendant had the capacity to appreciate the risk, although not aware of it at the time the conduct was engaged in. In common with the strict form of *Caldwell* recklessness, these forms of mens rea do not require a concomitant awareness of the risk of the outcome of the conduct, and so do not require a belief that the circumstances required for the outcome might exist at the time the conduct is engaged in. They are not accordingly vulnerable to Hailsham's ineluctable logic since his first premise, that the appropriate form of mens rea contains an element which is negated by the (mistaken) belief that the circumstances required for the outcome do not exist, no longer holds.

So only one of these forms of recklessness provides a logical equivalence to intention for the purposes of following Hailsham's ineluctable logic. If these other forms of recklessness are considered to be viable forms of mens rea, as we have suggested above they must be, then the preliminary issue to investigate is what form of recklessness constitutes an appropriate mens rea for rape. Again, the real issue of what is the basis for establishing culpability for rape has been avoided, and Hailsham is guilty of the elementary mistake of invoking logic before establishing his premises.

Seeking the appropriate mens rea for a particular offence is in part, as I have suggested in the previous section, an historical investigation. However, we recognised in chapter 1 that the present condition of legal materials may or may not provide us with clear and satisfactory answers to the questions we need to ask of the law. We may discover that the historical process furnishes inconsistent, incomplete, or even inadequate answers in the light of currently acceptable standards. The role of the courts may be as much to investigate what would be an appropriate form of mens rea for a particular offence, as to discover the form that has previously been established in the law. Accordingly it is essential to clarify the different forms available, and what practical implications each holds.

Certainly, Hailsham's spurious logic with its forced premises does not permit the court to undertake a meaningful role. Regrettably this episode cannot itself be consigned to history, despite the developments in the mens rea of rape that have moved beyond *Morgan*.[175] Among the cases cited by Lord Steyn in *R v G*, two recent House of Lords decisions[176] indicate that the compression of the mens rea issue into a doctrine of mistake still exerts a strong attraction on current Law Lords. The basic line of reasoning in both of these cases, which deal with indecent assaults on underage girls within statutory provisions which are silent as to mens rea, is as follows: (1) mens rea must be presumed in a statutory offence; (2) mens rea is now recognised as being subjective in nature; (3) a mistaken belief by the defendant will prevent mens rea occurring; (4) a mistake, no matter how unreasonable, will exclude liability.

Lord Nicholls in *B v DPP* provides a particularly clear example of the reasoning, and also clearly expresses the persisting influence of Hailsham's spurious logic, in his willingness to reiterate as its basis the defendant's mistaken belief negating *the intent* required by the offence.[177] The restrictive cognitivist approach to mens rea employed in this line of reasoning is clearly indicated by Bingham in the second case, *R v K*, in treating the belief of the defendant as a general 'element of mens rea',[178] and by Steyn's observation in the same case that the only alternative to the cognitivist forms of mens rea would be to regard the offence as being one of strict liability.[179] Although neither Bingham nor Steyn was bold enough to suggest in *R v G* that the real error in *Caldwell* was that their Lordships had turned criminal damage into a strict liability offence, it is evident that the authors of the two leading speeches in *R v G* had already fallen under the influence of *Morgan*.

Breaking the spell of *Morgan* allows full attention to be paid to the different forms of mens rea that are available. More particularly, this involves considering how different forms of recklessness relate to the culpability we wish to recognise for a particular offence. Although the cognitivist forms of mens rea (intention and *Cunningham* recklessness) only permit a finding of culpability when the defendant is aware of the possibility of his or her conduct causing harm to another, other forms of recklessness permit recognition of culpability in cases of inadvertence, when the defendant has failed to consider the risk of his or her conduct causing harm to another. There are two implications of broadening the

---

[175] See n 111 above.
[176] *B v DPP* [2000] 2 AC 428 and *R v K* [2001] UKHL 41; [2002] 1 AC 462.
[177] [2000] 2 AC 428, 462.
[178] [2001] UKHL 41 at [20].
[179] *ibid* at 34.

range of possible forms of mens rea in this way. The first and obvious one is that the very issue of inadvertence arrives on the agenda. The second is that finer considerations of what amounts to culpable conduct can be discussed in relation to each offence.

By allowing inadvertence to be considered as a basis for culpability, there is the possibility of recognising an obligation upon the defendant who is about to engage in particular conduct, at an earlier stage to the occurrence of the cognitivist obligation. The latter attaches to the state of awareness of the possibility of the conduct causing harm to another, and so is contingent upon that state of awareness being attained. Culpability is then attributed if the defendant who despite being aware of the risk, engages in the conduct during which the risk materialises, and causes harm to another.[180] When inadvertence is selected as the basis for culpability it imposes an obligation to consider and take account of the potential threat to the interests of others, at a point prior to the cognitivist contingency being reached. The inadvertence obligation is earlier and wider. It may be breached by the defendant who has failed to consider the risk that materialises, and so causes harm to another. Whether this prior obligation of inadvertence is a comparable basis for culpability to the subsequent contingent obligation of advertence depends upon the underlying criterion of culpability we select. We shall consider this more fully in the concluding section. For the moment, I want to explore how this additional option makes an impact by broadening the mens rea issue.

I have characterised as the mens rea issue the issue of what is the basis for establishing culpability for an offence. It has been acknowledged that this issue may, for some offences, be resolved by a process of historical enquiry, but for other offences where the state of legal materials provides inconsistent, incomplete, or inadequate answers, the courts may have to consider what form of mens rea is appropriate for a particular offence. The other side of the coin to an assessment of culpability is a determination of what conduct is considered to be blameless. Accordingly, the mens rea issue involves a judgement of what conduct can be expected of the defendant, what acts the defendant should undertake or refrain from in order to avoid criminal liability. Clearly then, a restriction to the cognitivist forms of mens rea establishes a barrier to expecting the defendant to refrain from anything other than what he or she has happened to consider might cause harm to another. As Hart pointed out,[181] this is not a natural restriction. It would be perceived as artificial and arbitrary if compared to normal practices of attributing blame in contexts outside the criminal law.

---

[180] This basic awareness of risk is common to both of the cognitivist forms of mens rea, intention and *Cunningham* recklessness, irrespective of which criterion of culpability (see n 173 above) is selected.

[181] Hart, above n 143, at 136.

That is not sufficient in itself to conclude that the cognitivist restriction is an inappropriate one for the criminal law to adopt, but it does indicate that some justification needs to be provided for considering it appropriate.

This is precisely what is missing in the cognitivist position, which, in ways that I have detailed above, purports to provide an absolute prohibition against considering anything other than the cognitivist forms of mens rea when dealing with specific offences—despite tolerating other forms of mens rea in offences not presently under consideration. If the cognitivist position is maintainable, it should be possible to demonstrate why it is that other forms of mens rea are inappropriate for each and every criminal offence. In practice, this means showing why it is that for the particular types of conduct that might lead to the harm prohibited in offence X, we should expect:[182]

(A)   D is to avoid any conduct that he has happened to consider might cause the prohibited harm to V;

but not expect:

(B)   D is to avoid any conduct that he might reasonably have considered might cause the prohibited harm to V

(or some such variation on the inadvertence theme).

The burden this imposes on the cognitivists is considerable, and can be spelled out by starting with an offence which inconsistently they make allowance for despite its breaching the restriction to cognitivist forms of mens rea. For a reckless driving offence, it is accepted that both (A) and (B) should be expected. That is to say, a person driving a car cannot avoid criminal liability for causing harm by claiming that he did not happen to consider the possibility, where he might reasonably have thought about the possibility that driving in such a way might cause harm to others—and so be expected to refrain from it. The apparently self-evident appeal (even to the cognitivists) of culpable inadvertence for a reckless driving offence boils down to an acceptance that persons wishing to engage in the conduct of driving a motor car should be expected to take some account of the interests of others in not suffering harm from that conduct.

If we next turn to the offence of rape, we can readily see that the cognitivist restriction, as adopted in *Morgan*, curtails the mens rea issue so that we cannot even address the possibility of culpable inadvertence taken up

---

[182] For the sake of simplicity, I am for the moment ignoring conduct which involves reasonably running the risk of bringing about the harm in question, such as a surgeon performing an essential but risky operation; or involves running a reasonable risk of bringing about the harm, such as where a very low risk is accepted as a normal aspect of everyday life. I use the term conduct to cover behaviour comprising both acts and omissions.

for a reckless driving offence. We are precluded from considering whether it is acceptable that persons wishing to engage in the conduct of sexual intercourse should be expected to take some account of the interests of their potential partners in not suffering the harm of having intercourse forced upon them without their consent.[183] The recent legislative reform to the offence of rape[184] indicates quite clearly not only that this is a possibility that should be carefully considered, but also that the outcome of such consideration can move the mens rea of the offence beyond the cognitivist restriction.

Finally, let us look again at an offence of criminal damage, whose mens rea has been pushed back by the Law Lords in *R v G* to those forms complying with the cognitivist restriction. Since this decision has been reached by adopting the flawed arguments supporting a general cognitivist position, the specific mens rea issue for criminal damage has been avoided. The possibility of culpable inadvertence recognised by the Law Lords themselves for reckless driving, and by Parliament for rape, has been taken off the agenda for criminal damage. Since there are a great number of types of conduct that might result in damaging another's property, it takes an enormous amount of presumption to conclude that we should not even consider whether persons who wish to engage in any conduct that might cause damage to another's property should be expected to take some account of the interests of others in not having their property damaged. One example will suffice to make the point, a variation on Hart's workman mending a roof who throws slates onto the street below.[185] Let us imagine that he has not bothered to check whether anyone has parked their car in the street below, that in his haste to finish the job he has not even given it a moment's thought. And one of the discarded slates crashes through the windscreen of a parked car. Can we be so confident that we do not even need to address the issue of whether the workman should be expected to take some account of the interests of users of the road below in not having their property damaged?

The Law Lords in *R v G* do not appear quite so confident. Both Lord Bingham and Lord Steyn emphasise that their rejection of *Caldwell* recklessness should not be regarded as letting off a defendant who 'closes his mind to a risk'.[186] These comments implicitly endorse the pre-Caldwellian doctrine of *Parker*,[187] that persons who effectively close their mind to an obvious risk are to be regarded as being aware of that risk. The problem of what amounts to *effectively* closing the mind is a

---

[183] For discussion of the acceptability of this position, see the sources cited in n 111 above.
[184] *ibid*.
[185] See text at n 146 above.
[186] [2003] UKHL 50 at [58] *per* Lord Steyn; cp Bingham at [39].
[187] [1977] 1 WLR 600, cited by Bingham, [2003] UKHL 50 at [14].

real one.[188] In *Parker* the defendant's rage when smashing a telephone handset was taken to suffice, but what other emotional or mental states should be regarded as effectively closing the mind to the obvious remains unclear. It was this very problem that led the Court of Appeal in *Stephenson*[189] to recognise that the *Parker* doctrine let in an objective test of recklessness, and led the majority of the House of Lords in *Caldwell*[190] to opt for a different route to that taken in *Parker*.

The wavering of Bingham and Steyn from a true cognitivist position in their endorsement of *Parker*, is not eased by the final and decisive reason given by Bingham for rejecting the Williams refinement to the *Caldwell* test,[191] requiring that the risk would have been obvious to the actual defendant if he or she had stopped to consider it. Bingham argues that juries or magistrates would find it far more difficult to speculate on what might have crossed the defendant's mind (if he had stopped to consider the risk) than on what did cross his mind (when he argues that he never considered the risk).[192] Since both exercises involve the task of constructing an awareness out of the obviousness of the risk and the perception of the defendant as capable of appreciating it, there is little or nothing to distinguish between constructing a hypothetical awareness and constructing a presumed actual awareness. But if this is so, Bingham's final reason is no reason at all against going all the way towards accepting a form of culpable inadvertence for criminal damage.[193]

Whether some form of culpable inadvertence should be accepted for all the types of harm prohibited by the criminal law is a question I shall consider more fully in the concluding section. What has been established by our reflections so far is that there are no grounds that have been put forward for excluding culpable inadvertence from the mens rea issue of any of the specific offences we have considered. In the final paragraphs of this section, I want to briefly consider the second implication of permitting culpable inadvertence into the range of possible forms of mens rea, that I introduced above, a finer appreciation of the offence-specific element of recklessness.

[188] The actual phrase used by the Court of Appeal in *Parker* [1977] 1 WLR 600, 604, is 'in effect, deliberately closing his mind to the obvious' (quoted in *R v G* [2003] UKHL 50 at [14]). This conveys a constructive closing of the mind, contrary to the best efforts of Glanville Williams (also quoted, *ibid*) to represent it in true cognitivist spirit as an actual closing of the mind accompanied by an awareness of what one was closing the mind to.
[189] [1979] 1 QB 695, 700, 704. Significantly, the point was conceded by counsel for the Crown (at 698).
[190] [1981] 1 All ER 961, 965–66.
[191] See n 131 above.
[192] [2003] UKHL 50 at [38]. The other two reasons given by Bingham have been dealt with above: text following n 130, and text accompanying nn 122–23, respectively.
[193] Lord Rodger shows more openness to adopting the form of culpable inadvertence consisting of the Williams' refinement to *Caldwell*, as adopted by the Magistrates in *Elliott v C*, *ibid* at [70].

Even with *Cunningham* recklessness there is an offence-specific element, in that conduct causing the harm prohibited by the particular offence will not be deemed reckless unless running the risk of causing that harm in that way is regarded as unreasonable.[194] What is considered to be an unreasonable taking of a risk will vary depending on how the conduct and its potential for harm is assessed in relation to each offence. For example, there are certain risks attached to driving a car, such as the risk of mechanical failure even after appropriate maintenance of the vehicle, which one is permitted to take without being regarded as criminally reckless. However, inasmuch as *Cunningham* recklessness establishes a cognitivist threshold for criminal liability at the point the defendant becomes aware of the risk, it is quite possible for investigation of the offence-specific element, of what would be regarded as reckless driving, to become suppressed by the cognitivist restriction to risks that the defendant is aware of.

This, it is submitted, is the true reason behind the position taken by the House of Lords in *R v G* in retaining *Caldwell* recklessness for driving offences.[195] Persons wishing to engage in the conduct of driving a car should not be allowed to avoid culpability for driving in a manner that would normally be regarded as reckless simply because they happen not to have considered the risk. It is certainly clear that this is precisely the reason behind the reform to the offence of rape,[196] that has been effected by abandoning the cognitivist restrictions of *Morgan*. A clearer view of what amounts to reckless conduct for rape can be reached once culpable inadvertence has been allowed into the range of the possible forms of mens rea for the offence. The detailed offence-specific element of recklessness is provided by allowing the question to be fully addressed, of what conduct we can expect D to refrain from when wishing to engage in sexual intercourse.

As for criminal damage offences, across a far greater variety of types of conduct, the offence-specific element of recklessness can also only clearly be refined by permitting the question of what conduct we can expect D to refrain from, to be first raised and then answered.

CONCLUDING REFLECTIONS

It is apparent from these observations on *R v G* that we are still some way from reaching a fair and coherent doctrine of recklessness in the English criminal law. What we have obtained through the great variety

---

[194] See n 182 above for a counter-example.
[195] [2003] UKHL 50 at [28], [69].
[196] For full discussion, see the sources cited in n 111 above.

of developments to recklessness in the appellate courts is a rich source of material from which a number of important lessons can be learned. Perhaps the most pressing lesson still to be learned about recklessness is what approach to it will yield a clearer grasp of the basis for establishing culpability in some of the more serious criminal offences. The failings of the appellate courts to contribute, after so many attempts, to a coherent body of knowledge in this area, indicate that something different may be needed to the basic approaches tried so far. Apart from lessons on recklessness, there are also more general lessons to be learned from this material. No effective discussion of recklessness can avoid dealing with the wider implications of the mens rea issue, and, in particular, dealing with the relationships between recklessness and other forms of mens rea. More widely still, the material on recklessness provides further opportunity to consider the nature of legal materials. Within this concluding section, I shall endeavour to draw out some of the more important lessons to be learned about recklessness itself, and these broader topics.

The Failings of Authority

There are two sources of authority that have been tried and been found wanting, during this period of instability in the law on recklessness. The first is the authority of the dictionary, or the use of ordinary language. The second is the authority of established legal doctrine, or precedent (as we have been dealing with judicial development of the law). We shall consider them in turn.

It is indisputable that different meanings for recklessness are to be found in the ordinary usage of the word as conveyed by a dictionary definition.[197] It is also clear from our discussion of developments in the criminal law's approach to recklessness that these different meanings are regarded as bearing significantly different connotations for determining criminal liability. If this were not so, the *Caldwell-Cunningham* divide would never have arisen, and the energies of counsel, judges, and academic commentators in relation to the cases discussed above and more[198] would have been expended elsewhere.

I think it is also beyond dispute that a wholesale adoption by the law of the complete range of meanings found in a dictionary definition would

---

[197] A singular dictionary definition should not be equated with a singular meaning for the word. Dictionary definitions frequently contain a range of disjunctive meanings for the word being defined, as the entries for a great number of common words reveal.

[198] Notably, concerning the dispute as to what form of recklessness is required for assault. The leading case is *Savage, Parmenter* [1991] 3 WLR 914, 924, upholding (on that point) the Court of Appeal in *Spratt* [1990] 1 WLR 1073, 1082–83. In their note prior to the Lords'

not be acceptable. This is so because that range includes 'carelessness', which is also given by the dictionary as a synonym for negligence.[199] And for the modern criminal law, there is a need to distinguish some sense of recklessness that differs from negligence or mere carelessness. This is required for one of two reasons, either to mark recklessness off from a lesser form of criminal culpability, or to mark it off from a form of non-criminal culpability.[200] Indeed, the need to recognise different levels of culpability may be regarded as a deep and virtually universal[201] problem of the criminal law, to which we shall return.

Given that some restriction to the range of dictionary meanings is required by the criminal law, there seem to be two routes available for restoring recklessness to a body of legal knowledge. One is to accept the comprehensive range of dictionary meanings available, and then leave the necessary qualification to be effected across the whole range by the tribunal of fact: making an assessment as to when the failure to take care is sufficiently culpable to require punishment. This amounts

---

decision, Andrew Ashworth and Kenneth Campbell pointed out the existence of other authority on the point derived from cases relating mistake to the negation of mens rea— 'Recklessness in Assault—and in General?' (1991) 107 *Law Quarterly Review* 187, 190. This is an important implication of the choice of recklessness to take into account, which as the authors observe (at 188) was lacking in *Caldwell*. For arguments in favour of a broader approach to recklessness for the assault offences, see CMV Clarkson, 'Violence and the Law Commission' [1994] *Criminal Law Review* 324, 330–31.

[199] See entries in the *Oxford English Dictionary*.

[200] See the problems faced by Lord Goff in distinguishing reckless from careless driving in *Reid* [1992] 1 WLR 793, 812, 815. His final resort to a requirement of mens rea ('a certain state of mind') at 815 leaves the job unfinished, since the requisite state of mind has not been properly defined. See also the efforts of Lord Atkin in *Andrews* [1937] AC 576, in seeking to distinguish the gross negligence required for manslaughter. He traces the exclusion of 'mere inadvertence' as a historical development (at 581–82) but does not consider that the use of mens rea is helpful in making the distinction (at 583).

[201] It can be traced back to the distinction between the two principal forms of fault, *dolus* (involving deliberate action) and *culpa* (carelessness) in Roman law, which has continued to exert an influence on modern legal systems. See, eg, George Fletcher, *Rethinking Criminal Law* (Boston, MA, Little, Brown & Co, 1978; republished, Oxford, OUP, 2000) 443–49. The basic Roman distinction was treated by Austin as corresponding to the distinction between intention (or malice), on the one hand, and negligence (more technically, negligence, heedlessness, and rashness), on the other hand. See John Austin, *Lectures on Jurisprudence* I (5th edn, London, John Murray, 1885; reprinted 1929) 430–33. Even in the radical proposal of Tadeusz Grygier, *Social Protection Code: A New Model of Criminal Justice* (South Hackensack, NJ, Fred B Rothman & Co, 1977), which dispenses with mens rea altogether, there still remains an attempted distinction (at §11(1)) between a less and more serious deviation from the standard of conduct.

The recognition of the need to make distinctions of this kind has not been attended by a clear recognition of how the distinction should be made. The Romans used the terms, *dolus* and *culpa*, in a variety of ways; recognised different degrees of *culpa*; and did not always see the distinction between the two as being hard and fast (despite Austin's contrivance to make it so). See Austin, *loc cit*; WW Buckland, *A Text-book of Roman Law*, Peter Stein (ed) (rev 3rd edn, Cambridge, Cambridge University Press, 1975) 556–59.

to taking the gross negligence route.[202] This withdraws the law's concerns to enumerating the offences to which recklessness should apply, and places confidence in those tribunals for determining issues of reckless culpability more effectively than we could hope for from a detailed legal definition of meaning(s) for recklessness. This may be regarded as a real-istic evaluation of the options.[203]

The other route is to furnish a restrictive but coherent definition of recklessness providing legal meaning(s), as a foundation for appropriate directions that can be clearly applied to different situations. This route relies on the second source of authority, established legal doctrine operat-ing through precedent, to provide the restricted legal definition. There has been a number of failings with this source of authority during the period we have been examining.[204] A major cause of these failings has been the neglect by the judiciary to ascertain the nature of the problem they have been dealing with, glaringly exhibited by Lord Diplock's reliance on a spurious single dictionary meaning for recklessness,[205] an error others have keenly followed.[206] However, this has been com-pounded by the opposing functions that recklessness has historically been called upon to perform in the English criminal law. On the one hand, in the case of recklessness as found in malice, it is performing the same func-tion as intention. A conscious decision to expose to harm is regarded as a common element of both states.[207] On the other hand, as a synonym for

---

[202] If done with sufficient indication that the grossness is an evaluation of all the circum-stances that the particular defendant was in, this need not be insensitive to the capacities of particular defendants to deal with risk. See the Law Commission proposal in Law Com No 237, discussed n 70 above. The qualification to be made by the tribunal of fact in this pro-posal is rendered by 'far below what can reasonably be expected of him in the circumstances'— cl 2(1)(c)(i). This broad perspective also overcomes the lacuna problem. See n 68 above and accompanying text.

[203] For further comment, see Simon Gardner, 'Manslaughter by Gross Negligence' (1995) 111 *Law Quarterly Review* 22.

[204] See text accompanying nn 105–15 above.

[205] See text following n 13 above.

[206] As examples, see the references to Lords Keith, Ackner, Goff, and Browne-Wilkinson in *Reid*, n 36 above, and Lord Mackay in *Adomako*, n 78 above.

[207] A relatively recent recognition of this connection is to be found in Lord Diplock's equa-tion of intention with foresight of a probable outcome of one's conduct in *Hyam* [1975] AC 55, 86. He finds the common element to be 'willingness to produce the particular evil consequence'. This is inaccurate, for the latter state of mind may not include this element (see further, my 'Intended Consequences and Unintentional Fallacies' (1987) 7 *Oxford Journal of Legal Studies* 104, 108). But both states of mind do share a willingness to produce the risk of the evil consequence, or, as I have put it, a conscious decision to expose to harm. It is clear that this lesser element did once suffice for intention in the criminal law. As Lord Edmund-Davies noted in *Caldwell* [1981] 1 All ER 961, 970, Austin recognised the modern (*Cunningham*) recklessness *as* intention. See Austin, above n 201, at 428–29, where intention is defined as involving 'a state of consciousness' as to a future event whose probability may be rated 'higher or lower'. This is seen to include subjective recklessness in the example that follows of pistol practice resulting in the undesired wounding of a passer-by, whom I am conscious 'may chance to be there'. Significantly, Austin informs his students that 'every

gross negligence it is used to raise the degree of carelessness[208] and it is not a conscious decision to expose to harm, but the degree of culpability for the exposure to harm that is uppermost.

It might of course have turned out that in performing these two functions the same concept of recklessness was used, but this clearly did not happen in English law. One way of breaking out of this awkward middle ground between two quite contrary positions, which the term recklessness has historically been left in, is to select a restrictive legal definition which bifurcates, recognising two substantially distinct forms of recklessness connoting different levels of culpability which could then be selected for different offences as appropriate. If this occurs, then for the sake of

wrong … supposes intention or negligence' (at 344), marking a division based wholly on the presence or absence of consciousness of the potential harm in the mind of the wrongdoer (at 428), for which an independent notion of recklessness is unnecessary. Austin's paradigm of the pistol practice, incidentally, is evidence against the depiction by Horder, above n 5, at 96, of 'the malice principle' as requiring conduct directed at an interest of the victim.

Contemporary dissatisfaction with Austin's broad approach to intention is found in FC Clark, *An Analysis of Criminal Liability* (Cambridge, Cambridge University Press, 1880; reprinted, Littleton, CO, Fred B Rothman & Co, 1983) 78, 100. Clark's preference (in ch VIII) for 'criminal knowledge' or 'virtual intention' does not, however, achieve greater clarity. Significantly, there is no mention of recklessness by Clark, nor in almost all of the efforts to codify the criminal law in the nineteenth century. The proposals of the 1833 and 1845 Criminal Law Commissioners settled for 'wilfulness' as covering intention and belief that a result was 'in any degree probable'. See ch I, s 3, Article 3 of the Draft Bill attached to the Fourth Report of the 1845 Commissioners, *Parliamentary Papers* (1847–8) XXVII, 1—discussed by Rupert Cross, 'The Reports of the Criminal Law Commissioners (1833–1849) and the Abortive Bills of 1853' in Peter Glazebrook (ed), *Reshaping the Criminal Law: Essays in honour of Glanville Williams* (London, Stevens & Sons, 1978) 14–16. The Indian Penal Code 1860 deals with intention or knowledge that an outcome is 'likely', eg, in the homicide provisions, ss 299 & 300. Sir James Fitzjames Stephen, *A Digest of the Criminal Law (Crimes and Punishments)* (3rd edn, London, Macmillan & Co, 1883) similarly uses intention or knowledge that an outcome is probable, in Article 223. In RS Wright's Draft Jamaican Criminal Code (C 1893, 1877), intention was defined extremely widely, in s 10(i)–(iii) to embrace purpose, belief that an outcome is probable, and even (presumptively) cases where such a belief would have been entertained if 'reasonable caution and observation' had been practised—discussed by ML Friedland, 'R.S. Wright's Model Criminal Code: A Forgotten Chapter in the History of the Criminal Law' (1981) 1 *Oxford Journal of Legal Studies* 307, 315; Keith Smith, *Lawyers, Legislators and Theorists* (Oxford, Clarendon Press, 1998) 151.

The exception where recklessness is mentioned is in s 174 (b) of the Draft Code appended to the Report of the Criminal Code Bill Commission (C 2345, 1879), which had been set up to consider the Criminal Code (Indictable Offences) Bill, 1878. (The proposals were then allowed to fall victim to a lack of parliamentary time.) This mentions recklessness in the definition of a form of murder satisfied by the offender meaning to cause a bodily injury known by him to be likely to cause death. That the offender 'is reckless whether death ensues or not' appears to add very little, as is confirmed by the discussion in the Report (at 24). Smith (at 150) suggests the term may have been borrowed from recent judicial usage (discussed by him at 162–64), though this is far from coherent. Smith (at 156) credits Kenny with making the term more acceptable. However, it is clearly used by Kenny, above n 5, in the first edition at 148, to cover a variant of intention, which is taken by Kenny (like Austin) to embrace subjective recklessness. Recklessness is only found enjoying a separate existence from intention, in the form approved by *Cunningham*, in subsequent editions.

[208] See the latter part of n 200 above.

clarity, it would be necessary to provide two distinct labels, and as a result we will have two technical legal definitions taken out of the popular range of meanings for recklessness.[209]

If it is ultimately decided that deliberate or conscious exposure of another to harm signifies the level of culpability which should be reserved for serious criminal offences,[210] then it follows that only a legal definition requiring conscious risk taking will suffice, from the range of possibilities that the use of recklessness provides. This is the rationale for Kenny's recklessness adopted in *Cunningham*. If, on the other hand, it is recognised that the level of culpability appropriate to serious criminal offences can be satisfied by demonstrating some sort of exposure to harm which is culpable on grounds other than that it is conscious,[211] then we will need to seek a way of bringing a broader notion of recklessness into the law. This is the move commenced but ineffectually made in *Caldwell*.

[209] Consider the earlier version of modern proposals for codification which drew up definitions of 'recklessness' and 'heedlessness'. See Law Com No 143 (HC 270, 1985), *Codification of the Criminal Law*, in cl 22 of the draft code. This did not survive the revised proposals, Law Com No 177 (HC 299, 1989), *A Criminal Code for England and Wales*, in cl 18 of the draft code. However, para 8.20 of the commentary on that proposal holds out the possibility of 'providing further key terms'. The need for such an additional fault term was proposed following *Reid* by LH Leigh, 'Recklessness after *Reid*' (1993) 56 *Modern Law Review* 208, 212, 217–18; and both 'recklessness' and 'gross carelessness' are found in the proposals in Law Com No 237 (nn 70, 202 above)—though their relationship is unclear (see n 211 below).

[210] Interesting comparative material on the use of conscious exposure to harm as the fundamental requirement for mens rea is provided by the Israeli Penal Code (in force since August 1995). The text of the draft and enacted code together with papers from a colloquium on the draft proposal are to be found introduced by Mordechai Kremnitzer, Preface (1996) 30 *Israel Law Review* 1. There is a general requirement of 'awareness' in the mens rea provision in s 20 of the Code (*ibid* at 13), which is constructed to cover both intention and recklessness (divided into 'indifference' and 'rashness'). For further discussion of more detailed problems raised by this provision, see Bjorn Burkhardt, 'Some Questions and Comments on What is Called 'The Mental Element of the Offence' *ibid* at 82, 84–93 (the article also contains comparative references to the English proposed code in Law Com No 177 and the German draft E 1962). For general discussion in favour of restricting recklessness to cases where there is awareness of risk, see James Brady, 'Recklessness' (1996) 15 *Law and Philosophy* 183. This position suffered a severe setback in *Reid*, in which it was abandoned mid-argument by counsel ([1992] 1 WLR 793 at 800, 804). For comment see Simon Gardner, 'Recklessness Refined' (1993) 109 *Law Quarterly Review* 21.

[211] The switch from conscious exposure to harm to culpable exposure to harm can be made in two ways: the first is to argue for an *equivalence* of culpability, that instances of inadvertent exposure to harm are equally as culpable as instances of conscious exposure; the second is to acknowledge the greater culpability of the latter but to argue that the *threshold* of culpability also accommodates the former. There is an ambivalence between these two positions in Law Com No 237 (n 70 above). Contrast paras 4.12—4.16 which justify bringing in inadvertence by arguing for an equivalence in culpability, with para 5.7 which justifies a separation of the offences of reckless killing and killing by gross carelessness on the basis of 'a clear distinction, in terms of moral fault' between advertence and inadvertence. It is important to clarify which of the two positions is being maintained, since the second position effectively lowers the threshold of culpability in a way which renders redundant argument over the special status of conscious exposure to harm in determining liability for serious criminal offences.

A Different Approach

If it were only the case of *Caldwell* itself that had proved troublesome, then there might still be reason for anticipating that the process of identifying its defects and proposing improvements would eventually bring the law into a condition that was generally acceptable. However, the analysis undertaken above of the way that *Caldwell* has been overruled in *R v G*, leaves us with no confidence that the law is following this path (quite apart from the various meanderings that have occurred in between these two House of Lords' decisions). In proposing a radically different approach to that tried so far, I want to emphasise what seem to me to be some of the important lessons still to be learned from the failed attempts to deal with this fundamental area of the criminal law. In summary, these lessons are as follows. (1) The mens rea issue allows us to ask the question of what is the basis for establishing culpability for a particular criminal offence. (2) Only a stunted response to the mens rea issue is possible if the very idea of mens rea is artificially and arbitrarily restricted before the mens rea issue is raised. (3) The strict subjectivist, or cognitivist, approach to mens rea produces just such a stunted response when it is advanced as a necessary restriction to the idea of mens rea, rather than put forward as a position historically adopted in the law, or advanced as a normative position that can be supported by argument. (4) The strict subjectivist, or cognitivist, approach has not been consistently adopted historically within the law; nor has it been cogently argued for as a normative position by its supporters. (5) The historical use of the term recklessness in the English criminal law has been varied and inconsistent. (6) Neither its relationship to the use of the term intention, nor its relationship to the use of the term negligence, has been constant or clear. (7) Part of the reason for this historical muddle has been a failure to recognise the different criteria of culpability that are capable of supporting the use of the terms, intention, recklessness, and negligence, when employed to express forms or levels of culpability. (8) There remains a need for forms or levels of culpability to be identified which are capable of distinguishing: (i) criminal from non-criminal culpability; and (ii) more and less serious criminal culpability.

Although these individual points have been raised in the preceding text, the order I have arranged them in here is suggestive of an alternative approach that I shall now amplify, by looking at point (7) in more detail, and by considering how the need identified in (8) might be met. The key characteristics of the approach to be developed here will be found, first, in providing an emphasis on criteria of culpability prior to consideration of mens rea forms, and secondly, in providing separate treatment of the external boundary of criminal culpability before working on internal divisions which mark out the differences between more and less serious offences.

There are three particular criteria of culpability[212] which have been used to undergird the use of the terms intention, recklessness and negligence, in the criminal law, for the purpose of expressing forms or levels of culpability.[213] These are the following:

(C1)   D is prepared by his conduct to bring about harm to V.
(C2)   D is prepared by his conduct to expose V to the unreasonable risk of harm.
(C3)   D is by his conduct unreasonably exposing V to the unreasonable risk of harm.

To clarify matters further, it is important to distinguish two variants of (C3):

(C3)(a)   where D has the capacity to appreciate and avoid that risk.
(C3)(b)   whether or not D has the capacity to appreciate and avoid that risk.

These criteria may be differentiated further by introducing a factor of seriousness, either to the harm involved, or to the risk of suffering the harm. So we could, for example, have three further variants of (C2):

$(C2)_{S1}$ to expose V to the unreasonable and serious risk of harm.
$(C2)_{S2}$ to expose V to the unreasonable risk of serious harm.
$(C2)_{S1+2}$ to expose V to the unreasonable and serious risk of serious harm.

The complexity of the combinations and permutations possible can be illustrated by considering what it is that turns negligence into gross negligence. If the move is effected by changing from a criterion of culpability appropriate for mere negligence, (C3)(b), to one that expresses a higher level of culpability, the question remains as to which. The dicta of Lord Atkin in *Andrews*[214] would seem to be satisfied by a move to $(C3)(b)_{S1}$ or $(C3)(b)_{S2}$—or perhaps to require $(C3)(b)_{S1+2}$.[215] However, the outcomes

---

[212] The distinctions between criteria of culpability is analytically significant even if there exists a general consensus on the other values to be adopted in society, and for the purpose of investigating these distinctions I ignore further variables introduced by recognising that what is considered to be 'reasonable' will at times be contentious within a particular society. For general discussion of the element of inherent incoherence in the law that this contributes to, see Andrew Halpin, *Reasoning with Law* (Oxford, Hart Publishing, 2001).

[213] See n 207, n 173 and accompanying text, n 180, above.

[214] See n 65 above.

[215] Although occasionally dicta can be found to support the seriousness factor being applied to one or both of the risk and the harm (see n 223 below), it is obviously not an exact science,

and dicta of Lord Taylor in *Prentice*[216] suggest a move to a form involving (C3)(a).

There may, of course, be different criteria of culpability employed in the use of a single term such as gross negligence: different ways of establishing that we have moved from mere negligence to something more gross. It is important to recognise here two quite different phenomena. On the one hand, there is the possibility of different compatible criteria being adopted, on the ground that they all satisfy a uniform threshold (they are all more serious than the criterion for mere negligence[217]), or that they can be regarded as in some way equivalent by satisfying a common requirement.[218] On the other hand, there is the danger of incompatible criteria being adopted for the same term at different times, creating incoherence in the law. For example, it would be possible to see the two approaches to gross negligence in *Andrews* and *Prentice*, mentioned in the preceding paragraph, as setting up a conflict between criteria involving (C3)(b) or (C3)(a).[219] Where this occurs, despite the use of the same term on the surface of the law, the underlying change to the criterion

and it may be more appropriate to seek a term which indicates the overall seriousness of the risk and the harm in the context of the defendant's conduct. See Jeremy Horder's discussion of 'indifference' and 'a great departure from an expected standard' as different ways of expressing the grossness of gross negligence in 'Gross Negligence and Criminal Culpability' (1997) 47 *University of Toronto Law Journal* 495. Consider also the Model Penal Code's definition of recklessness in §2.02(2)(c), which requires 'a substantial and unjustifiable risk' and also 'a gross deviation from the [normal] standard of conduct'. Joshua Dressler, 'Does One Mens Rea Fit All?: Thoughts on Alexander's Unified Conception of Criminal Culpability' (2000) 88 *California Law Review* 955, 958, suggests that the MPC is really dealing with a risk that is substantially unjustified (in the circumstances) rather than necessarily with a substantial risk. Although the seriousness factor is often loosely expressed, and it may at times be subsumed within the very unreasonableness of the risk taking, it is apparent that it also has a role to play in determining the relative culpability of offences, as we shall see below.

[216] See n 66 above and accompanying text.
[217] It is interesting to consider whether the two terms provided by Horder, n 215 above, relate to the same criterion of culpability or not. If so, then they may be regarded as helpful expressions relating to the different contexts of the ordinary person and the qualified person yet conveying the same underlying criterion. So the 'indifference' of the ordinary person would effectively express 'a great departure from' the 'expected standard' for an ordinary person in a particular context. Horder, above n 215, at 517–20, considers but rejects this possibility, yet his underlying criteria of culpability remain unclear, possibly because he does not directly address the capacity of the defendants (acknowledged at 520 n71). If Horder is taken as approving a form of (C3)(a) for ordinary persons but (C3)(b) for qualified persons engaging in their duties, this would seem to be a stricter approach than that taken in *Prentice* (see n 216 above, and n 219 below). However, there is some indication (at 520 n70) that Horder would not go so far. If not, then the role of the standard for the qualified person would seem to be more evidential than substantive.
[218] For an example of this in another context, see n 207 above. And for the importance of distinguishing between threshold and equivalence approaches, see n 211 above.
[219] Although Lord Taylor's dicta on gross negligence in *Prentice* are not exhaustive, further evidence that he is employing a (C3)(a) criterion is provided by his modification to the objective limb of *Caldwell* recklessness. See n 72 above.

of culpability indicates that the legal concept in question is being transformed by a process of gradual drift, or even abrupt dislocation.[220]

If we focus on the criteria of culpability that have been employed for the use of the terms intention and recklessness in the criminal law (for the moment simplifying things by overlooking the variants introduced by recognising the seriousness factor), then we obtain the following results:

(C1) INTENTION
(C2) INTENTION
        CUNNINGHAM RECKLESSNESS
(C3)(b) *CALDWELL* RECKLESSNESS (strict, as *Elliott v C*[221])

By using the common term intention in the law it is a simple matter to slip from (C1) to (C2). By focusing on (C2) as the criterion of culpability it is a simple matter to argue for the rational inclusion of recklessness, to reach the two cognitivist forms of mens rea, or the state of the law recognised by Austin and in the first edition of Kenny under the single term intention.[222] By using the common term recklessness it is a simple matter to slip from (C2) to (C3)(b). It is accordingly difficult to discern from the mere use of these terms fixed relationships to criteria of culpability which might assist in distinguishing: (i) criminal from non-criminal culpability; and (ii) more and less serious criminal culpability.

If we bring in the use of the term gross negligence, we can locate this as sharing the same criterion of culpability as strict *Caldwell* recklessness, as follows:

(C3)(b) *CALDWELL* RECKLESSNESS (strict, as *Elliott v C*)
        ANDREWS GROSS NEGLIGENCE

This expands the range of terms but does nothing to assist us in the task of seeing merely from the use of the terms where it is that the line should be drawn between criminal and non-criminal culpability, or more and less serious criminal culpability. Moreover, it suggests that we have to resort to the variants introduced by recognising the seriousness factor, in order to struggle towards the distinctions we need.[223]

---

[220] For further discussion of conceptual dislocation, see Halpin, above n 212, at 168–73.
[221] On appeal in the Divisional Court. The refinement to *Caldwell* recklessness preferred by the Magistrates in *Elliott v C*, and proposed by Glanville Williams (see n 131 above and accompanying text), falls under (C3)(a).
[222] See n 207 above.
[223] As did Lord Goff in *Reid* [1992] 1 WLR 793, 812: '*serious* risk of causing *physical* injury ... or *substantial* damage'. Consciousness of the need to distinguish careless and reckless driving may also account for the additional adjective provided by Lord Diplock in his model

Before concluding that no consistent, rational means for making these important distinctions is to be found either in the terms traditionally employed for forms of mens rea, or the criteria of culpability they have been related to, it is worth considering any special significance that might be possessed by (C3)(a). This criterion of culpability fits the type of negligence, or culpable inadvertence, proposed by Hart as being suitable for establishing criminal liability, which we discussed earlier. Although Hart's proposal was the product of a theoretical exercise rather than the investigation of practical legal doctrines, and, as I shall indicate below, may need further work before being adopted in practice, the criterion of culpability undergirding Hart's proposal does give it an extraordinary resonance with a number of practical developments in the law.

It is in fact possible to demonstrate that this criterion of culpability has been reached by qualifying positions originally expressed using all three of the mens rea terms (intention,[224] recklessness and negligence) and located in two of the other three major criteria of culpability, (C2) and (C3)(b). Reserving comment for the moment on the remaining criterion, (C1), the interesting point to consider is whether there is something of a gravitational pull towards (C3)(a) which indicates its particular significance for criminal culpability.

Let us consider the evidence for this in three practical developments which have taken different paths to reaching (C3)(a). The first is a straightforward modification to (C3)(b) employed in the strict form of *Caldwell* recklessness, proposed in the Williams' refinement and preferred by the Magistrates in *Elliott v C*: the risk would have been obvious to the actual defendant if he or she had stopped to consider it.[225] It is arguable that the Magistrates' position was subsequently vindicated by the approach taken by the House of Lords in *Reid*, but due to their reticence this can only be a matter of inference.[226] The second is a more subtle adjustment to *Andrews* gross negligence, which on the basis of Lord Atkins' dicta can also be regarded as employing (C3)(b).[227] The move to a form of mens rea employing (C3)(a) by the Court of Appeal in *Prentice* facilitated the appeals of two doctors and an electrician against convictions for manslaughter, by

direction in *Lawrence* [1981] 1 All ER 974, 982: 'an obvious and *serious* risk'. (All emphasis added.) Similarly, Lord Atkin in *Andrews* [1937] AC 576, 583, 585, employs the seriousness of the risk by speaking of the degree of negligence, in order to make both distinctions.

[224] Bearing in mind both the historical use of intention to cover *Cunningham* recklessness (see n 207 above and n 232 below) and the contemporary broadening of intention leading up to *Nedrick* (see n 133 above) which is probably best understood as employing (C2), certainly at its inception in *Hyam* (see n 207 above). For further discussion on the broad and varied use of intention, see Fletcher, above n 201 at 439–54.

[225] See n 131 above.

[226] See n 42 above.

[227] See n 214 above and accompanying text.

permitting reference to excuses or mitigating circumstances affecting the individual defendants as part of the process of assessing whether their negligence had been 'gross'.[228] The third, and most recent development is an amendment to (C2) effected by the House of Lords in *R v G* in embracing *Cunningham* recklessness, but with the qualification that it was to be applied together with the 'closed mind' doctrine from *Parker*: that persons who effectively close their mind to an obvious risk are to be regarded as being aware of that risk.[229] Although there may be room for doubt over what amounts to effectively closing the mind, it does seem clear that what is required by their Lordships in *R v G* is that the *particular* mind which is closed could otherwise be open,[230] and hence that their amendment takes us to (C3)(a) once more.

So although the criterion of culpability (C3)(a) has not been directly embraced in any of the leading cases in which forms of mens rea have been established in the English law, it has nevertheless made a forceful appearance in the way that leading approaches have been qualified in practice by the courts:

(C3)(a)   *CALDWELL* RECKLESSNESS (Magistrates in *Elliott v C*)
          ANDREWS GROSS NEGLIGENCE (*Prentice*)
          CUNNINGHAM RECKLESSNESS + *PARKER* (*R v G*)

If these practical qualifications to apparently very different approaches to mens rea all reach the same position in relation to the underlying criterion of culpability being selected, then this raises some significant questions. Do our traditional approaches to mens rea all inadequately convey a partial aspect, perhaps unduly emphasised, of the broader expanse of the mens rea issue? As we make adjustments to correct the overemphases present in different approaches, do we reach a synthesis in which initial differences are reconciled?

The suggestion that a modified *Caldwell* recklessness reaches the same position as a version of *Andrews* gross negligence is not a novel one, having been made by Lord Taylor in *Prentice*.[231] And although there seems a greater, and even bitter, divide between *Caldwell* recklessness and *Cunningham* recklessness, it seems that the *Parker* amendment to *Cunningham* recklessness was accepted by the House of Lords in *R v G*,

---

[228] See nn 66 & 67 above and accompanying text.
[229] See nn 186–89 above and accompanying text.
[230] [2003] UKHL 50 at [39] *per* Lord Bingham: '*he* did or must have done' (emphasis added); also at [58] *per* Lord Steyn. This circumvents the qualms felt by the Court of Appeal in *Stephenson* [1979] 1 QB 695, 704, that the closed mind doctrine may be ambiguous between a defendant with capacity to appreciate a risk who has closed his mind to it, and a defendant whose incapacity closes his mind to the risk. See further, nn 187–90 above and accompanying text.
[231] See n 67 above.

conscious that it was performing the same role that the objective limb of the *Caldwell* test had been called upon to perform in preventing 'the acquittal of those whom public policy would require to be convicted.'[232] Finally, even if we hold on to certain distinctive aspects of the traditional approaches, does the gravitational pull of (C3)(a) indicate that it possesses some sort of threshold importance for criminal culpability, such that we then have to justify why it is that a narrower more distinctive approach is suitable for a particular offence?

I shall attempt answers to these questions by considering whether Hart's suggestion for a form of criminal negligence can be used to express the mens rea issue at its broadest point, being potentially applicable to each criminal offence. I shall then consider what sort of policy considerations might prevail to limit the extent of the mens rea issue for a particular offence, or to set different limits for comparable offences in order to indicate the greater seriousness of the one relative to the other. At this stage I shall return to the neglected criterion of culpability, (C1), and consider the different roles that the term intention can play within the definition of an offence.

Remodelling Mens Rea

If our aim is to model the mens rea issue at its broadest point, then we will need to show how the boundary of criminal culpability can be drawn so as to set it apart not only from the non-culpable but also from that not considered *criminally* culpable. It must also be possible to relate within the boundary to each of the criteria of culpability employed for criminal culpability, and to contain within it each of the forms of mens rea used to express that culpability. A simple glance at Hart's proposal for criminal negligence[233] is sufficient to raise the problem that, even if it is accepted that Hart has captured the essence of culpable inadvertence, there is nothing in his approach to indicate that he has identified criminal rather than civil culpability—or, for that matter, legal rather than moral culpability. This can be addressed by adding a requirement to ensure that an appropriate level for criminal culpability has been reached. A second, less obvious, problem is that Hart's formulation is drafted with a focus on

---

[232] [2003] UKHL 50 at [39] *per* Lord Bingham; cp [58] *per* Lord Steyn. Should it be thought that the gravitational pull of (C3)(a) is merely a modern phenomenon, consider an example from the proposed reforms of the nineteenth century. In s 10(iii) of Wright's Draft Jamaican Criminal Code, above n 207, the presumptive intention in cases where the defendant using 'reasonable caution and observation' would have appreciated the risk, brings us within the scope of (C3)(a). It is clear from Wright's annotations that the individual defendant may rebut the presumption by demonstrating 'that he had such ground for believing that harm would not be caused'.
[233] See text at n 153 above.

the failure to take precautions, rather than on the culpable conduct engaged in. This is unfortunate in suggesting that the non-culpable conduct expected of the defendant would amount to carrying on the conduct in question with the precautions in place. This is too restrictive for two reasons. In some cases, the risk of causing harm to another is such that the conduct which runs the risk of that harm should be avoided altogether rather than engaged in with precautions in place. (Consider setting up an area for firearms target practice in the High Street, with warning notices to inform pedestrians and other road users.[234]) The second way in which Hart's formulation is unduly restrictive arises because of the particular topic he was investigating, culpable inadvertence. The mens rea issue extends to culpable advertence to risk and also culpably seeking to bring about the prohibited harm. In these cases the culpability of the defendant lies, again, not in a failure to take appropriate precautions[235] but in engaging in the conduct.

We can deal with the second problem by broadening the focus of the main provision to take in the defendant's conduct (understood as either an act or an omission). This can be regarded as covering behaving in a manner likely to cause the prohibited harm because the appropriate precautions have not been taken, or simply behaving in a manner that is likely to cause the prohibited harm (where precautions would not be appropriate in any event). We can then tentatively propose as a test of criminal culpability, at the broadest[236] threshold level:

(i)   Did the accused engage in conduct causing a prohibited harm which any reasonable man with normal capacities would in the circumstances have been expected to avoid?

(ii) Is the failure to avoid that conduct in those circumstances sufficiently serious to warrant criminal liability?

(iii) Could the accused, given his mental and physical capacities, have been expected to avoid that conduct?

[234] If that seems fanciful, consider the example of javelin practice in a public place in Justinian's *Institutes* IV.iii.4.

[235] The problematic cases of adverting to a risk and erroneously thinking that sufficient precautions have been taken, or erroneously assessing the risk as low enough to justify running, should be regarded as cases of inadvertence to the true risk. See discussion of the *Caldwell* lacuna, n 68 above; cp Austin, above n 201, at 429, discussing the impossible 'mongrel' case.

[236] The test is broad in the sense of being wide enough to encompass every offence, but also in the sense of being sufficiently general so as to avoid specific points of detail over which offence the defendant should be liable for (eg, such as arise in discussion of transferred malice). Similarly, the notion of 'causing a prohibited harm' should be understood at this stage as taking for granted any niceties in the exposition of a doctrine of causation; and as simply establishing a connection between the defendant's conduct and the proscribed harm, whether that harm is regarded more strictly as the result of the defendant's conduct or as constituted by the conduct itself. (*Note continues overleaf.*)

We will comment below on how this test may operate in relation to specific criminal offences, but first of all, some general comments. The distinction between culpable and purely accidental conduct is made at (i). The distinction between criminally culpable conduct and that which might give rise to moral or civil culpability is made at (ii).

Part (ii) of the test only partially determines the distinction between criminal culpability and moral/civil culpability, which will also be determined by the selection of prohibited harms as being appropriate for criminal offences. So, for example, there is an initial question as to whether the harm caused by stalking should give rise to a criminal offence, prior to the issue of what level of culpability should distinguish criminal liability for stalking.[237]

Justified conduct is distinguished from culpable conduct at (i), whereas excused conduct is distinguished at (iii).[238] The issue of whether some

---

The attempt to provide a general conception of criminal culpability by Larry Alexander, 'Insufficient Concern: A Unified Conception of Criminal Culpability' (2000) 88 *California Law Review* 931, provides an interesting comparison to the current project. One key difference is that Alexander is not concerned with the importance of relative culpability as distinct from threshold culpability (see Dressler, above n 215, at 963). The fundamental difference lies in Alexander's rejection of negligence as a possible basis for criminal culpability, on the spurious argument that some cases of obviously innocent, ignorant risk taking indicate all cases of inadvertence are non-culpable (at 949–51), and an insistence on choice as the basis of culpability without considering the choice of prioritising what one is prepared to advert to—impressing one's important guests rather than the safety of a young child in the bath (at 951 n57).

Bringing negligence into a broad approach to criminal culpability is also made problematical by Kenneth Simons, 'Dimensions Of Negligence in Criminal and Tort Law' (2002) 3 *Theoretical Inquiries in Law (Online Edition)* No 2 Article 2. Simons seeks to disassociate criminal negligence from conduct through a conception of 'cognitive negligence' focusing on deficient beliefs. However, a negligent belief does not ground culpability until acted upon (one may believe it is safe to leave a small child alone in the bath, but will not be culpable until one actually does so). Simons also invents a paradox (at 41–42) which makes it more difficult to take the different forms of mens rea together, but this rests on the false comparison between driving negligently (as to the possibility of harming the interests of others) and intentionally driving—rather than driving intentionally to harm the interests of others.

Jeremy Horder, 'Criminal Culpability: The Possibility of a General Theory' (1993) 12 *Law and Philosophy* 193, rejects the possibility of a uniform concept providing the basis for all principles of criminal culpability, and emphasises the role played by cultural values. Significantly, Horder insists on any theoretical explanation providing an account of criminal liability for negligence.

[237] Criminal and civil measures to deal with stalking were introduced by the Protection from Harassment Act 1997, following a consultation paper, *Stalking—The Solutions* (London, Home Office, 1996). For wider discussion, see Celia Wells, 'Stalking: The Criminal Law Response' [1997] *Criminal Law Review* 463.

[238] For general discussion of the distinction, see Fletcher, above n 201, at 759–817. The precise nature of the distinction has been the subject of much debate following the prominence given to it in Fletcher's work. See Kent Greenawalt, 'The Perplexing Borders of Justification and Excuse' (1984) 84 *Columbia Law Review* 1897; Joshua Dressler, 'Justifications and Excuses: A Brief Review of the Concepts and the Literature' (1987) 33 *Wayne Law Review* 1155. There remains disagreement over the classification of particular defences, such as duress. On this see, Peter Westen and James Mangiafico, 'The Criminal Defense of Duress: A Justification,

restraint other than punishment is appropriate remains open where (iii), but not (i), receives a negative answer.[239]

Normative standards enter each of the three parts of the test, in determining (i) what can be expected of the reasonable man;[240] (ii) what is sufficiently serious to warrant criminal liability; and (iii) which capacities of the accused will be considered relevant, and what importance will be attributed to them.[241]

The idea that we have here a general threshold test, or basic blueprint, for criminal culpability dependent on normative standards, seems

Not an Excuse—And Why it Matters' (2003) 6 *Buffalo Criminal Law Review* 833. Nevertheless, even if the analysis of the traditional defences is contestable and potentially multi-faceted, a distinction can be maintained between the two legal issues of what conduct is expected, and whether a particular defendant is accountable for a failure to act as expected. For some helpful recent discussion, see Mitchell Berman, 'Justification and Excuse, Law and Morality' (2003) 53 *Duke Law Journal* 1. Berman's insistence that the distinction in the criminal law tracks only a moral structure and not the substance of morality, supports the recognition of element (ii) in the three pronged test of criminal culpability provided above.

[239] See Fletcher, *ibid*, at 802. This allows for the possibility of social protection without mens rea, as advocated by Grygier, above n 201.

[240] Notably, in considering whether the view of the reasonable woman should be preferred. See on this, Forell and Matthews, above n 111. More generally, Moran in her illuminating study, *Rethinking the Reasonable Person*, above n 111, argues that the standard of the reasonable person needs to be linked to normative considerations of unacceptable indifference to the interests of others. The significance of the normative judgement for cases of indifference is brought out by Kenneth Simons, 'Does Punishment for "Culpable Indifference" Simply Punish for "Bad Character"? Examining the Requisite Connection Between Mens Rea and Actus Reus' (2002) 6 *Buffalo Criminal Law Review* 219, 297–315.

[241] This is a point acknowledged by Hart himself, above n 143, at 154–56. Nevertheless, AP Simester, 'Can Negligence be Culpable?' in Jeremy Horder (ed), *Oxford Essays in Jurisprudence, Fourth Series* (Oxford, Clarendon Press, 2000) 85, 92, 104, criticises Hart's test for failing to provide a proper link between the standard of the reasonable man and the capacity of the individual defendant, since it fails to investigate in detail the reasons why the defendant failed to meet that standard. Simester suggests, for example, that on the facts of *Elliott v C* it would be possible to apply Hart's test and find C culpable if we expected the reasonable man to recognise the risk and then found C could have recognised the risk if she had exercised a great deal of thought towards it. Simester makes the point that a finding of culpability requires us to decide that C could *reasonably* have been expected to pay attention to the risk, which requires us to know in detail why she failed to do so. Yet this second question of reasonableness governs just those factors in C's capacities we are prepared to take into account, and the standard of reasonableness adopted in the law at this point has to draw a line at a certain level of detail, effectively imposing the expectation of reasonable conduct on everyone above that line. As Hart (*loc cit*) mentioned, certain individual details are ruled out even by the cognitivist forms of mens rea, otherwise we would end up acquitting every defendant on the grounds of the specific point of detail that placed him or her in a less favourable position to the person behaving in a non-culpable manner. Cp Fletcher, above n 134, at 434: 'Duress is a defence to theft but greediness is not.' However, Moran, above n 111, at 240–57, raises concerns that Hart's account is ambivalent on whether his central issue of avoidability could let in claims of moral incapacity, and that Fletcher is over-reliant on customary or widespread community standards to set the limits. She herself proposes a critical egalitarian approach in order to establish the appropriate standards. Similarly, Samuel Pillsbury, *Judging Evil: Rethinking the Law of Murder and Manslaughter* (New York, NY, New York University Press, 1998) 182–84, argues that Hart's capacity test needs to be broadened into an analysis of indifference resulting from 'selfish and immoral priorities.'

contradicted by much of the discussion of traditional mens rea forms. This often proceeds on the basis that a technical understanding of the particular form of mens rea, rather than a normative evaluation, determines the extent of criminal culpability. The tendency is particularly marked in the case of intention.[242] In order to reject the suggestion that a technical rather than evaluative exercise lies at the heart of criminal culpability, it is important to see how the use of a particular mens rea form may satisfy one or more of the different parts of the test by exercising a normative presumption.

So where we take intention as the mens rea for an offence, *and* we have made the prior judgement that a particular harm is to be prohibited, then we assume that a defendant who intends to bring about a prohibited harm satisfies (i), because no reasonable person would intentionally bring about a prohibited harm. However, the presumption may be rebutted in exceptional circumstances, where the conduct is otherwise justified, as in self-defence. We may also generally presume in the case of intention that (ii) is satisfied, because once we have decided that no justification exists for engaging in the conduct at (i), the engagement in the conduct with the intention to bring about the prohibited harm will be sufficiently serious to warrant criminal liability. It is, indeed, the paradigmatic case of culpable conduct precisely because there is nothing (short of the *de minimis* doctrine) by which an evaluation that the defendant's conduct is somehow less serious could be made, and so disturb a presumption that this part of the test is satisfied. Similarly with (iii), if the defendant has the intention to bring about the prohibited harm, then the presumption will be that he or she had the capacity to avoid it, rebuttable only in exceptional excusatory circumstances, such as childhood or insanity.

In this light, the switch to one preferred conception of intention rather than another can be seen as activating a normative presumption, or (whether openly or not) making a normative judgement, in favour of setting the standard of normal conduct so as to find culpable what is covered by the conception preferred. So, preferring a conception of intention

---

[242] See Michael Moore, *Placing Blame: A General Theory of the Criminal Law* (Oxford, Clarendon Press, 1997) 55–59, ch 11 (an earlier version of ch 11 is found in Ruth Gavison (ed), *Issues in Contemporary Legal Philosophy: The Influence of H.L.A. Hart* (Oxford, Clarendon Press, 1987). The tendency is also found in discussions of recklessness. Consider, eg, the explications of recklessness as indifference by Alan White, *Grounds of Liability: An Introduction to the Philosophy of Law* (Oxford, Clarendon Press, 1985) 105–12 and *Misleading Cases* (Oxford, Clarendon Press, 1991) ch 3; and by Antony Duff, *Intention, Agency and Criminal Liability: Philosophy of Action and the Criminal Law* (Oxford, Blackwell, 1990) 165–73. The conflicting concepts of recklessness in terms of indifference offered by these authors rely heavily on their different technical understandings of indifference. By contrast, Horder, above n 215, employs indifference to express an overtly normative evaluation. Discussion of the failings of an overly technical approach to intention is provided by Alan Norrie, *Punishment, Responsibility, and Justice: A Relational Critique* (Oxford, OUP, 2000) 170–80.

that includes conscious exposure to risk of a certain kind, will effectively bring such risk taking within the presumptions that (i), (ii) and (iii) are satisfied. This is not necessarily an illegitimate move to make, for it may properly be considered that presumptively (outside exceptional justificatory or excusatory circumstances) a person who exposes the victim to a risk of that kind of suffering the prohibited harm, is engaging in conduct that any reasonable person would have avoided, in circumstances serious enough to warrant criminal liability, which he or she could have been expected to avoid. The problem here is that if the 'risk of a certain kind' cannot be clearly specified in advance, the pretence that a normative judgement[243] has already been made to set the standard of normal conduct by selecting this conception of intention, will give rise in practice to the reality that the normative issue is still to be determined.[244]

Where it is acknowledged that the kind of conscious exposure to risk that will presumptively satisfy the test cannot be clarified in advance, so as to treat it as a form of (or in the same way as) intention, then the questions posed by the test will have to be related to a separate mens rea form (such as the cognitivist form of recklessness). At least, parts (i) and (ii) of the test, as to whether a reasonable person would have avoided exposing the victim to the risk in that case, and whether failure to avoid doing so is serious enough to warrant criminal liability, will be opened up. This will occur because there is no longer perceived to be a tight fit between the prohibition of the law and the defendant's conduct. The conduct may now be regarded as being pursued for other, possibly legitimate, reasons, and the ocurrence of the prohibited harm may be regarded as a more or less remote probability in relation to that conduct. Such further factors may influence the response not only at (i) as to whether the conduct

---

[243] On the normativity of the judgement, see Norrie, *ibid*; and on the different normative approaches that can be taken, see the comparative study of *dolus eventualis* by Fletcher, above n 201, at 445–49. This study stresses that the judgement can be based on the finding of a 'particular subjective posture' towards the risk, rather than on a mere calculation of its probability. Fletcher points out (at 448–49) that there is no direct equivalent of *dolus eventualis* in the Anglo-American Common Law. The issue of oblique intention does, however, cover much of the same ground. This figures prominently in Moore, above n 242, *loc cit*. For extensive discussion, see Itzhak Kugler, *Direct and Oblique Intention in the Criminal Law: An inquiry into degrees of blameworthiness* (Aldershot, Ashgate, 2002).

[244] This is reflected in the difficulty of then specifying what conception of intention is being used. For discussion of the English experience, see Nicola Lacey, 'A Clear Concept of Intention: Elusive or Illusory?' (1993) 56 *Modern Law Review* 621; Jeremy Horder, 'Intention in the Criminal Law—A Rejoinder' (1995) 58 *Modern Law Review* 678; Nicola Lacey, 'In(de)terminable Intentions' (1995) 58 *Modern Law Review* 692. The underdetermination of the normative issue is described by Horder, at 687, in terms of leaving a certain amount of 'moral "elbow-room"'. Lacey (1995), at 694–95, questions just how much space this provides. For interesting discussion of how the selection of a conception of intention can create moral elbow-room by reference to the Court of Appeal judgments in *Re A (Conjoined Twins: Surgical Separation)* [2000] 4 All ER 961, see CMV Clarkson and HM Keating, *Criminal Law: Text and Materials* (5th edn, London, Sweet & Maxwell, 2003) 132–33.

should have been avoided, but also at (ii) as to whether the failure to avoid it is sufficiently culpable. However, the convention seems to be that if the exposure to risk were a conscious one, it can be presumed that (iii) is satisfied: the accused could have been expected to have avoided the risk. Although this is often presented as a matter of choosing to run the risk, the culpability of advertent risk taking needs to be unpacked further.

The association of advertence with a culpability of choice is dependent on something like the following line of reasoning. It is considered normal for humans with the capacity to appreciate a risk also to possess the capacity to avoid it. Being conscious of a risk indicates that one has the capacity to appreciate it. Therefore, one also possesses the capacity to avoid it. Yet this too displays a normative presumption (rebutted in standard excusatory circumstances), that no factor affecting the particular capacities of the defendant is such that he or she should no longer be expected to avoid the conduct in question.[245]

By contrast, when we consider a form of mens rea constituted by inadvertence, then a presumption does not even apply to part (iii) of the test. There are reasons for considering whether the defendant possessed the capacity to avoid the conduct (outside of the exceptional circumstances of excuse that applied to previous forms of mens rea[246]). Take, for example, a case similar in facts to *Prentice*, where a junior inexperienced doctor inadvertently exposes a patient to a risk. It may be judged appropriate[247] to consider the doctor's experience, training and present supervision in deciding whether he or she had the capacity to appreciate the risk, which a doctor with normal capacities would have avoided. These factors would not, however, be relevant in assessing culpability for a form of mens rea involving intention or advertence, at part (iii) of the test, because such forms presuppose a capacity to appreciate the risk.

Speaking still in general terms, we may then observe that the selection of different forms of mens rea linked to different criteria of culpability, makes the job of assessing criminal culpability more or less difficult, due

[245] For the general point, see n 241 above. For illustration of variation in normative judgement in a case where D was aware of the risk that his conduct contributed to (when driving a hitman to find a victim) but felt helpless to avoid the conduct, consider the majority and dissenting speeches in *Lynch v DPP for Northern Ireland* [1975] 1 All ER 913.
[246] Fletcher, above n 134, at 430–34, seeks to establish the underlying structural unity of negligent and intentional forms of culpability, and in doing so (at 434) suggests that the way intentional culpability takes account of some but not other excusing conditions amounts structurally to the same thing as the way negligent culpability assesses whether the defendant possessed the capacity to avoid the conduct in question. However, Fletcher does not explain why it is that the latter exercise roams more widely than the former.
[247] That this is a normative judgement becomes clear when considering an alternative, harsher standard which would not permit these factors to be taken into account: requiring all qualified doctors to take account of their known competence and not to practice beyond it. See further, Fletcher, above n 134, at 432; Horder, above n 215, at 515–17.

to the the normative presumptions that can be brought into play for these different criteria. It would be easiest to restrict ourselves to intention and (C1) simply because (outside of exceptional circumstances of justification or excuse) we can presume that all parts of the test will hold once we have established the basic element of purpose. In practice, however, different jurisdictions have in different ways expanded this simple category to cover part of the territory of (C2), whether intention or recklessness is used as the term to label the expanded form of mens rea.[248]

It is less easy to employ (C2), since the basic mens rea element of awareness of risk does not necessarily carry with it presumptions that parts (i) and (ii) of the test of culpability are satisfied. It is most difficult to employ (C3)(a), since this may additionally require further investigation into the satisfaction of part (iii) of the test. Nevertheless, ease or difficulty in satisfying the test should not be confused with satisfying the basic threshold test of criminal culpability at a higher or lower level.

One way of reinforcing the point that different forms of mens rea do not necessarily reflect different levels of culpability, is to show how the culpability of particular conduct can be made easier to demonstrate by altering the form of mens rea without changing the basic normative judgement as to culpability. An illustration is provided by considering the *Morgan* scenario, where the defendant claims that he believed the victim was consenting to sexual intercourse because he had been told so by a third party, who had also told him to discount her apparent objections as being part of a game she was playing. If we understand the mens rea of rape as being a form of recklessness or gross negligence covering culpable inadvertence, it will be necessary to respond to the three parts of the culpability test proposed above in order to determine that on the facts of this case the defendant should be regarded as possessing the mens rea required for a conviction of rape. The normative judgements required to be made, if a conviction is to follow, would be that in those circumstances: (i) a reasonable man would be expected to avoid the risk that the woman was not consenting by refraining from intercourse; (ii) the failure to do so is sufficiently serious to warrant criminal liability; and, (iii) the defendant possessed the capacities to appreciate and avoid the risk and could be expected to act otherwise. We only have to assume that the normative judgement in part (iii) would be made consistently for all male defendants other than those falling under general excusatory conditions,[249] and we can express exactly the same normative judgements with a different

[248] For discussion, see GR Sullivan, 'Intent, Subjective Recklessness and Culpability' (1992) 12 *Oxford Journal of Legal Studies* 380; Michael Gorr, 'Should the Law Distinguish between Intention and (Mere) Foresight?' (1996) 2 *Legal Theory* 359; and references in nn 201 & 243 above.
[249] If one were to find a category of male defendant to which this did not apply, it would be difficult to argue that the particular circumstances of the defendant, that were taken to

formulation of mens rea. We could reform the law of rape by providing a provision stating that the offence is committed where D has sexual intercourse with V when her consent to the intercourse has been communicated through a third party.[250] The mens rea for the reformed offence would be an intention (to have intercourse with V when her consent has been communicated through a third party), yet would be based on exactly the same normative evaluation of D's conduct as in the previous offence where a mens rea of recklessness or gross negligence had covered culpable inadvertence.

It would, of course, be easier to use the reformed version of the law because a mens rea in the form of intention would allow us to operate the normative presumptions in relation to the three parts of the culpability test, and so, outside of general justificatory or excusatory circumstances, the defendant's conviction would follow on proof of the relevant intention alone. In effect then, the reformulation of the offence with a mens rea of intention presents the law with the normative options determined that the formulation with a mens rea of recklessness or gross negligence leaves open. But once those options have been determined in a particular way, there is no difference in the culpability of the defendant, whichever of the mens rea forms is used.

There are important general points to be made here about the use of culpable inadvertence as a form of mens rea. First, and contrary to much received wisdom,[251] it does not necessarily indicate a lower level of culpability than the use of intention (and *a fortiori* a cognitivist form of recklessness). Secondly, it may be appropriate to use culpable inadvertence as a form of mens rea where the type of conduct involved does not lend itself to easy judgements about its criminality, typically because the

---

deprive him of the necessary capacities from which we could expect reasonable conduct for this offence, did not similarly prevent him from behaving reasonably in relation to other offences. In other words, this would be a general argument to expand the class of excusatory conditions, rather than the identification of a peculiar condition that was taken to deprive him of the capacity to behave reasonably with women.

[250] For discussion of a reform of this kind in s 273.1 of the Canadian Criminal Code, see Temkin (2002), above n 111, at 174–76. A less radical reform, providing only a presumption against belief in consent in certain specified circumstances, is to be found in s 76 of the Sexual Offences Act 2003.

[251] For discussion of 'the reigning hierarchy' of mental states, a critique, and a revision that nevertheless maintains the hierarchical structure, see Kenneth Simons, 'Rethinking Mental States' (1992) 72 *Boston University Law Review* 463. For a historical survey, see Paul Robinson, 'A Brief History of Distinctions in Criminal Culpability' (1980) *Hastings Law Journal* 815. An interesting attempt to harness the hierarchy in order to produce a schematic approach to homicide offences is made by Stanley Yeo, *Fault in Homicide: Towards a Schematic Approach to the Fault Elements for Murder and Involuntary Manslaughter in England, Australia and India* (Annandale, NSW, The Federation Press, 1997). The possibility of overlap within the hierarchical ordering is discussed in Douglas Husak, 'The Sequential Principle of Relative Culpability' (1995) 1 *Legal Theory* 493.

conduct involves possibly beneficial consequences as well as harmful ones (killing somebody by driving a motor car, as opposed to stabbing the victim with a knife). Thirdly, it may be appropriate to use culpable inadvertence as a form of mens rea because the type of conduct involved is engaged in by persons with significantly different capacities to appreciate and avoid the risk of harmful consequences.[252] Fourthly, it may be appropriate to use culpable inadvertence as a form of mens rea where, due to the rich and unpredictable diversity of human conduct, there may arise instances of conduct as yet not normatively evaluated and classified, but which may still give rise to the prohibited harm in a manner which is as culpable as conduct already recognised as criminal. And fifthly, the recognition of culpable inadvertence as a form of mens rea relates primarily to the recognition of the underlying criterion of culpability, (C3)(a), and not to which term (be it recklessness, gross negligence, negligence, or whatever) is used to label the mens rea of an offence.

So just what does this mean, when it comes to considering specific offences? There are three outstanding areas for comment. First, deferring discussion of the relative culpability of offences, there is the question of which of the criteria of culpability should be employed to specify the form(s) of mens rea required for a particular offence. To assert that an offence designed to prohibit a particular harm should have its mens rea fixed by (C1) and/or (C2) as a criterion of culpability would seem to arbitrarily restrict the protection offered by the law for that particular harm. It may also amount to shirking the difficulties involved in assessing where the limits of criminal culpability are to be found, when convenient presumptions do not provide easy answers. Might there, nevertheless, be legitimate grounds for making this sort of restriction in a particular case (bearing in mind we are still not considering the relative culpability of offences)?

One ground that might possibly be advanced is that the conduct bringing about the prohibited harm is invariably intentional, or at least that which would be considered sufficiently culpable to pass part (ii) of the test invariably is, so that nothing much is lost by restricting culpability to intentional conduct under (C1). It is difficult to think of an area of prohibited harm covered by the modern criminal law where this argument would succeed.[253] However, once we acknowledge the need to bring in

---

[252] This itself may be normatively contentious. See, eg, the discussion of whether different doctors should be treated as possessing significantly different capacities, n 247 above and accompanying text; and the discussion of the class of male defendants, text at n 249 above. The gist of the issue about significance is whether, despite individual differences, all members of the class can be expected to attain the threshold capacity to engage in the conduct appropriately or else to avoid it. If so, the differences remain insignificant.

[253] From the traditional harms of loss of life, injury to body, damage to or deprivation of goods, to the modern sophisticated harms caused by activities such as insider trading.

(C2) as an appropriate criterion of culpability, it is extremely difficult to resist the gravitational pull of (C3)(a), as has been documented above. An alternative ground that might then be advanced is the severity of the practical difficulties in applying (C3)(a), where the normative evaluation of the inadvertent conduct is extremely contentious within society, and no advantage can be taken of the normative presumptions that can be used with the other two criteria. Yet to fail to include inadvertent conduct under (C3)(a) in such a case is to take sides in the debate with those who normatively judge such conduct to be acceptable (or, at least, not criminally culpable). The recent history of the mens rea of rape in English law demonstrates all too clearly that where such a matter is open to debate then that debate needs to be aired. Actually debating the issue of inadvertence in relation to other areas of prohibited harm, might well give rise to a recognition of culpability that it is appropriate to criminalise.[254]

The second area for comment is the relative culpability of offences. One way of ranking the culpability of offences is to bring in the seriousness factor I have mentioned above.[255] People may be considered more culpable due to the greater degree of harm involved, or due to the greater degree of risk of bringing about a harm. The seriousness factor in relation to harm works across all forms of mens rea. An intentional killing is more culpable than an intentional assault. Yet the seriousness factor in relation to risk is sensitive to the form of mens rea. It works for recklessness and negligence, notably in assisting to make the transition from mere negligence to gross negligence, but is not employed for intentional conduct.[256] One intentional killing is not more culpable than another because the chance of succeeding in the assassination was higher. What is the reason for this?

A possible explanation is that killings carried out intentionally are characterised by a feature of culpability that reckless or negligent killings lack, which makes it redundant to consider the degree of risk involved.

---

[254] See the sentiment expressed by Fletcher, above n 134, at 437–38. Fletcher considers that the only plausible argument against admitting liability for negligence is a lack of resources.
[255] See text following n 213 above.
[256] Hyman Gross, *A Theory of Criminal Justice* (New York, NY, OUP, 1979) 82–88, seeks to establish a hierarchy of mens rea terms based on degrees of dangerousness exhibited by the conduct engaged in, during which (at 85) he asserts that more danger is exhibited by conduct done purposefully in a situation where a sleeping sailor is killed by asphyxiation when the ship's hold is fumigated, than by the same conduct done with indifference to the sailor's death. Yet, obviously, this is not so where both acts of fumigation are undertaken without checking whether the victim is sleeping in the hold. The risk, or danger, of his being there and being killed remains the same, irrespective of the intent of the fumigators. As pointed out by Brady, above n 210, at 194–95, some cases of reckless conduct may even exhibit a greater risk of harm than some cases of intentional conduct, and it is difficult to identify a single factor that will indicate a greater degree of culpability for the latter. He suggests that intentional conduct can be regarded as more culpable because it displays 'greater hostility', but refrains from exploring the notion further.

But if this is so, we should be able to point to some common metric of culpability that the intentional factor and the seriousness of risk factor are both capable of affecting. Otherwise, it would make sense to bring in the latter as well as the former to assess the culpability of intentional killings. A candidate for the common unit of measurement is to be found in the idea of disrespect, displayed in the culpable conduct, towards the legitimate interests of others. Culpable conduct may be more or less disrespectful, and so more or less culpable. And one way of indicating greater disrespect to the interests of others is to expose them to a greater risk of harm. If intentional conduct is generally considered more culpable in a way that overrides the calculation of risk, then it must be because we consider it displays more disrespect to the interests of others in seeking to harm those interests, than reckless or negligent conduct does in exposing them to the risk of harm, however great. According to this view, intentional conduct is regarded as showing not simply disrespect but something like contempt for the legitimate interests of others.

If this is accepted, then we do appear to have a basis for marking off intention as a distinctive form of mens rea, together with the criterion of culpability (C1), but this is subject to two crucial qualifications. First, the use of intention in this context should be recognised as differing from its role in satisfying the threshold test for criminal culpability. We have noted this special role in the context of working out how to indicate the relative culpability of different criminal offences. It is not, then, an argument for restricting the protection provided by the criminal law for any prohibited harm to intentional conduct alone. Secondly, copious historical and comparative evidence[257] demonstrates that this use of intention to signify a higher degree of culpability works only as a crude generalisation. Whether expressed as *'dolus'*, 'malice', or 'intentionally or recklessly', formulations of mens rea have been found to indicate a general recognition that some instances of exposure to risk of harm are as disrespectful and culpable (if not sometimes more so) than some instances of seeking to bring about the harm. Even in assessing relatively more serious degrees of culpability, there is an observable slippage from (C1) to (C2), which is disclosed by the evocative phrases employed to capture this greater degree of disrespect embracing instances of exposure to risk, such as 'extreme indifference to the value of human life', and 'wanton disregard for human life'.[258] And once this has been admitted, there is no barrier

---

[257] See references provided in nn 201 & 243 above.
[258] Discussed by Fletcher, above n 201, at 264–74 & 447–48. The phrases come from the Model Penal Code §210.2(1)(b), and the California Jury Instructions: Criminal (Supp to 3rd edn, 1976) §8.11, respectively. The latter phrase superceded the requirement of finding 'an abandoned and malignant heart' found in the California Penal Code §188. Under the proposals for codifying the Scottish criminal law, s 37 of the draft code includes a 'callous recklessness'

to admitting some instances of culpable inadvertence in (C3)(a) as displaying a heightened measure of disrespect.[259]

The third and final area for comment is the different roles intention can play in the definition of an offence. Apart from the role in satisfying the general threshold test of cupability, and the role in indicating a higher level of culpability through demonstrating greater disrespect for the interests of others, there exists another role that intention can play. This is to indicate the seriousness of the harm caused.[260] This can be found as a factor in determining whether there should be a criminal offence at all, which precedes the operation of part (ii) of the test of culpability.[261] It also has the potential to operate as a factor in demonstrating the relatively greater culpability of one offence over another.

As an example of the former, consider the role of an intention to permanently deprive in the statutory definition of theft in English law. Although this is regularly portrayed as simply one of the elements of the mens rea of theft,[262] it is arguable that it is not this element in the definition but rather the requirement of dishonesty that determines the culpability for the offence. The function of the intention to permanently deprive, by contrast, may be regarded as indicating the seriousness of the harm caused to the victim's property, to bring it under the appropriate scope of the criminal law: dishonest borrowings are culpable but not sufficiently serious to be considered a crime; dishonest deprivations are culpable and amount to a serious enough harm to be treated as criminal. Taking this line of reasoning a step further, it becomes plausible to suggest that this intention within the definition of theft operates as much as an element of the actus reus as of the mens rea of theft: the sort of appropriation required for theft is one that is intended to be permanent.

---

variant of murder, in preference to the existing formulation of 'wicked recklessness'. The Commentary makes it clear that the preferred phrase indicates an 'extreme disregard for human life' without imposing any technical restraints on how that is to be established, and that it covers instances of 'callous indifference' as well as cases where the risk is known and accepted. See Eric Clive, Pamela Ferguson, Christopher Gane and Alexander McCall Smith, *A Draft Criminal Code for Scotland with Commentary* (Edinburgh, Scottish Law Commission, 2003) 86–87.

[259] Arguably instances of this occur in the widening of the mens rea for murder in English law to include an intention to cause grievous bodily harm. As far as causing the *death* of the victim is concerned, the defendant may be only displaying culpable inadvertence. For discussion of other instances of negligent murder, see Robinson, above n 251, at 842–43; and for general discussion, see Pillsbury, above n 241, ch 9 and 193–95. For discussion of the modern English law, see Barry Mitchell, 'Culpably Indifferent Murder' (1996) 25 *Anglo-American Law Review* 64; William Wilson, 'Murder and the Structure of Homicide' in Andrew Ashworth and Barry Mitchell (eds), *Rethinking English Homicide Law* (Oxford, OUP, 2000).
[260] See text following n 213 above.
[261] This stage of the process was illustrated above with stalking. See n 237 above and accompanying text.
[262] See, eg, Sir John Smith, *The Law of Theft* (8th edn, London, Butterworths, 1997) 69ff.

Despite its status as a mental element, it operates as a qualification to limit what can constitute the actus reus.[263] Moreover, the status of this intention as an element of the mens rea can be doubted altogether, if we take mens rea, as we have been doing, as establishing the basis for culpability for the offence. For, clearly, an appropriation of another's property with an intention to permanently deprive will not be culpable if done honestly. Yet a dishonest appropriation will be culpable, even if not done with an intention to permanently deprive: it will simply not be criminal. This reinforces the suggestion that intention operates as a seriousness factor, qualifying the harm caused, rather than as an element of mens rea relating directly to culpability.[264]

An example of intention operating as a seriousness factor in relation to the harm caused, for the purpose of expressing relative culpability, is a rather rare occurrence in domestic law. Far more commonly it will express a higher degree of culpability by exhibiting (in the rather crude manner discussed above) a higher degree of disrespect to the victim's interests. However, we can consider an illustration from the Argentine Penal Code.[265] This provides for a form of aggravated homicide where anybody 'kills ... knowingly an ascendant, descendant or spouse'. The intention[266]

---

[263] Stephen Shute, John Gardner and Jeremy Horder, 'Introduction: The Logic of Criminal Law' in Stephen Shute, John Gardner and Jeremy Horder (eds), *Action and Value in Criminal Law* (Oxford, Clarendon Press, 1993) 13, recognise that the intention goes towards defining the nature of the wrong in theft but hold on to the view that it 'is plainly part of the *mens rea* of theft, if anything is.' The point that the intention qualifies the conduct so as to constitute it as a criminal wrong is also made by Horder, above n 244, at 681–82. Horder describes this role of intention as playing a part in constituting wrongs. In this respect Horder's analysis is compatible with that offered here, so long as a criminal wrong is understood as causing a harm or potential harm to another. (Horder leaves potential harm out of the discussion and so can set wrongfulness against harmfulness, for offences involving potential harms.) However, in another respect our analyses differ in a more significant manner. Horder strictly separates the assessment of a wrong from the assessment of culpability (at 682), whereas I allow for the severity of the wrong/harm to be a factor in determining (relative) culpability. Horder provides examples of offences other than theft where the intention operates in this way. For further discussion, see Jeremy Horder, 'Crimes of Ulterior Intent' in AP Simester and ATH Smith (eds), *Harm and Culpability* (Oxford, Clarendon Press, 1996).

[264] In determining the seriousness of the harm caused (or threatened), it may nevertheless *indirectly* affect the specific culpability of D's conduct, by making the failure to avoid it sufficiently serious to recognise criminal liability.

[265] Frederick Danforth (ed), *The Argentine Penal Code*, Emilio Gonzalez-Lopez (transl) (South Hackensack, NJ, Fred B Rothman & Co, 1963) Article 80. In international criminal law, this role for intention is far more common. It is required, eg, to establish that acts of homicide amount to the greater harm of genocide. For discussion, see Antonio Cassese, *International Criminal Law* (Oxford, OUP, 2003) 103–05, 167–68.

[266] I take an intention to do *x* with the knowledge that circumstance *y* applies, as being equivalent to an intention (to do *x* where *y*). This is the position taken by Glanville Williams, *The Mental Element in Crime* (Jerusalem, Magnes Press, 1965) 18. For discussion of the Model Penal Code's preference for a distinction between purposely and knowingly, and the objection to it from Glanville Williams (*op cit*, at 19), see Robinson, above n 251, at 847–48. Robinson considers that the MPC's distinction can be captured in terms of specific intent and intent.

to kill one's parent, for example, operates over and above the intention to kill required to establish culpability for homicide. Obviously, the more specific intention is taken to indicate a higher level of culpability, but it does so not by displaying more disrespect to the interests of others than negligent or reckless conduct would normally do to those same interests. This is the type of case already considered above. In the present case, the intention indicates a higher level of culpability by measuring a greater harm caused. The greater harm in the case of a matricide or parricide is brought about because another interest is threatened. An ordinary homicide threatens the victim's interest in life and the peaceable enjoyment of it. A matricide or parricide threatens, in addition, the interest of being able to trust those with whom one is in a particularly intimate relationship of trust and respect. The intention to kill one's parent demonstrates disrespect for this additional interest, and hence constitutes the greater harm, which would otherwise be difficult to find.[267] For this offence we may discern a compound intention[268] performing the twin roles of satisfying the threshold test of culpability and of indicating a higher level of culpability by demonstrating a more serious harm.

When we consider in general practical examples of the factors affecting levels of culpability, so as to settle the relative scope of two related offences, it is evident that these factors may vary considerably. Seriousness of risk, seriousness of harm, level of disrespect to the legitimate interests of others, certainly feature commonly in distinctions such as those between careless and reckless driving, or assaults causing actual bodily harm and grievous bodily harm, or murder and manslaughter. These factors will then inform consideration of the mens rea issue for a particular offence, determining what is the basis for establishing culpability for that offence. However, neither within the complex interplay of these factors, nor with a single factor taken in isolation, is there any ground for assuming that distinctions between less and more serious harms, between less and more culpable states, between less and more serious offences, can be drawn with great precision. Whether the distinctions employ overtly evaluative terminology, such as 'extreme

[267] One could imagine cases of intending to kill a victim whose identity was unknown being reckless as to whether that victim was one's parent. Where the probability was known by D to be extremely high, it might be possible to argue disrespect for the additional interest had been shown, and hence the greater harm had been done. This replicates the slippage noted above (text following n 257) between (C1) and (C2) when considering the role of intention to express a higher degree of culpability. All this assumes an approach to culpability based on the disrespect found in D's attitude, rather than a purely objective assessment of D's conduct. The curse meted out to Oedipus for parricide was earned otherwise. Its tragic quality was exhibited in his killing his Father completely unawares.

[268] Such an analysis was not required for theft due to the presence of dishonesty as a mens rea element. The analysis of a compound intention (relating to both actus reus and mens rea) can, however, be applied elsewhere, notably to offences of ulterior intent, discussed by Horder, above n 263.

indifference to the value of human life',[269] or seemingly technical terms, such as reckless and careless,[270] the working out of the distinction will require a contextual grasp of the sort of conduct involved and a sufficient familiarity with the range of conduct, to make it possible to recognise more and less serious instances.[271] This is intuitive rather than expository work. Intuitions may be shared: they may draw on common experiences and common sources of values. They may not be. Where not, the terms provided in the law will not indicate in themselves how exactly the distinction is to be made. The most we can hope for is that they narrow down the issues over which the precise boundaries will be drawn, and then in the responses to those issues there is gradually developed a coherent body of legal knowledge on how those distinctions are to be understood.

Perhaps it is not so important to argue over the most helpful terminology to use in the criminal law as it is to stress the uses to which that terminology is put. Overtly evaluative terminology may alert us more readily than apparently technical terminology to the normative judgement required in applying a term, but even evaluative phraseology may become legalistic. The crucial matter to focus on is what underlying issue the legal term relates to. In the employment of recklessness as a mens rea term in the criminal law, it is of fundamental importance to enquire whether the term is being used to designate satisfaction of the general threshold test of culpability, or is being used to designate a more serious level of culpability. In the former case, I think it can be concluded that whatever general term is employed, it should be understood to include instances of culpable inadvertence.[272] In the latter case, instances of culpable inadvertence are not ruled out,[273] but it is critical to relate the evaluative judgement that will include them or exclude them to the context. So (with the appropriate understanding in place) one might settle for 'recklessly damaging

---

[269] See text at n 258 above.

[270] See n 200 above.

[271] This is clearly evident in Lord Goff's method of working out the difference between careless and reckless driving, *ibid*, which relies on the grasp of such specific contextual matters as the distracting effect of 'a pretty girl in the car alongside' (at 812).

[272] If 'recklessness' is retained, the best formulation so far in English law seems to be the Williams' refinement to *Caldwell* recklessness (see text accompanying n 131 above), favoured by the Magistrates in *Elliott v C* but declined by the House of Lords in *R v G*. This does, however, suffer from restricting the enquiry to the narow issue of potential cognitive states. Although the potential to be aware of the risk might well be regarded as necessary to establishing that the threshold of culpability for failing to avoid the risk has been established, it does not follow that this is a sufficient factor. One may want to permit investigation of further factors in considering why that potential awareness was not realised and acted upon. In that respect, there are grounds for favouring the terminology of 'gross negligence', as the Court of Appeal did in *Prentice* (see text accompanying nn 65–67 above).

[273] See n 259 above.

another's property' for criminal damage, but prefer 'driving with reckless disregard for the safety of other road users' for reckless driving.

Finally, a brief comment on the wider lessons to be learned from the recent history of recklessness in the English criminal law. We need to recognise that the mens rea issue does not lend itself to neat solutions captured in straightforward definitions. We need to acknowledge that such body of legal knowledge we currently possess is incomplete, is open to development; and such guidance that it offers may pose questions to which the answers are contestable, as well as offering resolution to conflicting viewpoints. Certainly one lesson that is clear from this saga is that if we do not acknowledge these things, in preference for a simpler but less accurate portrayal of the state of legal materials, then we shall only learn the limits of our understanding by a far longer and a far harder path.

4

Some Problems with the Definition of Theft

INTRODUCTION

T HE PREVIOUS STUDY on recklessness raised some interesting issues about the definition of terms in the criminal law, but the subject of the study cannot be regarded as typical or representative for a number of reasons. The fact that recklessness is a mens rea term, and as such is used to establish culpability for an offence, immediately brings up several complicating factors. It performs an evaluative role in the process of attributing culpability for conduct, and the normative judgements it entails make the precise scope of the term dependent on the selection of a normative position from a potential plurality of conflicting positions. As one mens rea term among others, its particular role and precise meaning cannnot be understood in isolation from other mens rea terms, which only serves to magnify the task, given the historical confusion over the relationships between these different terms. As a mens rea term employed for a variety of offences, offence-specific variables may cloud any attempt to reach a clear understanding of how the term itself is used. Also, if we accept the suggestion made in the previous chapter that recklessness as a mens rea term may perform the distinct roles of establishing threshold criminal culpability, and of signifying a relatively more serious level of culpability, yet further complications may arise. Added to these factors which relate to recklessness being used as a mens rea term, we can recognise other complicating factors brought about by the attempt to establish the connection between legal usage of the term with ordinary usage as portrayed in the dictionary, where the dictionary definition of recklessness displays a disorganised collection of meanings. And finally, the judicial development of recklessness, as a common law concept, brings to the study a sense of instability due to the lack of a constant source for the term's definition, exacerbated by changing judicial attitudes prompting the selective treatment of earlier authorities.

Within this chapter I shall attempt a different study on the use of terms within the definition of a single offence. The offence is theft, and the two terms I wish to concentrate on here are dishonesty[1] and appropriation. This produces a number of contrasts with the previous study. Whereas that study dealt with the common law, mens rea, and the general part of the criminal law, this study deals with statute, both mens rea and actus reus, and a particular offence. One thing to consider will be how significant these differences turn out to be. However, we can note from the outset one feature of the present study which marks it out from the previous one. Although we examined the possibility of an offence-specific element in the use of recklessness, we found this operated by leaving certain considerations affecting the use of the term to be worked out in the setting of the particular offence after reaching a general understanding of the term.[2] In the present study, by looking at these two terms and their interrelationship within the definition of a particular offence, there is the opportunity for the offence-specific element to operate at a more basic level in determining how each term is understood. Indeed, an obvious motive for selecting these two terms for our study is that the definitions of the terms, and their interrelationship, have been particularly significant in working out the definition of theft.

THE TEST FOR DISHONESTY

The first task of this chapter is to investigate the test for dishonesty established in *Ghosh*.[3] Despite the longstanding authority of this decision in the criminal law of England and Wales, I want to suggest that the approach to defining dishonesty within the *Ghosh* test is unworkable. I shall seek to reinforce this view of the test by referring to how it has been modified by later appellate decisions, and by providing an illustration of the practical outworking of the test from the Guinness prosecutions. I shall then seek to shed further light on the problems that emerge from our consideration of the approach taken in *Ghosh*, by examining what sort of reform in this key area of the criminal law would be required in order to overcome them.

---

[1] Strictly speaking the term is adverbial in the definition of theft under s 1 of the Theft Act 1968: 'dishonestly appropriates property belonging to another with the intention of permanently depriving the other of it'. I shall generally use the less inelegant 'dishonesty' to refer to this term.

[2] By this I mean to say that the general understanding specifies the sorts of questions the term poses, which will receive specific responses in relation to a particular offence. This is perhaps more evident in the role performed by recklessness in satisfying the threshold test of culpability, but even where it is performing the role of assessing relative culpability there remains a general understanding that it is seeking to establish a particular level of culpability by drawing attention to an aggravated form of disrespect for the interests of others, the particular interest(s) and the nature of the aggravation being supplied by the context of the specific offence.

[3] [1982] 2 All ER 689.

The Background

The Criminal Law Revision Committee introduced the term 'dishonestly' as a means of making the law more intelligible to juries, rather than as effecting a substantive change.[4] However, by providing a word that is supposed to be intelligible to jurors the CLRC has, unwittingly perhaps, brought about a change in the role that this element of the offence performs. Since the ordinary usage of dishonesty employs the term as a standard, so the introduction of the term into the new offence of theft creates an ordinary standard where previously there had been a technical legal requirement. The point is clearly made in the judgment of Lawton LJ in *Feely*:[5]

> We do not agree that judges should define what 'dishonestly' means. This word is in common use whereas the word 'fraudulently' which was used in s 1(1) of the Larceny Act 1916 had acquired as a result of case law a special meaning. Jurors, when deciding whether an appropriation was dishonest can be reasonably expected to, and should, apply the current standards of ordinary decent people.

The switch through ordinary language to ordinary standards raises the crucial issue of how those standards are to be assessed. The decision of the Court of Appeal in the second Guinness appeal, which we shall examine in the case study below, demonstrates just how crucial this may be in establishing whether the conduct of a particular defendant will be pronounced criminal or not. The importance of having a clear test for dishonesty is not limited to its significance for offences under the Theft Acts.[6] It becomes all the more important in the light of the Law Commission's review of offences involving dishonesty, its willingness to consider broadening their scope, and its stated preference for retaining within the legal understanding of dishonesty the employment of standards of ordinary people.[7]

Statutory Amplification

The 1968 Act does provide some guidance in s 2 on how to assess the standards of honest conduct, but it is limited to particular situations. No

---

[4]Criminal Law Revision Committee (Cmnd 2977, 1966), Eighth Report, *Theft and Related Offences*, paras 35 and 39. (Hereinafter cited as, Eighth Report.)
[5][1973] 1 All ER 341, 345.
[6]As well as a number of offences under the Theft Act 1968, the requirement of dishonesty figures in the definition of the offences introduced by the Theft Act 1978.
[7]See Stephen Silber, 'The Law Commission, Conspiracy to Defraud and the Dishonesty Project' [1995] *Criminal Law Review* 461; Law Commission, LCCP No 155 (1999), *Legislating the Criminal Code: Fraud and Deception*; Law Commission No 276 (Cm 5560, 2002), *Fraud*—and the discussion in n 47 below.

attempt is made to furnish a general definition of dishonesty. Indeed, the CLRC were (somewhat ironically) divided as to whether any amplifying provision was required, since 'dishonestly' had been introduced on the basis that it was being used with its ordinary meaning.[8] The provisions in s 2 are fairly straightforward:

2. (1) A person's appropriation of property belonging to another is not to be regarded as dishonest—

   (a) if he appropriates the property in the belief that he has in law the right to deprive the other of it, on behalf of himself or of a third person; or

   (b) if he appropriates the property in the belief that he would have the other's consent if the other knew of the appropriation and the circumstances of it; or

   (c) (except where the property came to him as trustee or personal representative) if he appropriates the property in the belief that the person to whom the property belongs cannot be discovered by taking reasonable steps.

  (2) A person's appropriation of property belonging to another may be dishonest notwithstanding that he is willing to pay for the property.

What is intriguing is to speculate on whether it is possible to see within these particular instances, manifestations of a general concept of dishonesty that it falls to the courts to determine.[9] In each of the three cases covered by s 2(1), it is the defendant's own belief in the claim of right, etc that is material (not whether he did in fact have a legal right, etc). However, it is important to stress that his belief is only material because it is a type of belief that *the law* recognises as establishing that he was not dishonest. We cannot transfer an evaluation *of* the defendant's own beliefs to an evaluation *by* the defendant's own standards.[10] Exactly how the defendant's own beliefs should be regarded is a question the courts have had to grapple with.

A further insight is provided by the reason given for the inclusion of s 2(2). The CLRC considered the provision was required to make it clear that such behaviour could be dishonest where it might be argued otherwise.[11] This belies the simple assertion that everything can be

---

[8] Eighth Report, para 39.

[9] Suggested by *Woolven* (1983) 77 Cr App R 231.

[10] See the discussion of such faulty reasoning in *Ghosh* by Kenneth Campbell, 'The Test of Dishonesty in *R v Ghosh*' (1984) 43 *Cambridge Law Journal* 349, 354. The confusion is not limited to *Ghosh*. Alan White provides a further example of the confusion in his *Misleading Cases* (Oxford, Clarendon Press, 1991) 78.

[11] Eighth Report, Annex 2, Note on Clause 2, 125.

entrusted to the ordinary understanding of the term, and reveals that different and inconsistent views can be taken as to the meaning of dishonesty.

The Case Law

Although ordinary people may resort to using the term dishonesty, the standard that one ordinary person invokes the term to convey may differ from the standard of another. This poses the question of how instrumental the defendant's own views and beliefs are in selecting the particular standard by which his conduct is to be judged. At one extreme it is thought that it is only fair to find the defendant culpable when he has failed to live up to standards that he himself subscribes to—commonly referred to as a *subjective*[12] approach. At the other extreme it is thought necessary for society to impose standards upon its members irrespective of their own individual views and beliefs—an *objective* approach.

The courts in the past have been capable of taking a subjective or an objective approach to dishonesty. In June 1972, the Court of Appeal in *Gilks* upheld a direction to the jury to consider whether '[the defendant] thought he was acting honestly or dishonestly'.[13] Six months later, the Court of Appeal switched to an objective approach in *Feely*, where Lawton LJ required the jurors to make reference to 'the current standards of ordinary decent people'.[14]

The difference between the subjective and objective approaches here reflects not so much a conflict as a tension. In practice, we are sometimes prepared to judge behaviour in the light of a person's individual belief or viewpoint. On other occasions we insist on a standard being imposed that everybody must live up to. Resolving the tension may be more difficult in some cases than others: conscientious objectors during wartime; Sikhs being required to wear motor cycle helmets; a serial killer who claims to be on a divine mission to kill. The vacillation over dishonesty not only

---

[12] As we saw in the previous chapter, the terms *subjective* and *objective* are far from being unproblematical. For judicial reservations, see Lord Diplock in *Caldwell* [1981] 1 All ER 961, 966. For academic comment see, eg, Richard Tur, 'Subjectivism and Objectivism: Towards Synthesis' in Stephen Shute, John Gardner and Jeremy Horder (eds), *Action and Value in Criminal Law* (Oxford, Clarendon Press, 1993); and for critical doubts, Alan Norrie, 'Subjectivism, Objectivism and the Limits of Criminal Recklessness' (1992) 12 *Oxford Journal of Legal Studies* 45. However, for present purposes we can conveniently deploy the terms to signify the difference between approaches to dishonesty which do or do not, respectively, make allowance for the belief or viewpoint of the defendant himself. We shall look more carefully at this in the final section of this chapter, and refer to the broader issues raised by these terms in the next chapter.
[13] [1972] 3 All ER 281, 283.
[14] See text at n 5 above.

reflects this tension but may also be regarded as an effort to resolve it by reaching some sort of compromise.

The compromise reached by the Court of Appeal in *Ghosh* was to take the objective standard of dishonesty found in *Feely* based on the standards of ordinary decent people but to qualify it by the subjective requirement that the defendant must have been aware that his behaviour would be regarded as dishonest according to those standards. According to Lord Lane CJ, the compromise is designed to avoid two excesses. On the one hand, a purely objective approach would catch the foreigner who coming from a country where public transport is free fails to pay his bus fare. The further requirement of the *Ghosh* test that the foreigner must be aware of the ordinary standards prevents 'conduct to which no moral obloquy could possibly attach'[15] from being regarded as dishonest.

At the other extreme, a purely subjective approach would allow the ardent anti-vivisectionist to impose his own standards. This is prevented by insisting that he applies what he knows to be the standards of ordinary people:[16]

> ... a jury must first of all decide whether according to the ordinary standards of reasonable and honest people what was done was dishonest. If it was not dishonest by those standards, that is the end of the matter and the prosecution fails. If it was dishonest by those standards, then the jury must consider whether the defendant himself must have realised that what he was doing was by those standards dishonest. In most cases, where the actions are obviously dishonest by ordinary standards, there will be no doubt about it. It will be obvious that the defendant himself knew that he was acting dishonestly. It is dishonest for a defendant to act in a way which he knows ordinary people consider to be dishonest, even if he asserts or genuinely believes that he is morally justified in acting as he did. For example, Robin Hood or those ardent anti-vivisectionists who remove animals from vivisection laboratories are acting dishonestly, even though they may consider themselves to be morally justified in doing what they do, because they know that ordinary people would consider these actions to be dishonest.

The test established in *Ghosh*, depicted diagrammatically below,[17] provides two opportunities for the defendant to establish that he was not dishonest—in accordance with ordinary standards, or in accordance with what he regarded ordinary standards to be. Correspondingly, two requirements must be satisfied before a defendant's conduct can be pronounced dishonest.

---

[15] [1982] 2 All ER 689, 696.
[16] *ibid* at 696.
[17] A variation on the helpful diagram in Campbell, above n 10, at 351.

Twofold Test for Dishonesty

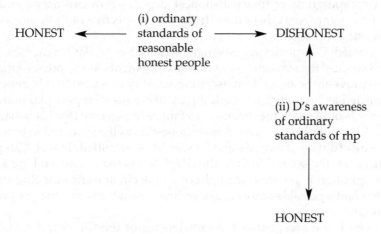

PROBLEMS WITH THE TEST

The appeal of the *Ghosh* test is precisely that it appears to strike an effective compromise. Upon further examination, however, we find within it not a stable compromise but a continuing tension between the subjective and objective approaches, concealed by the great assumption of the *Ghosh* test that there exists a set of ordinary standards of dishonesty. Once we accept that the common term dishonesty can be used to convey quite different standards then the *Ghosh* test collapses on its own foundation. For we can no longer confidently assert that every juror will have access to a uniform body of standards when interpreting dishonesty. Moreover, the subjective side of the compromise, which requires the defendant himself to be aware of those ordinary standards, is no longer restrained by the uniform body of standards whose general recognition within a society would only permit such a person as Lord Lane's paradigmatic foreigner to credibly express ignorance of them. Unrestrained, the subjective side of the compromise may fix on one of a number of views as to the ordinary standard of dishonesty, and not merely recreate the tension between subjective and objective approaches but intensify the tension by relocating it within the objective limb of the compromise.

The practical upshot is, as Edward Griew points out,[18] that far from precluding the values of Robin Hood or the ardent animal rights activist, the *Ghosh* test enables a 'Robin Hood defence' where the defendant believes, as a result of the conviction of his own moral or political beliefs, that 'ordinary people' will think he is acting correctly. A further

[18] Edward Griew, 'Dishonesty: The Objections to Feely and Ghosh' [1985] *Criminal Law Review* 341, 353.

practical consequence is that the *Ghosh* test may backfire in the case of a jury composed of 'ordinary dishonest jurors', whose ordinary standards may be regarded as dishonest (from the perspective of Professor Griew at least).[19]

Kenneth Campbell suggests that the fundamental flaw in the *Ghosh* test is to confuse the subjective and objective elements. If the point of the test is to prevent the defendant escaping liability in a case that is generally regarded as involving wrongdoing by using his own personal morality, then it is only when the defendant's failure to perceive that his behaviour would ordinarily be regarded as dishonest is itself considered to be excusable by ordinary standards that he should be acquitted. In fact, Campbell concludes, the second limb of the *Ghosh* test is redundant, so long as the first question is posed in the light of all the circumstances including the defendant's possible ignorance of ordinary standards and the reasons for that ignorance.[20]

Even if we accept that the deficiencies of the *Ghosh* test would be reduced by adopting this suggestion, we have not overcome the problem that there can be different views on what the reasonable honest man would decide. As Campbell himself comments:[21]

> But no one should be seduced into thinking that it is a test of pure social fact … It is a partially idealised test with a necessary component of moral evaluation which will vary from jury to jury.

Despite these criticisms the authority of the *Ghosh* test remains unchallenged in the courts. But given that the difficulties we have noted pose real practical problems, we must look at how dishonesty is in practice interpreted by the courts.

Dishonesty in Practice

Although the *Ghosh* test firmly places the issue of dishonesty in the hands of the jury, juries have to be directed, and judges' directions come to be scrutinised by appellate courts. The course that the test has taken in appeal cases provides some insight into its practice. It also demonstrates that the test has undergone significant modification.

The simplest way of making the modification arises when the test is not properly applied in the trial judge's directions, but the verdict is nevertheless upheld on appeal by applying the proviso to s 1 of the

---

[19] *ibid* at 346.
[20] Campbell, above n 10, at 354–56.
[21] *ibid* at 359.

Criminal Appeal Act 1968. This effectively substitutes the appellate court's determination for the jury's, by an evidential presumption, whilst still following the form of the test. In *Melwani*[22] and *O'Connell*[23] the Court of Appeal felt able to do this in cases involving bank and mortgage frauds, on the basis that a properly directed jury would have rejected the defendant's belief that he was acting honestly. By contrast, the conviction was quashed in *Boggeln v Williams*,[24] where the defendant had reconnected his electricity supply. In all three cases the defendant had indicated a belief that he would pay for what he had obtained, and the inference is that the application of the *Ghosh* test[25] must depend on the nature of the defendant's conduct: defrauding banks and building societies is just known to be dishonest. Yet the idea of there being no room for doubt on the outcome of applying the *Ghosh* test to particular conduct, is incompatible with the way the test is formulated.[26]

A second form of the modification occurs in *Roberts*,[27] where the defendant was convicted of handling stolen paintings for which he had endeavoured to obtain a reward from the insurers. The Court of Appeal held that the *Ghosh* test was not required, since the defendant had not raised the possibility that he thought that others would regard his behaviour as not being dishonest. This imposes a fairly light evidential burden on the defendant, to raise the belief that others would consider his behaviour to be honest, before the *Ghosh* test becomes applicable. However, the Court of Appeal in *Roberts* introduced a stronger aspect of the modification in taking a case of obvious dishonesty[28] as completely precluding the need

---

[22] [1989] *Criminal Law Review* 565.
[23] [1991] *Criminal Law Review* 771; (1992) 94 Cr App R 39.
[24] [1978] 2 All ER 1061.
[25] *Boggeln v Williams* was decided prior to *Ghosh*, but if anything the *Feely* test should be regarded as a more difficult barrier to overcome. In *Melwani*, above n 22, at 566, the two cases are regarded as expounding the same test.
[26] A point made by John Smith in his commentary on *O'Connell*, above n 23, at 773: 'Dishonesty under the *Ghosh* rule is determined by the standards of the jury which are not necessarily those of the Court of Appeal.'
[27] (1985) 84 Cr App R 117.
[28] The doctrine of obvious dishonesty is discussed by ATH Smith, *Property Offences* (London, Sweet & Maxwell, 1994) §§7–71-7–73; by Edward Griew, *The Theft Acts* (7th edn, London, Sweet & Maxwell, 1995) §2–133; and by Sir John Smith, *The Law of Theft* (8th edn, London, Butterworths, 1997) §2–122, text at n 4—cp *Archbold 2003*, vol 2, PJ Richardson (ed) (London, Sweet & Maxwell) §21–26. However, it is somewhat marginalised by each of these authors. Griew and John Smith both focus on the evidential requirement of the doctrine. ATH Smith in taking *Price* rather than *Roberts* as the leading case fails to address the stronger doctrine emerging in the latter case, though his subsequent comments on *Green* disclose more disquiet. More recently, ATH Smith, 'Offences Against Property' in David Feldman (ed), *English Public Law* (Oxford, OUP, 2004) has provided a stronger statement of the obvious dishonesty modification by attaching these comments directly to *Price* (at §26.47): 'The law would seem to be that a direction in *Ghosh* terms should [only] be given where it can plausibly be said that honest and ordinary people might think that whatever the defendant was doing was not dishonest.' Smith goes on to observe that this itself is a matter for

The Practice of Dishonesty

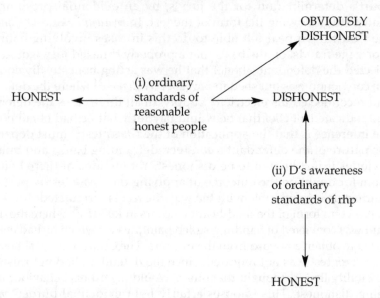

for the *Ghosh* test. Ironically, the idea of obvious dishonesty used in the *Ghosh* test itself[29] to convey how the test might in practice be applied, is cited in *Roberts* as authority for the proposition that there is no need to apply it.[30] This was followed in *Price*,[31] which involved issuing a number of worthless cheques; and *Forrester*,[32] where the defendant had forcibly taken property from his landlord to induce him to return the deposit, was decided similarly.

The practice of the courts goes beyond a simple application of the *Ghosh* test, which has effectively been restricted to cases where the court considers there is room to doubt whether the defendant's behaviour

doubt. A stronger view on obvious dishonesty from John Smith is to be found in his Comment on *Buzalek and Schiffer* [1991] *Criminal Law Review* 130, where the Court of Appeal treated conduct involving a lie as a case of obvious dishonesty so as to preclude the *Ghosh* test. Smith convincingly argues that the test should have been used.

Interestingly, in establishing liability for dishonest assistance in breach of trust, there appears to have been a retreat from a test of obvious dishonesty established by Lord Nicholls in the Privy Council case of *Royal Brunei Airlines v Tan* [1995] 1 AC 378 towards an approach modelled on the *Ghosh* test, following the House of Lords majority decision in *Twinsectra Ltd v Yardley* [2002] UKHL 12; [2002] 2 All ER 377. For helpful discussion, see Rosy Thornton, 'Dishonest Assistance: Guilty Conduct or a Guilty Mind?' (2002) 61 *Cambridge Law Journal* 524.

[29] Text at n 16 above.
[30] (1985) 84 Cr App R 117, 123.
[31] (1989) 90 Cr App R 409.
[32] [1992] *Criminal Law Review* 793.

could be regarded as dishonest. Notwithstanding the technical authority of *Ghosh*, the courts have taken a hard line by holding particular circumstances to amount to absolute dishonesty, thus permitting 'objective' standards to be imposed by the courts. The approach is represented in the diagram above.

The implications are twofold. First, the subjective element, which could operate in the *Ghosh* test to at least partially resolve the uncertainties over dishonesty in the defendant's favour can be excluded in a case of obvious dishonesty. Secondly, the clash of different standards of dishonesty may reappear in determining what is a case of obvious dishonesty. This leaves the possibility of the defendant seeking to establish his honesty in accordance with standards that are acceptable to himself, and perhaps also his peers, in a court that remains unsympathetic to his cause because in accordance with different standards his behaviour is regarded as obviously dishonest. The scenario arises in the following case study.

A Case Study: The Guinness Conundrum

Ernest Saunders allowed several million pounds of the assets of Guinness to be used for an illegal share support scheme without standing to gain a penny for himself. Thomas Ward accepted several million pounds of the assets of Guinness for himself in contravention of the company's articles of association. Why was Saunders convicted of theft and Ward acquitted? In both cases the guilt of the defendant turned on dishonesty.

The £5.2m success fee paid on the takeover of Distillers to Ward, an American corporate lawyer, had been agreed by a committee of Guinness directors (one of them Ward himself) rather than by the full board as the company articles required. On this basis summary judgment for the return of the money to Guinness was upheld by the House of Lords, where Lord Templeman criticised Ward's conduct in allowing personal interests to conflict with his duties as a director.[33] In these circumstances, it might have been anticipated that dishonesty would be established at the criminal trial, but Ward was acquitted. It is impossible to know what influenced the jurors, but one part of the evidence may have proved crucial. In describing the negotiation and size of his success fee, Ward informed the court that it was agreed in the manner in which he was used to operating in America.[34] It is quite possible that this convinced the jury of Ward's honesty—honest by the standards of ordinary American corporate lawyers. If so, it appears that we have found in Thomas Ward an

---

[33] *Guinness plc v Saunders* [1990] 2 AC 663, 694–95.
[34] *The Independent*, 2 & 3 February 1993.

instantiation of Lord Lane's paradigmatic foreigner, not riding on a bus but sitting on a board of directors.

Saunders was convicted of theft of the money used for the illegal share support scheme. Comments made by the trial judge, subsequently approved by Neill LJ in the first failed appeal to the Court of Appeal, indicate that Saunders had made no personal gain, and had behaved properly and honestly until he had 'got sucked into dishonesty by the ethos of the bitterly fought contested takeover'.[35] The clear implication is that the dishonesty of Saunders consisted solely in the fact that he was involved in breaching s 151 of the Companies Act 1985, even though perhaps not dishonest by the standards of ordinary company directors. The convicted Guinness defendants were widely reported in the media at the time as expressing astonishment that their practices should be regarded as dishonest.[36] And one of the grounds of the second appeal was that evidence of similar practices in the City, which had been withheld by the prosecution, substantiated this viewpoint.

In that appeal, the Court of Appeal accepted that the material should have been disclosed but nevertheless upheld the convictions, since there was 'ample evidence of a dishonest scheme'.[37] Although the Court elaborated on the 'scheme' as involving not merely a breach of s 151 but also false invoices and huge success fees,[38] the impact of the two failed Guinness appeals is to establish the possibility of constructive liability for theft whereby the infringement of company (or other) regulations may lead to a holding of 'obvious dishonesty'.[39]

Obvious and Not So Obvious Dishonesty

The idea of obvious dishonesty can relate to the *Ghosh* test in two ways. In the first case the full rigour of the test is not required because there exists a moral consensus in society over the conduct in question, such that even the rogue is aware that he is acting dishonestly. This does not operate as a qualification on the *Ghosh* test itself, but rather on the procedure for applying the test: there is no need to apply the second limb in asking whether the defendant was aware that his conduct would be regarded as dishonest, since it is a foregone conclusion that he was so aware.

---

[35] *Saunders, The Independent*, 17 May 1991—Transcript: Marten Walsh Cherer, available on *Lexis*.
[36] Less favourable evaluations of the conduct of Saunders are to be found in Peter Pugh, *Is Guinness Good for You?* (London, Financial Training Publications, 1987), and in the 'Slicker' column of *Private Eye*, 30 December 1994 and 13 January 1995.
[37] *Saunders (No 2)* [1996] 1 Cr App R 463, 522.
[38] *ibid*.
[39] Criticised by DW Elliott, 'Directors' Thefts and Dishonesty' [1991] *Criminal Law* Review 732.

In the second case, the test is modified. It is assumed as a matter of law that there exists a consensus. So, for example, we assume that all reasonable honest people would consider Robin Hood's conduct as being dishonest (and that all unreasonable dishonest people would realise this).[40] The crucial distinction consists in the fact that we have moved to a purely objective test. The defendant is now precluded from asserting that he himself thought that his behaviour would be regarded as honest even where he did.[41]

In general, we may depict four types of dishonesty in relation to the existence of a moral consensus, the view of the judge or jury, and the defendant's own view as to how his conduct will be regarded:[42]

Types of Dishonesty

1	actual moral consensus conduct dishonest	judge/jury aware conduct dishonest	defendant aware conduct dishonest
2	no moral consensus	judge/jury regard conduct dishonest	defendant believes conduct dishonest
3	no moral consensus fictional consensus	judge/jury regard conduct dishonest	fiction defendant aware conduct dishonest
4	no moral consensus	judge/jury regard conduct dishonest	defendant believes conduct honest

For the particular defendant involved, type 2 is not materially different from type 1.[43] The distinction between type 1 and type 3 is that between the two types of obvious dishonesty that we have identified, based on evident moral consensus or on legal fiction. If the consensus as to dishonesty is a legal fiction, but the law is itself relying on the consensus in order to establish dishonesty, the reasoning is entirely circular and wholly dependent on the caprice of the particular tribunal.[44]

In type 4 cases the defendant's own viewpoint as to the standards of reasonable honest people will be allowed to prevail, and the fiction to bring it in line with the tribunal's viewpoint will not be employed. This creates injustice for those who have been treated otherwise and have fallen victim to the fiction. To the injustice is added the impracticality of

---

[40] As Lord Lane in *Ghosh* did (text at n 16 above) in hypothetically *applying* the test.
[41] A marked illustration is provided in *Forrester*, above n 32, at 794, where the defendant stated that he regarded his conduct as not simply honest but also fair.
[42] In accordance with the standards of 'reasonable honest people', not necessarily his own standards.
[43] Note the court shares the defendant's views on the normal standards of (dis)honesty. Otherwise, he might be acquitted on the first limb of the *Ghosh* test.
[44] This seems to have been acknowledged by Farquharson LJ in *Green* [1992] *Criminal Law Review* 292, 293—discussed in ATH Smith (1994), above n 28, at §7–73.

determining whether a particular case should be treated by the tribunal as type 1, 3, or 4, once we allow in a doctrine of obvious dishonesty.

We may conclude that the operation of the doctrine of obvious dishonesty as a qualification on the *Ghosh* test is unworkable. Given the admission of a lack of moral consensus in the existence of the second limb of the *Ghosh* test, there is not a firm basis for founding a category of obvious dishonesty as fact, and there is no justification for finding it as a legal fiction. It is perhaps time to reconsider *Ghosh* itself.

POSSIBLE REFORMS

The refrain that echoes throughout this survey of the *Ghosh* test is the absence of a moral consensus within modern society over dishonesty. A call to abandon the *Ghosh* test in these circumstances is neither startling nor novel.[45] What the present study does underline is that for the test of dishonesty to be coherent the choice is limited to two options:[46] a wholly subjective approach, which would allow the individual defendant to limit his criminal liability by his own moral standards; or, a restricted legal definition of dishonesty. The first option may be coherent, but is nevertheless inconsistent in making the protection by the criminal law of a person's property depend on the moral outlook of the person seeking to interfere with it.[47] It also brings with it considerable evidential difficulties.

The second option should be given serious consideration. One attempt at this by Peter Glazebrook[48] builds on s 2 of the Theft Act 1968, broadening it out to a comprehensive definition of dishonesty.[49] This is compatible

[45] For previous calls for reform, see Griew, above n 28, at 80 n63.
[46] I ignore here the possibility of abandoning dishonesty altogether, as suggested by DW Elliott, 'Dishonesty in Theft: A Dispensable Concept' [1982] *Criminal Law Review* 395—for further comment, see n 55 below.
[47] Cp ATH Smith (1994), above n 28, at §§7–57, 7–58 & 7–60. Equally, an approach that left dishonesty to the jury to decide case by case, would bring inconsistency into the law, the outcome depending on the prevailing attitude within a particular jury. So even if the use of the jury's determination of dishonesty is motivated by a desire to soften the harder edges found elsewhere in the definition of theft, the device will produce an inconsistent approach incompatible with its rationale. It follows that the Law Commission's fondness for retaining such a role for the jury with this purpose in mind is misguided. See Law Com No 276, above n 7, Part V, and in particular paras 5.16–5.19 (though contrast para 5.43). For detailed criticism of the Law Commission's earlier failings to get to grips with the issue of dishonesty, see David Ormerod, 'A Bit of a Con? The Law Commission's Consultation Paper on Fraud' [1999] *Criminal Law Review* 789. Support for leaving the issue of dishonesty to the jury is provided by Richard Tur, 'Dishonesty and the Jury: a Case Study in the Moral Content of Law' in A Phillips Griffiths (ed), *Philosophy and Practice* (Cambridge, Cambridge University Press, 1985), but is premised (at 94) on any contentious cases after an application of common moral principles being dealt with by an acquittal.
[48] Peter Glazebrook, 'Revising the Theft Acts' (1993) 52 *Cambridge Law Journal* 191, 193.
[49] A comprehensive approach to dishonesty based on s 2 itself has been adopted in Hong Kong—discussed in ATH Smith (1994), above n 28, at §7–62.

with the partial approach in s 2(1), which sets *legal* borders around what states of mind will be recognised as not dishonest.[50] Glazebrook employs six categories in his proposed definition, but two relate to specific situations rather than a general approach, and I shall accordingly ignore them for present purposes.[51] This leaves the other four:

'Dishonesty'
  A person's appropriation of property belonging to another is to be regarded as dishonest unless—

(a)   done in the belief that he has in law the right to deprive the other of it, on behalf of himself or of a third person; or
(b)   done in the belief that he would have the other's consent if the other knew of the appropriation and the circumstances of it; or
(c)   done (otherwise than by a trustee or personal representative) in the belief that the person to whom the property belongs is unlikely to be discovered[52] by taking reasonable steps; or ...
(e)   the property is money, some other fungible, a thing in action or intangible property, and is appropriated with the intention of replacing it, and in the belief that it will be possible for him to do so without loss to the person to whom it belongs; or ...

However, category (e) does not so evidently cover cases of honest conduct as do the other three.[53] It is arguable that although some such cases are generally regarded as honest conduct, others would not be— specifically where the defendant is aware that the owner would not have consented to the taking of the property in all the circumstances that prevailed at the time, including the defendant's intention to repay and his belief that he could do so. This recognition is not only consistent with the qualified acceptance of the category in *Feely*,[54] but also conveniently permits the issue to be subsumed in the earlier category of belief in the owner's consent if he 'knew of the appropriation *and the circumstances of it.*'

  This modification of Glazebrook's proposal derives further support from a view that the underlying rationale of offences against property is

[50] See further, text preceding n 10 above.
[51] Property received in good faith and for value (s 3(2) of the 1968 Act); picking mushrooms, etc (s 4(3)).
[52] Modifying the 'cannot be discovered' of s 2(1)(c).
[53] This covers the *Feely* scenario, n 5 above, where the honesty was subject to the evaluation of the jury. However, support for the category does sometimes appear unstinted: John Smith (1997), above n 28, at §§2–123–2–124; and also in his Bracton Lecture, 'Reforming the Theft Acts' (1996) 28 *Bracton Law Journal* 27, 35–36.
[54] See previous note.

the protection of the owner's interests,[55] which include determining who shall be permitted to use the property.[56] It has a fortunate compatibility with the broad range of proprietary interests whose invasion may amount to an appropriation.[57] And quite simply, it accords with an ordinary notion of what dishonest treatment of another's property entails—treating it in a way that would not be agreed to.

We could go further and suggest that this is the paradigm case of dishonesty in relation to another's property. In this light, the other two cases borrowed from s 2(1) are merely a qualification and a development of the paradigm case. The qualification is made to acknowledge the superior authority of the law over the consent of the owner, and the development takes us to a case where it is not regarded feasible to discover the person whose consent would otherwise (subject to the qualification noted) be material. We may then propose a modified version of Glazebrook's suggestion as a general definition of dishonesty, giving the paradigm case due prominence, and emphasising the importance of the particular circumstances of the defendant's situation,[58] as follows.

Proposed General Definition of Dishonesty
for Property Offences

1. The way a person deals with the property of another is to be regarded as dishonest where it is done without a belief that the other would consent to it if he knew of all the circumstances, unless the person believes that way of dealing with the property is permitted by law.
2. The way a person deals with the property of another is not to be regarded as dishonest if done (otherwise than by a trustee or personal representative) in the belief that the person to whom the property belongs is unlikely to be discovered by taking reasonable steps.

---

[55] This is illustrated in Elliott's proposed substitute for dishonesty, above n 46, at 406–410: 'detrimental to the interests of the other in a significant practical way'. The advantage of the present proposal is that it earths what is significantly detrimental in what the owner would not consent to, rather than leaving it an open issue—see John Smith (1997), above n 28, at §2–124. The use of the term dishonest to cover the category of wrongful treatment of property that may amount to theft, is a secondary issue. Smith, *loc cit*, suggests Elliott's substitute could be regarded as a definition of dishonesty.

[56] Seen in s 2(2) of the 1968 Act, which upholds the possibility of a finding of theft although the defendant is willing to pay for the property. Significantly, it has been suggested that whether or not the defendant is to be regarded as dishonest revolves around whether he believed the owner would consent: John Smith (1997), above n 28, at §2–120; cp ATH Smith (1994), above n 28, at §7–77.

[57] Theft Act 1968, s 3(1), following *Morris* [1983] 3 All ER 288 and *Gomez* [1993] 1 All ER 1.

[58] This is done by stressing *all* the circumstances. The point is also important in establishing dishonesty in a case involving deception, like *Lawrence* [1971] 2 All ER 1253, where the taxi

This has the appeal of conceptual tidiness, but is it desirable in practical terms? The defendant in *Feely*, faced with a general prohibition against borrowing from the till, would have to argue that *in all the circumstances* of his case he believed that his employer would have made an exception, and consented. Or else, that he believed he had a legal right to the money. It does not seem too harsh to hold that a defendant who takes money from his employer's till, aware that he has no legal right to take it, and aware that his employer will not consent to it even in the particular circumstances in which he finds himself, is behaving dishonestly by taking the money.[59]

The same test would be faced by a defendant taking food to feed a starving child,[60] and might be satisfied by showing a belief that in the extreme circumstances the owner would have consented if he had known about them, or else a belief in some lawful defence of necessity.[61] As to the Guinness defendants, Saunders and his co-defendants would have found the issue of dishonesty sharply drawn on whether they believed that the company would have consented, which, in the circumstances of their efforts to conceal the scheme from the other directors,[62] might have led to a swifter and more straightforward resolution of the issue. On the same approach, Thomas Ward might have found it more difficult to mount a successful defence against the criminal charge. And the Guinness conundrum might well have never been. By contrast, Lord Lane's bus riding foreigner would have a ready defence based on belief in consent or legal right.

driver knew that the student would not have consented if he had known about all the circumstances, including what the correct fare was.

[59] The case of where D is *unsure* as to whether he has a legal right, or whether his employer would consent, is problematical. However, the problem can be resolved by the way the test of dishonesty is formulated: D is dishonest unless he had the belief in consent (or legal right); or, D is only dishonest where he had the belief that the owner would not consent. Glazebrook's formulation takes the first approach, which can be justified on an underlying premise that one should not interfere with another's property unless one has a positive belief that it is right to do so.

In effect, the alternatives suggested here reflect whether the underlying mens rea for theft involves an element of intention (the positive belief in an absence of consent amounts to an intention to engage in the conduct without consent) or an element of inadvertence (the lack of a belief in consent amounts to recklessly engaging in the conduct without consent). Thus this use of dishonesty as a mens rea term can be made to fit the threshold test discussed in the previous chapter. For discussion of the further problem of a defendant who entertains wholly unreasonable grounds for a belief in his own honesty, see n 110 below and the concluding section of this chapter.

[60] Considered as a plausible case of conduct that would not be regarded as dishonest by ATH Smith (1994), above n 28, at 276 n44.

[61] *ibid loc cit* and at §7–30.

[62] The application of the proposed test might, however, lead to a different result where the board of directors were agreed to the infringement of company regulations, and so could be taken to be expressing the consent of the company. This does away with the constructive liability noted, text at n 39 above.

Animal rights activists would not presumably raise a belief in the consent of the owner of the beagles, and would accordingly have to convince the court of a belief in a legal right (perhaps to prevent the commission of an offence of cruelty to animals). And if aware that the law failed to protect animals in such cases, these defendants would be found guilty of theft of the beagles through interfering with the lawful exercise of the rights of the beagles' owner, which makes their criminal liability turn on a consistent application of the law's determination of these issues[63] rather than on a particular moral viewpoint.[64]

This would also leave Robin Hood a thief. A conclusion that is not at all surprising. One would expect an oppressive regime to brand someone who stood against it as an outlaw. The point about Robin Hood is not that he was not a thief but that he was a good thief.[65]

THE APPROPRIATE APPROPRIATION

The structure of the definition of theft within the Theft Act 1968 appears deceptively straightforward. We are provided with a concise definition in s 1, which contains five key elements. In the following five sections, each of those elements is amplified. The very fact that the amplifying provisions were considered necessary belies the confident assertion made on behalf of the reforms introduced by the 1968 Act, that they were drawing on a readily intelligible, ordinary usage of language.[66] Further concerns about the potential vagaries of ordinary language usage, and its suitability as a resource for clarifying the definition of theft appear when we look a little more carefully at the amplifying provisions found in ss 2–6 of the Act. It is clear that there is not a fixed pattern in the relationship between each of the definitional elements in s 1 and the respective amplifying provision that appears in the following sections. The relationship may be comprehensive (as with the provision on property in s 4) or partial (as with the provision on dishonesty in s 2). The amplifying provision may confirm ordinary usage (eg, s 2(1)(b): not dishonest to take something where you think owner would consent), restrict ordinary usage (eg, s 4(2): land is not property), or artificially extend ordinary usage (eg, s 6(1): a person who does not intend to permanently deprive is to be taken as having that intention ...).

[63] Of course it is open to argue that the law is wrong not to provide protection to animals in such circumstances, but this is to challenge the law as it presently exists, not to suggest that the law says otherwise.

[64] Cp John Smith (1997), above n 28, at §2–122.

[65] I am indebted to a discussion held some years ago now with my children, for this conclusion.

[66] The opinion the CLRC expressed about appropriation, in particular, was that the term could be 'easily understood even without the aid of further definition'—Eighth Report, para 34.

The story of how the courts have responded to the need to clarify the definition of appropriation (the key actus reus element of theft) and of the use they have made of the statutory amplification provided in s 3, features the sort of baffling relationships between House of Lords' decisions that were encountered in our study of recklessness in chapter 3. It also provides a further illustration of judicial reluctance to confront the complexities of ordinary language usage, its interaction with legal definitions, and the precise roles that definitional material may be performing. A quartet of House of Lords' decisions strains the intellectual muscles of those who have tried to make sense of this area of the law, though, to be fair, the problems can be traced back to the original selection of statutory material. Before examining this in detail, it is worth providing an overview of the key judicial developments in the House of Lords.

The four cases, *Lawrence*,[67] *Morris*,[68] *Gomez*,[69] and *Hinks*,[70] can be portrayed as establishing the following sequence of propositions.

(1)   Appropriation may occur where the victim consents to it.

(2)(a) Any interference with the rights of ownership may amount to an appropriation.

(2)(b) Appropriation must be something unauthorised by the victim.

(3)(a) Any interference with the rights of ownership may amount to an appropriation.

(3)(b) Appropriation may occur where the victim consents to it.

The numbers relate to the positions adopted in the first three cases above. The progression between the third case, *Gomez*, and the fourth, *Hinks*, was not a matter of advancing the accepted state of the law, but of putting more of it into practice.

I shall argue below that the key to unravelling the confusion found within the judicial development of the law is to be found in concentrating on the specific context of the two propositions (2)(a) and (2)(b) established in *Morris*; that this in turn explains the relationship between *Morris* and *Lawrence*; and that the failure to acknowledge the importance of the context of (2)(a) and (2)(b) has contributed to the continuing dissatisfaction with the current state of the law.[71] Underlying the argument is an

---

[67] [1971] 2 All ER 1253.
[68] [1983] 3 All ER 288.
[69] [1993] 1 All ER 1.
[70] [2000] 3 WLR 1590.
[71] The dissatisfaction is far from comprehensive, but even those who are prepared to approve the outcome of *Hinks* display some unease over the manner in which it has been reached. See Stephen Shute, 'Appropriation and the Law of Theft' [2002] *Criminal Law Review* 445 (leaving open doubts about its genealogy in *Gomez*); Alan Bogg and John Stanton-Ife,

insistence on recognising the complex usage of appropriation within ordinary language, and an implied accusation that the CLRC were willing to take advantage of the width of the term without concerning themselves with the potential confusion this entailed.

The complexity and confusion were swiftly reached. The widespread response to being called upon to reconcile propositions (1) and (2)(b) following *Lawrence* and *Morris*, was bewilderment, found in the remarks of academic commentators and judges alike. In the sixth edition of his commentary on the Theft Acts, Edward Griew found it necessary to insert a disclaimer: 'This central topic … remains quite beyond my capacity to expound both simply and accurately.'[72] And in the Court of Appeal, Parker LJ remarked upon, 'The difficulties caused by the apparent conflict between the decisions.'[73] Others resorted to various desperate devices to avoid the apparently stark contradiction between what the Lords said in *Lawrence* about the possibility of conduct amounting to an appropriation even where the victim had consented to it,[74] and what the Lords said in *Morris* in requiring that the conduct amounting to an appropriation should be unauthorised by the victim.[75] Dicta in the former case were pronounced obiter,[76] notwithstanding that the remarks were made by the House of Lords in direct answer to the question certified for appeal. A rather reluctant, and ultimately unsuccessful, attempt was made at drawing a subtle distinction between consent and authority in order to try to reconcile the two cases.[77] And there was even resort to the device that has proved popular elsewhere in the criminal law, when the failure to find coherence and consistency in the judgments of the appellate courts seems overwhelming: the exact meaning of the term is left to the jury to determine.[78]

'Protecting the vulnerable: legality, harm and theft' (2003) 23 *Legal Studies* 402 (endorsing the protection provided against exploitation but querying whether this is best effected within the offence of theft). The generally hostile reception to *Hinks* is fully reviewed within these two articles, including the more stringent criticisms, collected by Shute, at 450 n29.

[72] Edward Griew, Preface to *The Theft Acts 1968 and 1978* (6th edn, London, Sweet & Maxwell, 1990). Cp John Smith, Preface to *The Law of Theft* (6th edn, London, Butterworths, 1989).
[73] *Dobson v General Accident plc* [1990] 1 QB 274, 281.
[74] [1971] 2 All ER 1253, 1256 *per* Viscount Dilhorne.
[75] [1983] 3 All ER 288, 293 *per* Lord Roskill.
[76] Smith, above n 72, at § [32].
[77] A possibility considered by Parker LJ in *Dobson v General Accident plc* [1990] 1 QB 274, 285, but not with unbridled enthusiasm (see further at 281C–F). It was unfavourably received by John Smith in his Comment on *Dobson* [1990] *Criminal Law Review* 273, 274, and rejected by the Court of Appeal in *Gomez* [1991] 3 All ER 394.
[78] Simon Gardner, 'Is Theft a Rip-Off?' (1990) 10 *Oxford Journal of Legal Studies* 441. For comment in favour of the device being employed for recklessness, see Di Birch, 'The Foresight Saga: The Biggest Mistake of All?' [1988] *Criminal Law Review* 4, 14. For comment against the use of the device, in relation to intention see Andrew Halpin, 'Intended Consequences and Unintentional Fallacies' (1987) 7 *Oxford Journal of Legal Studies* 104, 111–13. And for general

Less ambitiously, the tendency in appeals heard during this period was to take sides with either *Lawrence* or *Morris*,[79] an obviously unsatisfactory state of affairs which reached its zenith when the Court of Appeal in *Gomez* acknowledged that the House of Lords in *Morris* did not regard itself as being in conflict with *Lawrence* but then proceeded to invoke *Morris* and utterly ignore *Lawrence*.[80] This clearly flawed strategy was harshly criticised,[81] and ultimately rejected by the House of Lords on appeal. Before examining the response made by the Lords in *Gomez* (and applied further in *Hinks*), I want to consider how a more careful consideration of the complex usage of appropriation might shed light on the relationship between *Lawrence* and *Morris*.

The Senses of Appropriation

There is much in Lord Roskill's speech in *Morris* that is allusive or vague, but two things are stated quite unequivocally at the beginning. Lord Roskill clearly upholds the earlier decision of the House in *Lawrence*,[82] and he points out that the House of Lords which was invited in *Lawrence* to consider the general definition of theft in s 1 was not concerned in that case with the application of s 3(1) of the Theft Act 1968.[83] Since we also find Lord Roskill consistently qualifying his own comments on appropriation with a reference to s 3(1),[84] the relationship between these two provisions of the 1968 Act becomes crucial to any understanding of how the two cases can be reconciled.

There are two factors affecting the relationship between s 1 which establishes appropriation as a definitional element of theft, and s 3 which seeks to amplify the meaning of appropriation for the purpose of defining theft. The first factor is what meaning or meanings the term

---

discussion, see Edward Griew, 'Consistency, Communication and Codification: Reflections on Two Mens Rea Words' in Peter Glazebrook (ed), *Reshaping the Criminal Law: Essays in honour of Glanville Williams* (London, Stevens & Sons, 1978) 57–59.

[79] For details see Griew, above n 72, at §2-73 and n 7; Smith, above n 72, at § [33] and Preface.
[80] [1991] 3 All ER 394. The Court of Appeal's decision to quash a conviction for theft, where D brought about the sale of electrical goods in a shop with worthless cheques, conflicts with two central points found in *Lawrence*: (1) an appropriation may occur in the obtaining of goods by deception (and thus there is an extensive overlap between s 15 and s l of the Theft Act 1968)—[1971] 2 All ER 1253, 1255f & 1256c–e; (2) an appropriation of another person's property may occur within the course of a contractual transaction which conveys that property to the thief—*ibid* at 1255f–h.
[81] The criticism was particularly unrestrained in *Archbold 1992*, vol 2, PJ Richardson (ed) (London, Sweet & Maxwell) §§21-49a–21-49c.
[82] [1983] 3 All ER 288, 292f–h.
[83] *ibid* at 292h.
[84] *ibid* at 293d, 293f & 293j.

appropriation may bear in its ordinary usage, which, all other things being equal, we might expect to be introduced into the definition of theft by the mention of the term in s 1. The second factor is the manner in which the amplifying provision, s 3, operates on the term introduced in s 1.

If we look to the CLRC's Eighth Report for guidance on the precise relationship between s 3 and the definitional element appropriation found in s 1, it would appear that the Committee inserted s 3 into their draft Bill for the avoidance of doubt,[85] though there is additionally a hint that one particular set of circumstances required especial provision in s 3(1), so possibly providing an artificial extension to ordinary usage.[86]

It follows that s 3 could be regarded as confirming that one particular meaning of appropriation taken from ordinary usage was to figure in the definition of theft, and, accordingly, that s 3 provided only a partial amplification on one of a number of meanings that the term appropriation may bear for the purpose of defining theft. Even if s 3 is regarded as introducing an artificial extension to the meaning of appropriation, it may still be treated as providing a partial amplification, in relation to that artificial meaning rather than the other meanings found in the ordinary usage of the term.

The plausibility of the suggestion that s 3 provides only a partial amplification of appropriation in dealing with one particular meaning (or an artificially delineated subset of meanings), depends upon what meaning or meanings the term appropriation may bear in its ordinary usage. The CLRC were clearly of the opinion that the term appropriation was sufficiently wide to embrace conduct that would fall under all the former offences of larceny, embezzlement and fraudulent conversion,[87] but the Committee did not discuss in detail the precise meaning(s) of the term.[88]

The ordinary usage of appropriation as attested to by the dictionaries is sufficiently complex to provide us with more than one meaning for the word. For it covers not only making something completely one's own property but also diverting something to a particular purpose (eg, as in an Appropriation Bill in Parliament). It covers not only a dealing with property that is consented to by the party from which the property has been taken (eg, the transference of tithes to a religious corporation) but

---

[85] Eighth Report, para 34. It would seem to be clear from this paragraph that one thing the CLRC wished to avoid any doubt on was that appropriation could cover obtaining by deception, for it cites Sir James Fitzjames Stephen twice to the effect that it covered obtaining by false pretences.

[86] *ibid* at para 36 (dishonest retention after honest acquisition, explicitly mentioned in s 3(1)). There is apparently in s 3(2) a possible restriction on ordinary usage—see *ibid* Annex 2, at 125.

[87] *ibid* at para 33.

[88] Familiarity with ordinary usage was presumably considered sufficient—see n 66 above.

also a dealing with property that is wholly opposed to the wishes of the party from which it has been taken (eg, 'The rapacious appropriation of the abbey lands').[89]

Whether we regard it as employing one of a number of meanings to be found in ordinary usage, or as an artificially created subset of meanings under the Act, we may therefore treat s 3 as dealing with a particular sense of appropriation expressed by the formula 'any assumption of the rights of the owner.' And it would not be unreasonable to suggest that the particular flavour of appropriation conveyed by the use of 'assumption' in this formula was one that involved a dealing with property that was opposed to the wishes of the party from which the property was taken.[90] By contrast, the remaining ordinary usage of the term would allow us to find in s 1 the term appropriation covering cases of dealing with the property in a manner consented to by the party from which it is taken.[91]

Lord Roskill's insistence upon unauthorised conduct in *Morris* can therefore be taken to refer specifically to a sense of appropriation found in s 3(1), and to have no bearing upon what the House of Lords upheld in *Lawrence*: the possibility of consensual appropriation within the ordinary usage of appropriation to be found in s 1.

A Rationale for the Dual Approach

The idea that the difference between *Lawrence* s 1 appropriation and *Morris* s 3 appropriation can be explained solely in terms of whether or not the appropriation was consensual would be utterly unconvincing. For the paradigm theft involves the taking of a person's property without his consent, and nobody would doubt that this falls under the general definition provided by s 1 without recourse to s 3. However, *Lawrence* did not hold that all s 1 appropriation must be consensual, merely that s 1 appropriation may be consensual. If follows that non-consensual appropriation can be found in s 1 as well as s 3 and cannot be the basis for the distinction between the two forms of appropriation.

The factors identified above as being at play in the different senses of appropriation concerned not only whether the appropriation was consensual or not but also whether the appropriation governed the complete taking of the property or merely the diversion of the property to a particular

---

[89] All of this is to be found in the *Oxford English Dictionary*.

[90] Usurpation, one of Lord Roskill's favoured synonyms for assumption ([1983] 3 All ER 288, 293d, 293j, 295f), is also used by the OED in the entry for assumption.

[91] Contrary to the doubts expressed by John Smith over the possibility of a consensual appropriation (eg, Smith, above n 72, at § [32]), this is borne out not only in general usage found in the dictionary but also in another legal usage with which he would have been familiar as an author of a leading text on contract: Sale of Goods Act 1979, s 18 r 5(1).

purpose. It is by bringing this latter factor into the picture that we can make sense of the difference between s 1 appropriation and s 3 appropriation. We may regard s 3 as dealing with something less than the appropriation found in the paradigm theft where the thief in appropriating the other's property is in practice divesting the other completely of his enjoyment of ownership of that property. The appropriation in s 3 is something less than this either because the thief has already acquired some aspects of the enjoyment of property that is properly the owner's (eg, he has been given possession of the property prior to the theft) or because the thief's conduct is only partially intruding upon the owner's enjoyment of his property (eg, he is making some use of the property which, for the moment at least, falls short of completely taking it away from the owner).

This rendering of s 3 appropriation accords with Lord Roskill's interpretation of s 3(1) as covering the assumption of any of the rights of ownership rather than the assumption of full ownership.[92] This has been criticised for confusing any assumption of the rights of ownership (which the Act does state) with the assumption of any of the rights of ownership (which the Act does not state), and for involving the absurdity of treating any interference with the property of another, such as kicking another's camel, as appropriation.[93] But this criticism can be rebutted.

The force of the first point assumes that the 'of' linking the assumption to the rights of ownership should unambiguously be taken to indicate an exhaustive connection, whereas it might as easily indicate a partitive one.[94] If the eating of sweets before meals is forbidden, it is no excuse for a child to say that he only ate one sweet. Similarly, the assumption of some rights may be regarded as satisfying the requirement of assumption of rights if 'of' is taken partitively. In this case it is correct to regard any assumption of rights as covering the assumption of any rights.

The force of the second point is dissipated once we acknowledge that appropriation alone does not amount to theft. Even if kicking a camel can be regarded as appropriating the camel on the basis that it involves an assumption of one of the rights of the owner,[95] this will not be theft as there will be no intention to permanently deprive the owner of his

---

[92] [1983] 3 All ER 288, 293a–b.
[93] LH Leigh, 'Some Remarks on Appropriation in the Law of Theft after *Morris*' (1985) 48 *Modern Law Review* 167, 170. Cp John Smith, Comment on *Morris* [1983] *Criminal Law Review* 815, 815–16.
[94] See further, entry XIII for 'of' in the *Oxford English Dictionary*.
[95] There are actually grounds to doubt this. Leigh's 'interference with a thing' (above n 93, at 170) does not necessarily amount to Lord Roskill's 'interference with ... the owner's rights' ([1983] 3 All ER 288, 293j). Kicking your camel interferes with your camel but not necessarily with your rights of ownership, in that it does not prevent you from exercising your rights over the camel, to kick it or otherwise.

camel—unless the camel is being kicked for some ulterior purpose, such as to prod it into movement towards the herd of camels owned by the thief.

But even if Roskill's interpretation can be squared with the text of s 3, is there any rationale for singling out this form of appropriation and insisting that it should be carried out without the authority of the owner? Theft in general may be regarded as serving the purpose of protecting an owner's enjoyment of his property, but only where the threat to that enjoyment has reached a certain level of seriousness (so, a mere borrowing is not theft). In cases where the rogue divests all control that the owner may have had over his property, the threat to the owner's enjoyment is the same whether the rogue effects this by conduct that is consented to by the owner or not. However, there may be a lesser threat in those cases where the rogue does not remove all control over the property from the hands of the owner, but merely diverts the property to a particular purpose. In these cases, whilst the conduct of the rogue is consistent with what the owner has authorised, the owner will still retain some control over his property, although there is a burgeoning threat to his future enjoyment. But when the conduct of the rogue crosses into what is unauthorised by the owner, the threat to the owner's enjoyment of his property becomes more substantial, for the owner is now losing any effective control over his property he might have from knowing what is happening to it. At this point, the threat may be regarded as sufficiently serious to count as theft.

Consider some illustrations of this scheme of appropriations from the supermarket. **(i)** If the rogue walks undetected out of the supermarket with a tin of salmon in his pocket, then he has removed all control over the salmon from the supermarket and divested the supermarket of all enjoyment of the salmon. This occurs without the consent of the supermarket. The same net result occurs **(ii)** where the rogue walks out with the tin of salmon with the consent of the supermarket, having given a dud cheque to the cashier for the goods. These cases, irrespective of consent, should be regarded as s 1 appropriations.

Suppose, however, that the rogue is still inside the supermarket. **(iii)** He intends to take a tin of salmon and leave without paying for it, as in the first scenario. With this intention, he picks up a tin of salmon from the shelf and puts it in a supermarket basket. Already, there is some threat to the enjoyment of that property by the supermarket, but it is minimised by the fact that the supermarket is still exercising a degree of control over it. The property is still on supermarket premises, and is being dealt with in a way authorised by the supermarket which makes it possible for the supermarket to exercise control over it and to ensure enjoyment of the property by getting a price paid for it: the rogue will have to pass the checkout on his way out, and the assistant will require payment for any goods in the basket. But once **(iv)** the rogue slips the salmon into his pocket, despite the fact that the property is still on supermarket premises the effective control over the property is lost because the rogue is now dealing with the property in an unauthorised way which will frustrate the normal procedures of the supermarket which are designed to ensure their enjoyment of the property by getting a price paid for it. This provides grounds for treating the latter unauthorised conduct, but not the former authorised conduct, as a s 3 appropriation.

I am not arguing here that this is an approach to theft that is necessitated once we introduce the term appropriation into our definition of the offence, for it would be possible to employ within our definition of theft the sense of appropriation which couples an element of diversion (rather than a complete taking) together with an element of consent to the conduct involved, if we wished to impose liability at an earlier stage, such as in the third of the four supermarket scenarios. I am arguing that this is a plausible approach to theft, and that it can provide a coherent picture of the law as found in the House of Lords' interpretation of s 3 in *Morris*, while being compatible with the doctrine established in *Lawrence*.[96] The most important point to make is that any proposed scheme for understanding the use of appropriation in the definition of theft must make due allowance for the potentially complex usage of that term, and clarify just how the term is to be understood within this particular legal setting. This point has not, however, been taken up by the House of Lords in the final two cases dealing with appropriation in theft.

THE CHANGE MADE BY *GOMEZ*

Instead of confronting the range of meanings potentially covered by the term appropriation in the definition of theft, the House of Lords in *Gomez* treated the issue before them as turning on a simple conflict between their two earlier decisions in *Lawrence* and *Morris* regarding the possibility of admitting consensual appropriations within the offence of theft. In taking this narrow view of the issue, a decision to uphold *Lawrence* amounted to a decision to overrule that part of *Morris* which required an adverse interference with or usurpation of some right of the owner.[97] Nevertheless,

---

[96] For further detailed discussion of how this scheme of appropriations would fit with the scenarios arising in other cases, see Andrew Halpin, 'The Appropriate Appropriation' [1991] *Criminal Law Review* 426, 431–32.

[97] [1993] 1 All ER 1, 4, 12–13 *per* Lord Keith with whom Lords Jauncey, Browne-Wilkinson and Slynn concurred. Lord Lowry dissented, expressing a preference for *Morris* over *Lawrence* (as the Court of Appeal effectively had also done), and for a uniform meaning for appropriation within the 1968 Act that requires conduct engaged in without the consent of the owner from whom the property is stolen (*ibid* at 22b, 25j, 33h, 35f, 38b). Lowry's viewpoint

with regard to another aspect of *Morris*, that under s 3(1) the assumption of any of the rights of the owner could amount to an appropriation, their Lordships expressed approval.[98]

The two points decided in *Gomez* combined not simply to clarify the law as between two previously conflicting viewpoints, but to expand it in a direction that it had not previously taken. For by adopting a uniform approach to the possibility of consensual appropriations, the Law Lords took the *Lawrence* doctrine into a wider setting than the House had actually considered in that case, since the *Morris* understanding of the significance of s 3(1) appropriations was yet to come. And by upholding the *Morris* understanding that an assumption of any of the rights of the owner could amount to an appropriation but rejecting the *Morris* qualification that the appropriation had to be without the owner's consent, the Lords in *Gomez* increased the range of partial intrusions on the rights of ownership that would be counted as appropriations for the purposes of theft.

In terms of the numbered propositions provided in the introduction to the previous section,[99] they severed (2)(a) from (2)(b) in *Morris*, upheld it alongside (1) from *Lawrence*, and so created a combination, (3)(a) and (3)(b), which had never previously been recognised in the law. In terms of the supermarket scenarios considered at the end of the previous section, they expanded the scope of appropriation to bring scenario **(iii)** into the law of theft. This, however, remained purely abstract and unaddressed in *Gomez*, for that case, where the defendant acquired full control of electrical goods from a shop by using worthless cheques, involved a scenario **(ii)** type case, not a scenario **(iii)** type.

Remaining Problems

The kind of situation that had, in the abstract, been let into the offence of theft by the Lords in *Gomez* subsequently arose in the case of *Gallasso*, and the response made by the Court of Appeal in that case is particularly illuminating. The case concerned a nurse caring for severely mentally handicapped adults, who, as part of her normal duties, was entrusted to pay

---

is based upon elevating the wishes of the majority of the CLRC not to have an overlap between theft and obtaining by deception (*ibid* at 21, citing para 38 of the Eighth Report) over the language they adopted. The desire to restrict appropriation to non-consensual conduct finds its origin in the perceived popular understanding of the distinction between obtaining by false pretences (consensual) and theft (non-consensual). However, as Lowry himself points out (*ibid* at 20, citing the passage of the Eighth Report referred to in n 85 above), the CLRC recognised that the prior legal use of the term clearly indicated it could cover those very forms of consensual conduct which arose in obtaining by false pretences.

[98] *ibid* at 9.
[99] See text following n 70 above.

money belonging to patients into their bank acccounts. On one occasion she paid a patient's cheque into an account she had opened for him, which was regarded as being done with the owner's consent, but there was evidence to indicate that she had selected this particular account with a view to making it easier for her to withdraw the money later for her own use. This provided a dishonest motive to accompany the consensual diversion of the owner's property into his own bank account. Her conviction for theft thus provided a clear example of scenario **(iii)** being recognised by the law, and was wholly compatible with the position taken by the Lords in *Gomez*. Notwithstanding this, on appeal the Court of Appeal in *Gallasso* quashed the conviction, on the grounds that a dishonest motive could not turn something into an appropriation which would otherwise not be one.[100]

This nicely illustrates the difficulty of turning the abstract position on appropriation taken by the Lords in *Gomez* into an actual recognition of appropriation in practice. The failure of the Court of Appeal to do so betrays an entrenched position on appropriation which is not moveable to the scenario **(iii)** type case. By treating the factor of dishonesty as turning something from what was not an appropriation into an appropriation, the Court of Appeal discloses a mindset in which scenario **(iii)** is not appropriation and requires transforming (presumably into scenario **(iv)**) before it can become appropriation. Whereas, in accordance with the scheme approved by the Lords in *Gomez*, **(iii)** is already an appropriation and the dishonesty is not required to turn it into an appropriation, but to recognise the appropriation as theft.

The technical incompatibility of *Gallasso* with *Gomez* led John Smith to dismiss it as *per incuriam*.[101] The wider significance of the case is that it shows the weakness of the doctrinal position taken in *Gomez*. For the doctrine is delivered without contemplating the practical implications that follow from it. When a practical illustration does surface in the later case of *Gallasso* the Court of Appeal shrinks from following through the doctrine. This might be seen as raising doubts over the extent to which scenario **(iii)** has been embraced as a case of appropriation for the definition of theft, and certainly indicates the residual strength of a traditional, intuitive grasp of the parameters of the offence. The pull of conservative conventions on the boundaries of theft, in the period after *Gomez*, has not been felt only in a rejection of scenario **(iii)** type cases. In *Hinks* doubts were raised within the House of Lords itself over the extent to which a scenario **(ii)** type case could be accepted as an appropriation.

The underlying problem is again a conflict between linguistic opportunity and intuitive recognition. In the abstract, the House in *Gomez* had

---

[100] (1992) 98 Cr App R 284.
[101] John Smith, Comment on *Gallasso* [1993] *Criminal Law Review* 459, 460.

opened up appropriation for theft to cover all four scenarios. In practice, it had only confirmed a shift in the intuitive grasp of theft to accept a case of obtaining by deception within a scenario **(ii)** type case. We have seen that the Court of Appeal in *Gallasso* rebuffed the stretching of traditional sensibilities to take in a scenario **(iii)** type case of a partial diversion of property with the owner's consent. In *Hinks*, the issue was whether the intuitive boundary could be moved to take in another instance of a scenario **(ii)** type case, where the owner had been dishonestly cajoled into making gifts to the defendant.

The defendant in *Hinks* befriended the victim, a 53-year-old man of low intelligence, and acted as his main carer. Within a period of seven months she obtained a number of gifts from him of a total value of about £60,000, representing most of his savings. Lord Steyn delivered the speech propounding the majority viewpoint.[102] This used a straightforward application of *Lawrence* and *Gomez* to find appropriation in the case of a consensual gift,[103] and upheld the jury's finding that the defendant had 'acted dishonestly by systematically raiding the savings in a building society account of a vulnerable person who trusted her.'[104]

Two dissenting speeches were delivered by Lord Hutton and Lord Hobhouse. Hutton accepted the majority viewpoint on appropriation,[105] but considered that there was an outstanding issue of dishonesty on the grounds that a valid gift from the victim would bring s 2(1)(b) of the 1968 Act into play: a person cannot be regarded as dishonest where he believes the owner would consent in the circumstances.[106] Hobhouse considered that there was neither an appropriation nor dishonesty in the case of a valid gift. At the heart of his dissent lies the contention that *Hinks* can be distinguished from *Lawrence* and *Gomez*, which he took pains to uphold.[107]

To deal with the dishonesty point first, it is clear from *Lawrence* that the s 2(1)(b) provision, which only establishes an absence of dishonesty where the defendant can establish belief in the owner's consent on the basis that the owner 'knew of ... the circumstances', becomes inoperative in a case of fraud precisely because the owner was not aware of the circumstances of the fraud.[108] However, this qualification can be regarded as applying to

---

[102] Lord Slynn and Lord Jauncey concurred.
[103] [2000] 3 WLR 1590, 1599, 1601. Steyn also reiterated the position taken in *Gomez* in relation to the scope of s 3(1) appropriations (at 1599). (The case of *Gallasso* was not cited in argument nor in any judgment in *Hinks*.)
[104] *ibid* at 1602.
[105] *ibid* at 1603.
[106] *ibid* at 1604–05, 1607–08.
[107] *ibid* at 1616.
[108] This is acknowledged by Hutton (*ibid* at 1605) and Hobhouse (*ibid* at 1617), both citing the relevant passage from *Lawrence*.

the facts of *Hinks*, even if it is presumed for the sake of argument that there was a valid gift in this case. In the words of Lord Dilhorne from *Lawrence*, which Hobhouse is so keen to emphasise, the defendant can only take advantage of s 2(1)(b) if he can show that he believed the owner would have consented *'with full knowledge of the circumstances'*.[109] Yet the position of the victim in *Hinks* when making the gifts was far from having full knowledge of the circumstances. He considered that he was engaged in the appropriate activity of making a gift to a genuine friend, whereas the truth of the matter (as the jury clearly found) was that the defendant was exploiting him.[110]

As for appropriation, Hobhouse's principal strategy is to revert to the traditional notion that appropriation in theft already bears a tainted connotation of conduct engaged in without the owner's consent.[111] He considers the earlier trio of House of Lords cases can be fitted in because the consent was defeated either by fraud (*Lawrence* and *Gomez*) or by acting in an unauthorised manner (*Morris*).[112] Quite apart from the point that the presence of exploitation might reasonably be considered to

---

[109] *ibid* at 1617.

[110] The deplorable conduct of the defendant in exploiting the victim is common ground to all the speeches in *Hinks*. The facts of *Hinks* can be distinguished from the hypotheticals considered by Lord Steyn, [2000] 3 WLR 1590, 1599–1600, where, in a number of ways, the defendant takes advantage of the owner giving consent to the transaction which would not have been given if he had been aware of all the circumstances (such as a dealer buying a valuable painting from someone who does not appreciate its true value at a bargain price). In these cases, as Steyn points out, the defendants could argue against dishonesty on another ground, a belief that they were lawfully entitled to the property, which under the *caveat emptor* mentality of an advanced capitalist society is a sound belief to entertain. This point is overlooked by ATH Smith (2004), above n 28, at §26.15, in expressing the view that such a case post-*Hinks* turns entirely on the jury's view of dishonesty. Admittedly, the distinction with *Hinks* depends on the assumption that Hinks did not entertain any ground for the belief that she was legally entitled to fleece a vulnerable person who trusted her. Were the contrary to be so, and it was still considered desirable to provide the protection of the criminal law for such a case, then the belief in a legal right as a basis for negating dishonesty in s 2(1)(a)—or, in the proposed definition of dishonesty provided earlier in this chapter— would have to be qualified with a requirement of reasonableness, making it less subjective. Technically speaking, such a qualification would also be needed for the defendant under a s 15 charge of obtaining property by deception, who took an extreme and mistaken view of how much *laissez-faire* was entertained by the law.

The deplorable conduct of just how much protection the law does provide against undue influence, and the related danger that the scope of a defence to theft can get tied up with the technicalities of the civil law. But even in Hobhouse's dissenting speech in *Hinks*, there is the recognition that some circumstances are such as to provide a common sense recognition that there would be no legal right to fleece the vulnerable, approving, *ibid* at 1622, the decision in *Kendrick and Hopkins* [1997] 2 Cr App R 524. See further, the concluding section of this chapter, and also n 59 above.

[111] [2000] 3 WLR 1590, 1616.

[112] *ibid* at 1620. In order to get round the answer to the certified question in *Lawrence*, Hobhouse resorts at this point to the distinction between a limited and fully informed consent. But, as pointed out in the text, it could just as easily be argued that consent induced by exploitation is a limited, and not a fully informed consent.

defeat consent for the purposes of appropriation (as much as it might for the purposes of dishonesty), there is one key element of the Theft Act material which starkly contradicts Hobhouse's preferred contextual[113] reading of appropriation. It is found within one of the subsections central to Hobhouse's argument, s 2(1)(b). As mentioned, this provides that there will be no dishonesty where the defendant believed that the owner would have consented. The significant point is that the Act refers to just such a case of consensual conduct as 'appropriation'.[114]

That consensual appropriations are referred to in the Theft Act itself, in other criminal law contexts noted by the CLRC in its Report,[115] in other legal contexts familiar to commentators,[116] and in general usage of the term,[117] might be thought evidence enough to avoid the possibility still being in dispute in the fourth House of Lords case to deal with the matter. However, this is to really miss the point of the protracted controversy. Because the usage of appropriation is so complex, to open up the possibility of consensual appropriations as the House of Lords did in *Lawrence*, or to indicate the inclusion of some non-consensual appropriations as the CLRC were keen to do in what became s 3, is inadequate to deal with all the possible cases of appropriation that may emerge, of a consensual or non-consensual character. The controversy has endured because of a

[113] Two supporting arguments of Hobhouse's contextual approach can be mentioned in passing. One is to bring in the mechanisms of s 5 together with a technical grasp of the passing of property from the civil law. Hobhouse argues ([2000] 3 WLR 1590, 1611–13) that where a gift is made and then taken up by the donee, property passes at the gift-making stage and so the property then *appropriated* by the donee would not be property belonging to another. (Hobhouse himself refers to consensual appropriations without any conscious effort in these pages of his speech.) He makes much of s 5(4)'s redressing this problem in the case of a mistake (presumably including one induced by fraud) by artificially holding that the property is to be understood as still belonging to the donee, but completely overlooks the far wider artificial extension of 'belonging to another' provided in s 5(1), which would cover the donor who still has possession of the gift. The full extent of the artificiality of ownership created by s 5 for the purposes of defining theft is sufficient to counter any suggestion that the technicalities of the civil law are being relied upon. A more plausible contextual interpretation would be to take a common sense understanding of the whole transaction including the fraud or exploitation, the agreement to give the property, and the acquisition of the property—and treat this as involving an appropriation of property belonging to another. This is a possibility Hobhouse himself recognises (at 1617H), and was used in *Lawrence* [1972] AC 626, 632, without the need to rely on s 5(4).
The second argument is to insist on a compound definition of theft which is narrower than the sum of its parts, eg, [2000] 3 WLR 1590, 1623. In reality, the insistence on treating 'dishonestly appropriates' as 'a composite phrase' simply draws attention to the way that some of the elements within the definition may have a qualifying effect on others, but does not allow one to beg the question of how each of those elements is to be understood. Hobhouse's own views on appropriation under s 3(1) or dishonesty under s 2(1) that he then refers to (*ibid*), do not gain any further credence by being joined in a compound definition.
[114] Appropriation or the cognate verb is referred to generally, and then specifically in each of the three cases of honest appropriations, under s 2(1).
[115] See n 85 above.
[116] See n 91 above.
[117] See text at n 89 above.

failure to confront those complexities of usage in preference for adopting an approach that will dispose of the case at hand. Even now, the practical reach of appropriation in theft in a scenario **(iii)** type case is in doubt after *Gallasso*, and dissent remains in the House of Lords over which examples of a scenario **(ii)** type case should be admitted.

One might seek to attribute responsibility for this particular problem in the definition of theft to the other members of the CLRC who failed to heed the caution expressed by Glanville Williams about the potential reach of the term.[118] But a more important lesson can be learned from the history of appropriation in the law of theft. The future reach of language runs beyond the stretch of present concerns.[119] As with our earlier studies of recklessness and dishonesty, we can see that appropriation was selected as a term in order to provide the opportunity to deal with certain concerns in a particular way, but that selection opened up further opportunities to deal with other concerns as yet presently undecided. It is not credible that the selection of some alternative term would have wholly precluded such further opportunities.

And when these opportunities arise, the response is not to be determined by our understanding of the term but by the use we wish to make of the term. The explication of terms replicates at a more specific level the application of rules, we considered in chapter 1. As rules do not necessarily come with a recognisable and comprehensive rationale to provide authoritative determination of every application, neither do terms come with a fixed use in the form of a static definition that predetermines every instance. The study of appropriation in theft demonstrates again how ordinary usage of a term may not be tied down to one particular meaning. It also shows that the relationship between legal and ordinary usage may be left hanging loose.

In these circumstances, the response to be made at the level of applying a rule involves (as we saw when first considering the majority view in *Hinks*[120]) the selection of an appropriate rationale. Exactly the same process of selection operates in choosing the use of a term, when the opportunity arises. Lord Steyn is keen to provide as a rationale for theft the need to deal with such 'dishonest and repellent conduct'[121] as the defendant displayed in exploiting the property of others, whereas Lord Hobhouse considers theft should be limited to dealing with conduct that is dishonest and morally reprehensible, *and* known to involve a technical

---

[118] Related by John Smith, 'The Sad Fate of the Theft Act 1968' in William Swadling and Gareth Jones (eds), *The Search for Principle: Essays in Honour of Lord Goff of Chieveley* (Oxford, OUP, 1999) 100.

[119] For more detailed discussion, see Andrew Halpin, *Reasoning with Law* (Oxford, Hart Publishing, 2001) chs 6–9.

[120] See ch 1 above, text at nn 52–54.

[121] [2000] 3 WLR 1590, 1600.

invasion of property rights.[122] In this way he brings theft closer to the conventional paradigm of taking the property of another.[123] Yet neither of these competing rationales comes close to providing us with a comprehensive view of the offence.

CONCLUDING REMARKS

Working out a rationale for theft clearly relates to the use that will be made of both of the terms we have been studying. The extent to which this will be an ongoing process depends on the condition in which the definition of the offence, or at a more detailed level the definition of the terms, is found. I suggested earlier[124] a way of reforming the definition of dishonesty which would reduce the need to continue this process by clarifying the issues over which the meaning of dishonesty would be decided, and by taking up an agreed position on these issues as far as possible. Can a similar reform be proposed for the definition of appropriation?

As far as clarifying the issues goes, this is assisted by fully confronting the possible usage of the term. The issues that emerge deal with the question of how much interference with the enjoyment of ownership we want the law of theft to protect, and what sort of interference we want that part of the law to respond to. A concrete representation of these issues was provided by the range of scenarios, **(i)–(iv)**, in the supermarket, and I suggested how a rationale could be found for excluding **(iii)** but including the others. This would amount to upholding the decision though not the reasoning in *Gallasso*. If this were to reflect an agreed position for reforming the law of theft, then an amplifying provision on appropriation could be proposed to include the following.[125]

---

[122] *ibid* at 1610 (cp 1624). Hobhouse's requirement of an 'inherent illegality' must be construed as requiring a breach of civil law property rights which the owner would still be entitled to enforce. If not, his allegation that the majority view treats 'otherwise lawful conduct as criminal' is simply a question begging assertion that the conduct is not criminal. The real point of conflict with the majority arises due to Hobhouse's insistence that because the defendant cannot be dishonest where he believes he has the legal right to the property, the trial judge's direction must include a technical explanation of the basis for establishing the transfer of title by means of a valid gift. For further discussion, see concluding section.

[123] By insisting that D is aware of the fact that the gift was invalid due to the incapacity of V, and hence the property still belonged to V at the time D acquired it, it is possible to fit the acquisition into the standard profile of taking the property of another.

[124] Text following n 58 above.

[125] The full provision could also provide in additional subsections the material dealing with the particular circumstances currently covered by the second part of s 3(1) and s 3(2).

Proposed Amplifying Provision for Appropriation

An appropriation will be recognised as occurring when—

(a)   a person deals with the property of another in a way which completely deprives the other of the enjoyment of that property; or

(b)   a person deals with the property in an unauthorised manner amounting to some lesser assumption of the rights of the other over that property.

If both of these proposals for reform had been accepted, would the issue in *Hinks* never have arisen? No. But a clearer view of the outstanding issue would have emerged. It would have been clear from clause (a) in the reformed provision on appropriation that an appropriation had occurred, because Hinks had, by cajoling her victim into giving her his property,[126] dealt with the property in a way which completely deprived him of the enjoyment of it. No certified question would, then, have been framed in relation to appropriation. However, an outstanding issue does remain.

When we consider dishonesty, even under the reformed state as proposed above, there is a problem, not with the consent point because we have required a belief that the defendant believes the victim would have consented in the knowledge of all the circumstances, and it is implausible he would have done so if he had been aware that his 'friend' was in fact taking him for a ride. The problem arises with a possible belief that the defendant's dealing with the victim's property is permitted by law.

The reason why this point is problematic but the consent point is not, is that we can be confident in asserting that *nobody* would believe that an owner would consent to being deprived of his property by exploitation (or fraud)—that is the very reason why exploitation (or fraud) has to work in the dark. However, it is plausible to suggest that a perpetrator of exploitation could believe that the victim had transferred the legal entitlement to the property, for this is a common occurrence in some cases of exploitation in the commercial realm, where one party takes advantage of the other party being deprived of all the relevant information in order to strike a favourable bargain, that the other party would not otherwise have consented to.

There is then a spectrum of exploitation of the ignorance of others, from the unlawfully fraudulent to the lawful use of commercially sensitive information. Somewhere along this spectrum lies the unlawful

---

[126] A mere acceptance of the property by way of gift would have sufficed for clause (a), but it is important to provide a full description of D's conduct for the purpose of considering the next stage.

use of undue influence, or the exploitation of an incapable victim, which would render a transaction void. But also along this spectrum lies the use of a power of persuasion which would obtain a favourable outcome for the persuader but not an unlawful one. These distinctions are far from being clear cut, as is apparent from the cases upon them. However, even Hobhouse is prepared to recognise cases 'vitiated by incapacity … which would lead both the man in the street and the law to say that the transfer was not a true gift'.[127] Subsequently,[128] he draws the line between the facts of *Mazo*[129] (gifts to a maid by an 89-year-old lady of a reduced mental state) and the facts of *Kendrick and Hopkins*[130] (liquidation of assets of a blind 99-year-old lady by owners of a residential home using power of attorney). However, if the latter case is a case of 'obvious dishonesty' in a more specialist setting, such that there need be no discussion of whether the defendant had the belief that he was acting lawfully (or with the victim's consent[131]), and the former case is not, so that the trial judge's failure to direct on this specific point will vitiate a conviction, the question arises as to which of the two the facts of *Hinks* are closer to.

However this question is answered, we are left with the general problem that there is no clear consensus here either on where exactly the defining point of obvious dishonesty is to be found. The trial judge's general direction on dishonesty in *Hinks* was upheld by the majority in the House of Lords, more on the basis that if the facts alleged were accepted it would amount to a case of obvious dishonesty, rather than on a detailed consideration of the technicalities.[132] Hobhouse's dissent requires that on the facts of *Hinks* the technical issue of whether the defendant believed she was acquiring valid title to the gifts should be put to the jury,[133] and in making this requirement he is prepared to invoke the criteria for a valid gift established in *In re Beaney, Deceased*.[134] Yet these criteria are stated to demand different levels of understanding on the part of the donor, depending on 'the particular transaction'.[135]

---

[127] [2000] 3 WLR 1590, 1610.
[128] *ibid* at 1621–22.
[129] [1997] 2 Cr App R 518.
[130] [1997] 2 Cr App R 524.
[131] Although s 2(1)(b) is the preferred limb in Hobhouse's discussion, I treat this as weaker than the belief in lawful right under s 2(1)(a), because it requires a belief in consent on the understanding that the victim knew of the circumstances. I have argued above that the full significance of this requirement has been neglected. If this argument is not accepted, the discussion in the main text here in relation to 2(1)(a) can equally be applied to 2(1)(b).
[132] [2000] 3 WLR 1590, 1602 *per* Lord Steyn. Cp Lord Slynn at 1592.
[133] *ibid* at 1621–24.
[134] [1978] 1 WLR 770.
[135] *ibid* at 774. Where the donor was giving away her 'only asset of value' the standard required to be met included an understanding of the implications of her action. For the view that the criteria for a valid gift were not met on the facts of *Hinks*, see Law Com No 276, above n 7, at para 7.65.

Although Hobhouse's motivation is clearly to avoid the possibility of the jury confusing a defendant whose conduct was regarded as morally reprehensible by the standards of good neighbours but was still commercially acceptable and lawful, with a defendant whose conduct was morally reprehensible and unlawful,[136] it is not at all clear that transferring the issue to a consideration of the criteria for a valid gift will harden this distinction. The boundaries of capacity and valid gift making are themselves open to argument.

It is not then inconceivable that the outer limits of lawful gift making will be fixed by a consideration of the appropriate level of understanding it is thought that the donor should possess, at just that point where exploitation of the absence of that level of understanding would be considered morally reprehensible and obviously dishonest. Hobhouse found just such a coincidence on the facts of *Kendrick and Hopkins*. But neither way of framing the issue guarantees a clear grasp of when exactly the point is reached.

Disagreement over how the issue is to be framed has obscured another important feature of the way this sort of case has been discussed. Although the wording of s 2(1) clearly indicates that it is the defendant's belief that is under consideration (whether as to consent or to lawfulness), the discussion by Steyn of how the jury viewed the dishonesty of the conduct of Hinks,[137] or by Hobhouse of what the 'man in the street'[138] thought of the validity of a gift, indicate the absence of a concern with the defendant's own perspective.

I have suggested that this utilises the device of 'obvious dishonesty' in a more specialist setting. In any case, there is here, as with the earlier more general deployment of the device, a strained invocation of a common standard where what is effectively going on is the setting of a uniform standard. To suggest that this is simply an objective standard of dishonesty would be to fail to learn from the study of recklessness in the previous chapter. A richer and potentially more illuminating description of this use of dishonesty would be to take it as an instance of culpable inadvertence. It may be culpable inadvertence primarily related to standards rather than to conduct,[139] but it still ultimately impacts on the interests of the victim. By failing to give proper consideration to those grounds for concluding that he is acting against the consent of the victim and in an unlawful manner,[140] the defendant is unreasonably taking the risk of acting in a dishonest manner, which disrespects the legitimate interests of

---

[136] [2000] 3 WLR 1590, 1610, 1624.
[137] *ibid* at 1602.
[138] See text at n 127 above.
[139] For this, see ch 3, text following n 213 and subsequent discussion.
[140] Cp nn 59 & 110 above.

the victim. One would also have to add the qualification that the defendant had the capacity to give proper consideration to those grounds, if one were maintaining the parallel with culpable inadvertence in relation to conduct.[141]

In a society where rogues were inclined to disrespect the legitimate interests of others *and* given to doubt their own dishonesty in doing so, it would, accordingly, be necessary to revise the proposed definition of dishonesty given above[142] in the following manner: ... without a *reasonable* belief that the other would consent to it if he knew of all the circumstances, unless the person *reasonably* believes that way of dealing with the property is permitted by law. And it should be further understood that the assessment of a reasonable belief needs to take into account the capacity of the individual defendant to appreciate the nature of what he was doing.

Admittedly, this still leaves open the issue of the precise boundaries of the assessment that the accused behaved in a manner which any reasonable person with normal capacities would in the circumstances have been expected to avoid.[143] It does, however, clarify just what remains at issue in the law of theft.

[141] See text cited in n 139 above.
[142] See text following n 58 above, for the definition; for earlier discussion of this point, see n 110 above; and for similar discussion, see Law Com No 276, above n 7, at para 7.69.
[143] Cp ch 3, text following n 236.

5

Definition in the Criminal Law

I T WOULD BE presumptuous on the basis of the limited studies undertaken here, and actually contrary to the approach developed within this book, to suggest that a comprehensive account of defini-tion in the criminal law could be provided. Although the inherent aim of definition is to provide greater clarity in our understanding, the precise nature and practice of definition themselves elude clear understanding.[1] Nevertheless, much of what takes place within both the practice of the criminal law and the criticism which that practice attracts, relies on cer-tain assumptions about the role of definition in the criminal law. Revealing and questioning these assumptions has been a principal aim of this book.

An assumption made in turn for this investigation has been that the practice of definition within the law is intimately linked to the use that is made of legal materials. If this is so, then the complex and contentious nature of legal materials, and the very different perspectives that can be taken on them (which we explored in chapters 1 and 2) should be illumi-nated by examining at a more detailed level the workings of definitions. More specifically, the mixture of doctrinal restraint and social critique which, it was suggested, characterises the use of legal materials; the absence of specialist or privileged attributes among those who work with legal materials together with a recognition of the privileged position given to the preference of the judge; the relationship between the criminal law and a particular vision of social needs and the extent to which the one may be reformed by the other; the room for disagreement over underly-ing values and wider legitimacy; and the technical capability of the crimi-nal law—all of these should be made more apparent through examining the detailed workings of definition in the criminal law.

And on these issues the reader should by now be in a better position to form a view. More than this, the process of tracing the irregularities and controversies attending the uses of definitions within the criminal law should be capable of unearthing the suppressed assumptions and check-ing the unsound assumptions of current practices. Beyond that, there lies

---

[1] For a general picture, see Richard Robinson, *Definition* (Oxford, Clarendon Press, 1954).

the possibility of suggesting more helpful practices, or, at least, drawing attention to the limitations of existing ones. Within these concluding pages I shall attempt to draw out some brief observations on current practices, and consider how they might be improved.

Both the intellectual apparatus conventionally employed in the criminal law, and the ideological aspirations conventionally attributed to the criminal law, rely heavily on a particular view of how definitions work within it. Simply put, definitions are required to place conduct neatly into given categories. Definitions are needed to inform us that the conduct of the defendant fits the crime. Definitions are needed to establish the mens rea elements in order to be sure of convicting a culpable defendant of the crime. They are needed, moreover, to distinguish different forms of mens rea so as to be able to work out how culpable the defendant is within a hierarchy of culpable states, so as ultimately to ensure that the punishment fits the crime.

This view of definition as providing access to established categories which then indicate the significance of the conduct classified within them (as criminal, culpable, or more culpable), endorses the rational character of the criminal law. The enterprise of improving the criminal law is essentially seen as one of increasing its rationality through acquiring better definitions, which are capable of placing conduct more clearly in the appropriate categories. Such improvement is not limited to the technical aspect of the enterprise. It impacts also on the ideological aspirations of the criminal law, to ensure that only conduct which is truly culpable will be found criminal (*actus non facit reum nisi mens sit rea*), and that punishment will only be meted out in accordance with the law (*nulla poena sine lege*).[2]

There is, however, within the conventional practice of definitions a particular tell-tale sign that something other than providing access to established categories is at work. This is found in the diversity of ways in which definitions are made to work, in providing or refusing recognition to a potential member of a category. Three different ways can be noted, perhaps best expressed as different types of test to see whether something fits the defined category or not. The exclusive feature test requires that the contender possesses that feature on pain of being otherwise excluded from the category. The feature of awareness of risk found in the strict subjectivist, or cognitivist, definition of recklessness furnishes an example. This kind of definition produces a recognisable uniformity among members of the category which will each display the required feature in order to gain recognition as members.

The second test is the threshold test. This requires that contenders meet the threshold but does not stipulate the manner in which this is

---

[2] Extensive discussion of the first maxim took place within the latter part of chapter 3. For further comment on the principle of legality, see n 13 below.

done, or the extent to which the threshold is exceeded. Consequently there may be great variety among members, since no single common feature will necessarily mark them out as members. An example is provided by the threshold test for mens rea proposed in chapter 3, or, from existing law, we could mention the definition of gross negligence provided by the House of Lords in *Andrews* or by the Court of Appeal in *Prentice*.

The third test is the paradigm test. This requires contenders to establish sufficient resemblance to a recognised paradigm in order to join it inside the category. The similarity between members is potentially stronger here than in the exclusive feature test, since it is possible to require resemblance to be displayed in a number of features in order to establish sufficient connection to the paradigm and so to gain entry into the category. However, there is also the possibility for less uniformity to occur with this test, when weaker requirements are set for fitting the features displayed by the paradigm. And where the paradigm is sufficiently complex in character, a weaker use of the paradigm test may create diversity among the membership due to different members only resembling the paradigm in one of a number of different ways. We only need to add the possibility of a paradigm shift from the original to another paradigm, or indeed the growing recognition of multiple paradigms, in order for this approach to produce a category readily analysable in terms of family resemblances between members straight out of one of Wittgenstein's language games.[3] Before reaching this point of deterioration, however, a paradigm test may exert a strong influence on membership of the category. An example is found in the definition of appropriation preferred by the Court of Appeal in *Gallasso*, which excludes a contender lacking both the feature of taking and the feature of non-consensual conduct associated with a paradigmatic case of theft.[4]

What is given away by recognising this variety of kinds of tests within the conventional practice of definition? Well, just the possibility of choosing one approach to definition rather than another defeats the idea that there is something in the process of definition itself that neatly orders the members into a category. Having, for example, selected an exclusive feature test to arrange the members of a particular category,

---

[3] For discussion of Wittgenstein's insights, and their limitations, see ch 7 of Andrew Halpin, *Reasoning with Law* (Oxford, Hart Publishing, 2001); developed further in 'Or, even, What the Law Can Teach the Philosophy of Language: A Response to Green', forthcoming *Virginia Law Review*.
[4] An interesting analysis of the doctrine of breaking bulk established in *The Carrier's Case* (1473) (whereby a bailee became liable for larceny if he broke into the goods in his possession, as an exception to the possessorial immunity he would otherwise have enjoyed) in terms of paradigmatic influence is provided by George Fletcher, *Rethinking Criminal Law* (Boston, MA, Little, Brown & Co, 1978; republished, Oxford, OUP, 2000) 83–84.

what is to stop the switch to a threshold test throwing that particular ordering into disarray by allowing in other members who satisfy the threshold by displaying different features? If there is not a fixed definitional test to establish each category, the choice of definitional test will determine what category we end up with.

The point can be demonstrated by considering the switch from *Cunningham* to *Caldwell* recklessness. The category of legal recklessness is changed by the switch of definitional test, but since there is no way of establishing prior to the choice of test which definition is to be used, the definition itself cannot be relied on for establishing the category. It is the choice of definition that is decisive.

Once we recognise the possibility of choice on the large scale between different kinds of tests, it is a small matter to acknowledge the role of choice at a more detailed level in working through how exactly the test will operate, as new contenders are considered for entry into the category. The fundamental point to make is that the process of definition simply does not work as the conventional assumptions require. The idea that armed with the correct definition we can determine precisely what is and what is not recognised as a member of the category—and hence what conduct is criminal, culpable, or more culpable—presumes first of all that there is a correct definition, and secondly that all possible contenders have already been sorted as members or non-members by that definition. The reality is, as the studies undertaken in chapters 3 and 4 reveal, we do not know which definition to adopt and how precisely to apply it until *after* we have had the opportunity of considering the contenders for the category we are constructing. This is demonstrated most dramatically in the definitional changes made for the category of legal recklessness, particularly most recently in *R v G*, but is evident elsewhere, in, for example, Lord Lane's concern to keep the ignorant foreigner out of the dishonesty category in *Ghosh*, or Lord Steyn's concern to keep the defendant inside the category of appropriation in *Hinks*.

There are other aspects of the process of definition that we have encountered in our studies which tell against the conventional assumptions, but before recalling them I want to address one significant omission from the variety of tests we have been considering. I have not included an ordinary usage, or dictionary test as a way of providing a definition of a term. The reason for this is quite simple, and became particularly apparent in the studies on recklessness and appropriation. Ordinary usage may be complex and, correspondingly, dictionary definitions may cover a range of different meanings. To put it another way a single word may act as the entrance to a number of quite distinct categories. (The range of meanings may be so diffuse that even in the generous imagery of Wittgenstein's language game, it may take a number of games to encapsulate them all.) There is then a qualitative difference between 'a dictionary definition' which records the variety of ordinary usage, and a technical definition which seeks to establish the members of a particular category. The failure to recognise this difference led to much unnecessary confusion both with the development of *Caldwell* recklessness (to the point that the basic status of the *Caldwell* test as a definition or a direction was left in doubt), and with the use of appropriation in the law of theft.

Far from offering the basis for a definitional test to establish membership of a category, the complexities of the ordinary usage of language may increase the confusion over how exactly the category is to be constructed. A multiplicity of ordinary uses for a particular word produces a diversity of choices over which category to adopt, and as we clearly saw in the studies on recklessness and appropriation the choice made will alter the possibilities of what may count as criminal, culpable, or more culpable.[5] This choice, the choice of how to relate our legal usage of a term to the existing ordinary usage of a word, may then be regarded as potentially another choice to be made, alongside the choice of definitional test.

I have also mentioned a role for choice in working through the process of definition at a more detailed level when considering new contenders for membership of the category. In part, this arises due to the general condition of language,[6] but more particularly we have seen in our studies on the general mens rea terms and dishonesty the need for choice arising when the category in question has been selected for an explicitly evaluative purpose. If the evaluative project is still ongoing, ie certain instances of conduct are still to be evaluated as falling inside or outside the category, then an evaluative choice will still have to be made. Some of these choices may be controversial because there is not a detailed consensus within society on how that evaluative issue is to be decided, and if so the selection of an evaluative term to head up the definitional test is not going to provide us with a clear category, as the use of dishonesty in the definition of theft has demonstrated.

In such cases, a more effective strategy may be to limit the work of the evaluative term by rendering its technical use more restricted by reference to non-evaluative conditions, as was suggested in chapter 4 in the proposed reform of the definition of dishonesty. Nevertheless, as was recognised at the end of that chapter, there may still remain evaluative work to be done at the margins of the category which this strategy cannot wholly exclude.

[5] Similarly, one of the failings of Wittgenstein's approach, noted *loc cit* n 3 above, is that it does not offer any basis for determining which language game we should play from a number of possibilities open to us, despite the significance of choosing one rather than another.
[6] For further discussion, see chs 6 & 9 of Halpin (2001), above n 3.

Indeed, the strategy of approaching a category with an evaluative purpose by providing an apparently non-evaluative term, or stipulating a non-evaluative use for a term, is likely to backfire, as we saw in chapter 3 when considering the cognitivist approach to mens rea terms. The deployment of cognitive states to cover evaluative categories served only to suppress the underlying evaluative issue, which then broke out as the process of definition continued, wreaking havoc with the attempts to construct the category in an inappropriate manner.[7]

A more general point can be made here about the purpose of the category under construction. It is not simply that suppressing an evaluative purpose by a non-evaluative one will prove ineffective. We also learned from our studies in chapter 3 that mistaking one evaluative purpose for another will also cause problems. I suggested that it is of particular importance to recognise the difference between an evaluative project to establish a threshold level of culpability, and one to establish a relatively more or less serious level of culpability. In either case, the definitional process will be made easier by considering the underlying issue that needs to be confronted for the project in question. In neither case does the definitional process flow smoothly by falsely regarding it as the mere unpacking of the established meaning of a term.

The insistence on recognising the scope for choice throughout the process of definition flies in the face of a reliance on the definition itself to place conduct neatly into given categories. One possible response to these observations is to express a blanket scepticism about the value of definition in the criminal law. Such scepticism was encountered within the heterodox or critical approaches to the criminal law considered in chapter 2. More widely, it can be detected in a growing enthusiasm for particularism, insisting on a closer contextual assessment of particular instances, opposed to general categories, general definitions, and even doubting the existence of a general part to the criminal law.[8]

---

[7] For further discussion of this point, see VF Nourse, 'Hearts and Minds: Understanding the New Culpability' (2002) 6 *Buffalo Criminal Law Review* 361.

[8] Particularistic tendencies of different strengths, and supporting quite different perspectives on the criminal law, are to be found in Alan Norrie, 'From Criminal Law to Legal Theory: The Mysterious Case of the Reasonable Glue Sniffer' (2002) 65 *Modern Law Review* 538, and *Punishment, Responsibility, and Justice: A Relational Critique* (Oxford, OUP, 2000); John Gardner, 'On the General Part of the Criminal Law' in Antony Duff (ed), *Philosophy and the Criminal Law: Principle and Critique* (Cambridge, Cambridge University Press, 1998), and 'Criminal Law and the Uses of Theory: A Reply to Laing' (1994) 14 *Oxford Journal of Legal Studies* 217; Nicola Lacey, 'General Principles of Criminal Law? A Feminist View' in Donald Nicolson and Lois Bibbings (eds), *Feminist Perspectives on Criminal Law* (London, Cavendish Publishing, 2000). See further, ch 2 n 94.

An ambitious attempt to advance particularism more generally within the law has been made by David Jabbari, 'Reason, Cause and Principle in Law: The Normativity of Context' (1999) 19 *Oxford Journal of Legal Studies* 203; 'Radical Particularism: A Natural Law of

The problem with a resort to particularism is that viewing each instance in isolation does not preclude the need to pass judgment[9] upon it. In the case of the criminal law this will involve determining the same outcomes as were served by the discredited general definitions. Was this instance of conduct criminal, culpable, more culpable? Extreme particularism would deny this possibility by avoiding any comparison with any criterion that could be employed to make these judgments. The need to be sensitive to context and individual differences must be matched with some sense of the general for it to be possible to make judgment at all.[10]

The process of definition identified in this work offers a path between sham generalisations and excessive particularisations by insisting on greater attention being paid to the complexities of the material being defined, and more careful reflection over the exact issue the definition is responding to. In addition, the recognition that further complexity may unravel and deeper reflection become possible as the underlying issue is examined in new settings, calls for a consciousness of the developing (and often unfinished) nature of the work of definition. Within this broader and more dynamic understanding of the process of definition, it is possible to recognise general issues, while at the same time acknowledging that there may be responses to those issues that require attention to the particular. Responses may have to be offence-specific (as we saw with recklessness), or, conduct specific where the issue identified is itself sensitive to particular features of conduct (as we saw when we came to considering the dishonesty issue in *Hinks*).

This account of definition is in some respects less tidy than the role conventionally assumed for definition. Unleashing the issue contained by the category may discredit the definitional test that sought to keep the category closed, and even disrupt the category itself. Related classifications may become casualties, as we saw when the mens rea issue was opened up in chapter 3 and the conventional actus reus/mens rea and subjective/objective distinctions became less secure. The detailed study of the

Context' (1999) 50 *Northern Ireland Legal Quarterly* 454. An interesting discussion of the difficulties of steering a course between particularism and subjectivism is to be found in Mayo Moran, *Rethinking the Reasonable Person: An Egalitarian Reconstruction of the Objective Standard* (Oxford, OUP, 2003) 305–14.

Dissatisfaction with conventional representations of the general part of the criminal law has provoked considerable debate, found within the contributions to Duff (ed) (1998) above, and Stephen Shute and AP Simester (eds), *Criminal Law Theory: Doctrines of the General Part* (Oxford, OUP, 2002). See also Alan Norrie, 'Legal and Moral Judgment in the "General Part"', Shaun McVeigh and Peter Rush, 'Cutting our Losses: Criminal Legal Doctrine', both in Shaun McVeigh, Peter Rush and Alison Young (eds), *Criminal Legal Doctrine* (Aldershot, Ashgate, 1997); Victor Tadros, 'The system of the criminal law' (2002) 22 *Legal Studies* 448.

[9] And, quite possibly, *judgement*.
[10] See the discussion in ch 3 n 241.

working of the definition of theft in chapter 4 cast further doubts on the strength of these conventional classifications.[11] If *the* general issue for the criminal law is the assessment of criminal culpability in such terms as were suggested in the threshold test proposed in chapter 3, then there is no clear divide between actus reus and mens rea, nor between explicitly evaluative elements within the definition of an offence and apparently technical elements whose determination will necessarily contribute to the resolution of the general evaluative issue. It should not then surprise us to see an evaluative issue being at stake when the argument is being conducted over the definition of an actus reus term, such as appropriation. Moreover, the manner in which the proposed threshold test was formulated made it clear that a more subtle approach to the subjective-objective distinction would be needed than conventional understanding provided. A point confirmed when we considered that distinction further in examining dishonesty in chapter 4.

It would, however, be wrong to assume that untidiness is the hallmark of the approach to definition developed here. The disturbance of apparent tidiness is also the opportunity for working towards a more effective ordering of the materials of the criminal law. This has implications for attempts to expound the law, to reform, to codify[12]—and even to exalt the

---

[11] Doubts about the stability and value of these classifications have been expressed on a number of occasions. On the actus reus/mens rea distinction, see Rupert Cross, 'The Mental Element in Crime' (1967) 83 *Law Quarterly Review* 215, 226; ATH Smith, 'On Actus Reus and Mens Rea' in Peter Glazebrook (ed), *Reshaping the Criminal Law: Essays in honour of Glanville Williams* (London, Stevens & Sons, 1978); Celia Wells, 'Swatting the Subjectivist Bug' [1982] *Criminal Law Review* 209; Martin Gardner, 'The *Mens Rea* Enigma: Observations on the Role of Motive in the Criminal Law Past and Present' (1993) *Utah Law Review* 635; Paul Robinson, 'Should the Criminal Law Abandon the *Actus Reus-Mens Rea* Distinction?' in Stephen Shute, John Gardner and Jeremy Horder (eds), *Action and Value in Criminal Law* (Oxford, Clarendon Press, 1993), and *Structure and Function in Criminal Law* (Oxford, Clarendon Press, 1997), which incorporates material from Robinson's earlier essay; Nicola Lacey, Celia Wells and Oliver Quick, *Reconstructing Criminal Law: Critical Perspectives on Crime and the Criminal Process* (3rd edn, London, Butterworths, 2003) 43–60.

On the subjective/objective distinction, see the references provided in ch 4 n 12. Different attempts to move beyond conventional subjective/objective positions are made by Jeremy Horder, 'Cognition, Emotion, and Criminal Culpability' (1990) 106 *Law Quarterly Review* 469, and Victor Tadros, 'Recklessness and the Duty to Take Care' in Stephen Shute and AP Simester (eds), *Criminal Law Theory: Doctrines of the General Part* (Oxford, OUP, 2002).

[12] The merits of codification are often seen in terms of avoiding the failings of an uncodified body of law. For example, the recent Scottish proposals are motivated by concerns that the judiciary cannot be relied upon to bring about the reform and clarification that the existing common law body of law requires. See Pamela Ferguson, 'Codifying Criminal Law (1): A Critique of Scots Common Law' [2004] *Criminal Law Review* 49. Support for an English and Welsh code has been premised on a code being able to provide respect for the principle of legality, or promotion of wider human rights concerns, that the uncodified law is unable to give. See ATH Smith, 'Judicial Lawmaking in the Criminal Law' (1984) 100 *Law Quarterly Review* 46; Mrs Justice Arden, 'Criminal Law at the Crossroads: The Impact of Human Rights from The Law Commission's Perspective and the Need for a Code' [1999] *Criminal Law Review* 439. Assessing the positive merits of a particular code may require more careful

legality of the criminal law.[13] For all of these enterprises depend on the practice of definition. And all of these enterprises will be conducted more

consideration. For a serious attempt to compare the merits of the different American state criminal codes, see Paul Robinson, Michael Cahill and Usman Mohammad, 'The Five Worst (and Five Best) American Criminal Codes' (2000) 95 *Northwestern University Law Review* 1.

The criteria used to evaluate a code, and the expectations that can legitimately be made of a code, remain contestable, and as Celia Wells has pointed out, there is a danger that codification will be undertaken with certain key assumptions of the project unexplored— 'Codification of the Criminal Law: Restatement or Reform?' [1986] *Criminal Law Review* 314. Continuing debate over what can actually be technically achieved by a code provides strong argument against any assumption that the deficiencies of precodified law can be dealt with by merely engaging in the codification process. See, on the Model Penal Code, George Fletcher, 'Dogmas of the Model Penal Code' (1998) 2 *Buffalo Criminal Law Review* 3; Paul Robinson, 'In Defense of the Model Penal Code: A Reply to Professor Fletcher' (1998) 2 *Buffalo Criminal Law Review* 25; Don Stuart, 'Supporting General Principles for Criminal Responsibility in the Model Penal Code with Suggestions for Reconsideration: A Canadian Perspective' (2000) 4 *Buffalo Criminal Law Review* 13. And, more generally, see Robinson (1997), above n 11; Jeremy Horder, 'Criminal Law and Legal Positivism' (2002) 8 *Legal Theory* 221.

A clear grasp of the potential roles and limitations of definition in the criminal law is essential to any attempt to evaluate codification in general, or the advantages of a particular codification project.

[13] Concerns with the principle of legality have been heightened following the implementation of the Human Rights Act 1998, as the Law Commission's recent discussion on the possibility of a general dishonesty offence has demonstrated. See Law Commission No 276 (Cm 5560, 2002), *Fraud*, paras 5.29–5.33. Nevertheless, the precise relationship between that principle and a requirement of certainty in the definition of criminal offences remains unclear. In surveying recent decisions of the European Court of Human Rights (including *SW and CR v UK* (1996) 21 EHRR 363—the aftermath of the abolition of the marital rape exemption in *R v R*), the Law Commission suggests, at paras 5.32–5.33, that the principle of maximum certainty sets a higher threshold than the requirements of Article 7 of the ECHR. An illuminating discussion of the historical development of the principle of legality within the criminal law is provided by Finbarr McAuley and J Paul McCutcheon, *Criminal Liability: A Grammar* (Dublin, Round Hall Sweet & Maxwell, 2000) 42–56, and a helpful comparative study on the principle is provided in ch 10 of Ben Emmerson and Andrew Ashworth, *Human Rights and Criminal Justice* (London, Sweet & Maxwell, 2001). What is evident from this discussion, and from the stance taken by the European Court of Human Rights in *SW and CR v UK* (at 399), in permitting judicial developments that are 'consistent with the essence of the offence and could reasonably be foreseen', is that some sort of allowance for judicial clarification of offences must be made by the principle of legality. The crux of the matter is how much and on what basis.

Treating the process of definition as involving the clarification of issues may help to shed some light on this problem. We could in general regard the 'essence' of the offence as the issue which the definition of the offence has already restrictively set for further clarification (though it is not easy to see how this applies to the state reached by the law under consideration in *SW and CR v UK*—see ch 3 n 116). Some support for this perspective is provided from the deliberations of the International Criminal Tribunal for the former Yugoslavia in the case of *Krstić* (ICTY Case No IT-98-33-T) (2 August 2001), discussed by Antonio Cassese, *International Criminal Law* (Oxford, OUP, 2003) 104–05. The Trial Chamber was concerned with the definition of genocide in circumstances where there had been a massacre of 7–8,000 Muslim men of miltary age in the limited area of Srebrenica, and felt able to clarify the issue of what amounted to the *physical or biological destruction* of part of a protected group by holding that limitations as to geographical area or men of military age did not prevent a finding that there was intent to destroy part of the protected group of Bosnian Muslims. However, the Chamber explicitly cited the principle of legality in holding that they were unable to effectively by being able to recognise the issues that are to be confronted, the progress that has been made in resolving them, and the work they still require to be done. Improved definition in the criminal law is less about the care with which we choose words. It is more about obtaining a clearer focus on the issues.

consider the issue of the *destruction of cultural or sociological characteristics* of a group as falling under the definition of genocide.

Bibliography

AESCHYLUS, *Eumenides* in the Loeb edition, *Aeschylus* II, with translation by Herbert Weir Smyth (London, William Heinemann, 1926)

LARRY ALEXANDER, 'Insufficient Concern: A Unified Conception of Criminal Culpability' (2000) 88 *California Law Review* 931

LARRY ALEXANDER and EMILY SHERWIN, *The Rule of Rules: Morality, Rules, and the Dilemmas of Law* (Durham, NC, Duke University Press, 2001)

PETER ALLDRIDGE, *Relocating Criminal Law* (Aldershot, Ashgate, 2000)

American Law Institute, *Model Penal Code* (Official Draft and Explanatory Notes: Complete Text of Model Penal Code as Adopted at the 1962 Annual Meeting of the American Law Institute, 24 May 1962) (Philadelphia, PA, American Law Institute, 1985), also in Dubber (2002)

Archbold 2003, PJ Richardson (ed) (London, Sweet & Maxwell); *Archbold 1992*

MRS JUSTICE ARDEN, 'Criminal Law at the Crossroads: The Impact of Human Rights from The Law Commission's Perspective and the Need for a Code' [1999] *Criminal Law Review* 439

ANDREW ASHWORTH, 'The elasticity of mens rea' in Tapper (ed) (1981)

ANDREW ASHWORTH, Editorial [1986] *Criminal Law Review* 1

ANDREW ASHWORTH, 'Belief, Intent, and Criminal Liability' in Eekelaar and Bell (eds) (1987)

ANDREW ASHWORTH, 'Interpreting Criminal Statutes: A Crisis of Legality?' (1991) 107 *Law Quarterly Review* 419

ANDREW ASHWORTH, *Principles of Criminal Law* (4th edn, Oxford, OUP, 2003); (3rd edn, 1999)

ANDREW ASHWORTH and KENNETH CAMPBELL, 'Recklessness in Assault—and in General?' (1991) 107 *Law Quarterly Review* 187

ANDREW ASHWORTH and BARRY MITCHELL (eds), *Rethinking English Homicide Law* (Oxford, OUP, 2000)

FERNANDO ATRIA, *On Law and Legal Reasoning* (Oxford, Hart Publishing, 2001)

JOHN AUSTIN, *Lectures on Jurisprudence* I (5th edn, London, John Murray, 1885; reprinted 1929)

JM BALKIN, 'Deconstruction' in Patterson (ed) (1996)

REZA BANAKAR and MAX TRAVERS (eds), *An Introduction to Law and Social Theory* (Oxford, Hart Publishing, 2002)

KIT BARKER, 'Understanding the Unjust Enrichment Principle in Private Law: A Study of the Concept and its Reasons' in Neyers, McInnes and Pitel (eds) (2004)

M CHERIF BASSIOUNI and GAMAL M BADR, 'The Shari'ah: Sources, Interpretation, and Rule-Making' (2002) 1 *UCLA Journal of Islamic and Near Eastern Law* 135

JOHN BELL and GEORGE ENGEL, Cross's *Statutory Interpretation* (3rd edn, London, Butterworths, 1995)

SEYLA BENHABIB, *Critique, Norm, and Utopia: A Study of the Foundations of Critical Theory* (New York, NY, Columbia University Press, 1986)

MITCHELL BERMAN, 'Justification and Excuse, Law and Morality' (2003) 53 *Duke Law Journal* 1

DERYCK BEYLEVELD, RICHARD KIRKHAM and DAVID TOWNEND, 'Which presumption? A critique of the House of Lords' reasoning on retrospectivity and the Human Rights Act' (2002) 22 *Legal Studies* 185

DI BIRCH, 'The Foresight Saga: The Biggest Mistake of All?' [1988] *Criminal Law Review* 4

DI BIRCH, 'Rethinking Sexual History Evidence: Proposals for Fairer Trials' [2002] *Criminal Law Review* 531

DI BIRCH, 'Untangling Sexual History Evidence: A Rejoinder to Professor Temkin' [2003] *Criminal Law Review* 370

PETER BIRKS, 'The Early History of Iniuria' (1969) 37 *Tijdschrift voor Rechtsgeschiedenis* 163

PETER BIRKS, *Harassment and Hubris: The Right to an Equality of Respect*, the Second John Maurice Kelly Memorial Lecture (Dublin, Faculty of Law, University College Dublin, 1996)

ALAN BOGG and JOHN STANTON-IFE, 'Protecting the vulnerable: legality, harm and theft' (2003) 23 *Legal Studies* 402

CHRISTINE BOYLE, MARIE-ANDRÉE BERTRAND, CÉLINE LACERTE-LAMONTAGNE and REBECCA SHAMAI, *A Feminist Review of Criminal Law* (Ottawa, Ministry of Supply and Services, 1985)

JAMES BRADY, 'Recklessness' (1996) 15 *Law and Philosophy* 183

JOHN BRAITHWAITE, 'Rules and Principles: A Theory of Legal Certainty' (2002) 27 *Australian Journal of Legal Philosophy* 47

SCOTT BREWER, 'Exemplary Reasoning: Semantics, Pragmatics, and the Rational Force of Legal Argument by Analogy' (1996) 109 *Harvard Law Review* 923

ADRIAN BRIGGS, 'Judges, juries and the meaning of words' (1985) 5 *Legal Studies* 314

WENDY BROWN and JANET HALLEY, 'Introduction' in Brown and Halley (eds) (2002)

WENDY BROWN and JANET HALLEY (eds), *Left Legalism / Left Critique* (Durham, NC, Duke University Press, 2002)

ROGER BROWNSWORD, *Contract Law: Themes for the Twenty-First Century* (London, Butterworths, 2000)

WW BUCKLAND, *A Text-book of Roman Law*, Peter Stein (ed) (rev 3rd edn, Cambridge, Cambridge University Press, 1975)

BJORN BURKHARDT, 'Some Questions and Comments on What is Called "The Mental Element of the Offence"' (1996) 30 *Israel Law Review* 82

KENNETH CAMPBELL, 'The Test of Dishonesty in R v Ghosh' (1984) 43 *Cambridge Law Journal* 349

TOM CAMPBELL, 'Rationales for Freedom of Communication' in Campbell and Sadurski (eds) (1994)

TOM CAMPBELL and WOJCIECH SADURSKI (eds), *Freedom of Communication* (Aldershot, Dartmouth, 1994)

PETER CANE, *Responsibility in Law and Morality* (Oxford, Hart Publishing, 2002)

PETER CANE and MARK TUSHNET (eds), *The Oxford Handbook of Legal Studies* (Oxford, OUP, 2003)

ALBERT CARDARELLI and STEPHEN HICKS, 'Radicalism in Law and Criminology: a Retrospective View of Critical Legal Studies and Radical Criminology' (1993) 84 *Journal of Criminal Law and Criminology* 502

PAUL CARRINGTON, 'Of Law and the River' (1984) 34 *Journal of Legal Education* 222

ANTONIO CASSESE, *International Criminal Law* (Oxford, OUP, 2003)

EMILIOS CHRISTODOULIDIS, *Law and Reflexive Politics* (Dordrecht, Kluwer Academic Publishers, 1998)

EC CLARK, *An Analysis of Criminal Liability* (Cambridge, Cambridge University Press, 1880; reprinted, Littleton, CO, Fred B Rothman & Co, 1983)

CMV CLARKSON, 'Violence and the Law Commission' [1994] *Criminal Law Review* 324

CMV CLARKSON and HM KEATING, *Criminal Law, Text and Materials* (5th edn, London, Sweet & Maxwell, 2003)

ERIC CLIVE, PAMELA FERGUSON, CHRISTOPHER GANE and ALEXANDER McCALL SMITH, *A Draft Criminal Code for Scotland with Commentary* (Edinburgh, Scottish Law Commission, 2003)

JULES COLEMAN and SCOTT SHAPIRO (eds), *The Oxford Handbook of Jurisprudence and Philosophy of Law* (Oxford, OUP, 2002)

HUGH COLLINS, *The Law of Contract* (4th edn, London, Butterworths, 2003)

JOANNE CONAGHAN, 'Wishful Thinking or Bad Faith: A Feminist Encounter with Duncan Kennedy's *Critique of Adjudication*' (2001) 22 *Cardozo Law Review* 721

DRUCILLA CORNELL, *The Imaginary Domain: Abortion, Pornography & Sexual Harassment* (New York, NY, Routledge, 1995)

DRUCILLA CORNELL, MICHEL ROSENFELD and DAVID CARLSON (eds), *Deconstruction and the Possibility of Justice* (London, Routledge, 1992)

KIMBERLÉ CRENSHAW, 'Race, Reform, and Retrenchment: Transformation and Legitimation in Antidiscrimination Law' (1988) 101 *Harvard Law Review* 1331

Criminal Code Bill Commission (C 2345, 1879), *Report of the Royal Commission appointed to consider The Law Relating to Indictable Offences: With an Appendix containing a Draft Code embodying the Suggestions of the Commissioners*

Criminal Law Revision Committee (Cmnd 2977, 1966), Eighth Report, *Theft and Related Offences*

RUPERT CROSS, 'The Mental Element in Crime' (1967) 83 *Law Quarterly Review* 215

RUPERT CROSS, 'The Reports of the Criminal Law Commissioners (1833–1849) and the Abortive Bills of 1853' in Glazebrook (ed) (1978)

FREDERICK DANFORTH (ed), *The Argentine Penal Code*, Emilio Gonzalez-Lopez (transl) (South Hackensack, NJ, Fred B Rothman & Co, 1963)

CHARLES DEBATTISTA, 'Is the end in sight for chartering demise clauses?', *Lloyd's List*, 21 February 2001, 5

LORD DENNING, *The Discipline of Law* (London, Butterworths, 1979)

IAN DENNIS, 'The Critical Condition of Criminal Law' (1997) *Current Legal Problems* 213

JACQUES DERRIDA, 'Letter to a Japanese Friend' in Wood and Bernasconi (eds) (1985)

JACQUES DERRIDA, 'Force of Law: The "Mystical Foundation of Authority"' in Cornell, Rosenfeld and Carlson (eds) (1992)

JACQUES DERRIDA, *Points ...: Interviews, 1974–1994* (Stanford, CA, Stanford University Press, 1995)

JACQUES DERRIDA, *On the Name* (Stanford, CA, Stanford University Press, 1995)

MARTIN DOCKRAY (ed), *City University Centenary Lectures in Law* (London, Blackstone Press, 1996)

JOSHUA DRESSLER, 'Justifications and Excuses: A Brief Review of the Concepts and the Literature' (1987) 33 *Wayne Law Review* 1155

JOSHUA DRESSLER, 'Does One Mens Rea Fit All?: Thoughts on Alexander's Unified Conception of CRIMINAL CULPABILITY' (2000) 88 *California Law Review* 955

MARKUS DUBBER, *Criminal Law: Model Penal Code* (New York, NY, Foundation Press, 2002)

ANTONY DUFF, *Intention, Agency and Criminal Liability: Philosophy of Action and the Criminal Law* (Oxford, Blackwell, 1990)

ANTONY DUFF, Introduction to Duff (ed) (1998)

ANTONY DUFF, 'Principle and Contradiction in the Criminal Law: Motives and Criminal Liability' in Duff (ed) (1998)

ANTONY DUFF (ed), *Philosophy and the Criminal Law: Principle and Critique* (Cambridge, Cambridge University Press, 1998)

NEIL DUXBURY, *Patterns of American Jurisprudence* (Oxford, Clarendon Press, 1995)

NEIL DUXBURY, *Jurists and Judges: An Essay on Influence* (Oxford, Hart Publishing, 2001)

NEIL DUXBURY, *Frederick Pollock and the English Juristic Tradition*, forthcoming (Oxford, OUP, 2005)

RONALD DWORKIN, *Taking Rights Seriously* (London, Duckworth, 1977)

RONALD DWORKIN, 'In Praise of Theory' (1997) 29 *Arizona State Law Journal* 353

RONALD DWORKIN, 'Thirty Years On' (2002) 115 *Harvard Law Review* 1655

HARRY EDWARDS, 'Collegiality and Decision Making on the D.C. Circuit' (1998) 84 *Virginia Law Review* 1335

JOHN EEKELAAR and JOHN BELL (eds), *Oxford Essays in Jurisprudence, Third Series* (Oxford, Clarendon Press, 1987)

DW ELLIOTT, 'Dishonesty in Theft: A Dispensable Concept' [1982] *Criminal Law Review* 395

DW ELLIOTT, 'Directors' Thefts and Dishonesty' [1991] *Criminal Law* Review 732

DW ELLIOTT, 'Endangering Life by Destroying or Damaging Property' [1997] *Criminal Law Review* 382

EVELYN ELLIS (ed), *The Principle of Proportionality in the Laws of Europe* (Oxford, Hart Publishing, 1999)

BEN EMMERSON and ANDREW ASHWORTH, *Human Rights and Criminal Justice* (London, Sweet & Maxwell, 2001)

TIMOTHY ENDICOTT, *Vagueness in Law* (Oxford, OUP, 2000)

SUSAN ESTRICH, 'Rape' (1986) 95 *Yale Law Journal* 1087

JIM EVANS, 'Controlling the Use of Parliamentary History' (1998) 18 *New Zealand Universities Law Review* 1

JIM EVANS, 'Questioning the Dogmas of Realism' [2001] *New Zealand Law Review* 145

LINDSAY FARMER, 'The Obsession with Definition: The Nature of Crime and Critical Legal Theory' (1996) 5 *Social and Legal Studies* 57

LINDSAY FARMER, *Criminal law, tradition and legal order: Crime and the genius of Scots law, 1747 to the present* (Cambridge, Cambridge University Press, 1997)

DAVID FELDMAN (ed), *English Public Law* (Oxford, OUP, 2004)

PAMELA FERGUSON, 'Codifying Criminal Law (1): A Critique of Scots Common Law' [2004] *Criminal Law Review* 49

JOHN FINNIS, *Natural Law and Natural Rights* (Oxford, Clarendon Press, 1980)

JOHN FINNIS, 'On "The Critical Legal Studies Movement"' (1985) 30 *American Journal of Jurisprudence* 21, also in Eekelaar and Bell (eds) (1987)

STANLEY FISH, *The Trouble with Principle* (Cambridge, MA, Harvard University Press, 1999)

OWEN FISS, 'The Death of the Law' (1986) 72 *Cornell Law Review* 1

PETER FITZPATRICK and ALAN HUNT (eds), *Critical Legal Studies* (Oxford, Basil Blackwell, 1987), a reprint of (1987) 14(1) *Journal of Law and Society*

GEORGE FLETCHER, 'The Theory of Criminal Negligence: A Comparative Analysis' (1971) 119 *University of Pennsylvania Law Review* 401

GEORGE FLETCHER, *Rethinking Criminal Law* (Boston, MA, Little, Brown & Co, 1978; republished, Oxford, OUP, 2000)

GEORGE FLETCHER, 'The Fall and Rise of Criminal Theory' (1998) 1 *Buffalo Criminal Law Review* 275

GEORGE FLETCHER, 'Dogmas of the Model Penal Code' (1998) 2 *Buffalo Criminal Law Review* 3

CAROLINE FORELL and DONNA MATTHEWS, *A Law of Her Own: The Reasonable Woman as a Measure of Man* (New York, NY, New York University Press, 2000)

CHRISTOPHER FORSYTH (ed), *Judicial Review and the Constitution* (Oxford, Hart Publishing, 2000)

ML FRIEDLAND, 'R.S. Wright's Model Criminal Code: A Forgotten Chapter in the History of the Criminal Law' (1981) 1 *Oxford Journal of Legal Studies* 307

LON FULLER, *Legal Fictions* (Stanford, CA, Stanford University Press, 1967)

DONALD GALLOWAY, 'Nothing If Not Critical' (1997) 36 *Alberta Law Review* 273

JOHN GARDNER, 'Criminal Law and the Uses of Theory: A Reply to Laing' (1994) 14 *Oxford Journal of Legal Studies* 217

JOHN GARDNER, 'On the General Part of the Criminal Law' in Duff (ed) (1998)

MARTIN GARDNER, 'The *Mens Rea* Enigma: Observations on the Role of Motive in the Criminal Law Past and Present' (1993) *Utah Law Review* 635

SIMON GARDNER, 'Is Theft a Rip-Off?' (1990) 10 *Oxford Journal of Legal Studies* 441

SIMON GARDNER, 'Recklessness Refined' (1993) 109 *Law Quarterly Review* 21

SIMON GARDNER, 'Manslaughter by Gross Negligence' (1995) 111 *Law Quarterly Review* 22

RUTH GAVISON (ed), *Issues in Contemporary Legal Philosophy: The Influence of H.L.A. Hart* (Oxford, Clarendon Press, 1987)

RAYMOND GEUSS, *The Idea of a Critical Theory, Habermas and the Frankfurt School* (Cambridge, Cambridge University Press, 1981)

MARIANNE GILES, 'Judicial Law-Making in the Criminal Courts: the case of marital rape' [1992] *Criminal Law Review* 407

PETER GLAZEBROOK (ed), *Reshaping the Criminal Law: Essays in honour of Glanville Williams* (London, Stevens & Sons, 1978)

PETER GLAZEBROOK, 'Revising the Theft Acts' (1993) 52 *Cambridge Law Journal* 191

PETER GLAZEBROOK, 'Still No Code! English Criminal Law 1894–1994' in Dockray (ed) (1996)

ROBERT GOFF, 'The Search for Principle' (1983) 69 *Proceedings of the British Academy* 169

LORD GOFF, 'Judge, Jurist and Legislature' (1987) 2 *Denning Law Journal* 79

ROBERT GOFF, 'The Mental Element in the Crime of Murder' (1988) 104 *Law Quarterly Review* 30

MICHAEL GORR, 'Should the Law Distinguish between Intention and (Mere) Foresight?' (1996) 2 *Legal Theory* 359

KENT GREENAWALT, 'The Perplexing Borders of Justification and Excuse' (1984) 84 *Columbia Law Review* 1897

EDWARD GRIEW, 'Consistency, Communication and Codification: Reflections on Two Mens Rea Words' in Glazebrook (ed) (1978)

EDWARD GRIEW, 'Dishonesty: The Objections to Feely and Ghosh' [1985] *Criminal Law Review* 341

EDWARD GRIEW, *The Theft Acts* (7th edn, London, Sweet & Maxwell, 1995); (6th edn, 1990)

HYMAN GROSS, *A Theory of Criminal Justice* (New York, NY, OUP, 1979)

HYMAN GROSS and ROSS HARRISON (eds), *Jurisprudence: Cambridge Essays* (Oxford, Clarendon Press, 1992)

TADEUSZ GRYGIER, *Social Protection Code: A New Model of Criminal Justice* (South Hackensack, NJ, Fred B Rothman & Co, 1977)

AG GUEST (ed), *Oxford Essays in Jurisprudence* (Oxford, Clarendon Press, 1961)

JEROME HALL, 'Negligent Behaviour Should Be Excluded from Penal Liability' (1963) 63 *Columbia Law Review* 632

ANDREW HALPIN, 'Intended Consequences and Unintentional Fallacies' (1987) 7 *Oxford Journal of Legal Studies* 104

ANDREW HALPIN, 'More Comments on Rights and Claims' (1991) 10 *Law and Philosophy* 271

ANDREW HALPIN, 'The Appropriate Appropriation' [1991] *Criminal Law Review* 426

ANDREW HALPIN, 'The Test for Dishonesty' [1996] *Criminal Law Review* 283

ANDREW HALPIN, *Rights and Law – Analysis and Theory* (Oxford, Hart Publishing, 1997)

ANDREW HALPIN, 'Definitions and directions: recklessness unheeded' (1998) 18 *Legal Studies* 294

ANDREW HALPIN, Review of Christodoulidis' *Law and Reflexive Politics* (2000) 4 *Edinburgh Law Review* 107

ANDREW HALPIN, *Reasoning with Law* (Oxford, Hart Publishing, 2001)

ANDREW HALPIN, 'Or, even, What the Law Can Teach the Philosophy of Language: A Response to Green', forthcoming *Virginia Law Review*

BV HARRIS, 'Final Appellate Courts Overruling Their Own "Wrong" Precedents: The Ongoing Search for Principle' (2002) 118 *Law Quarterly Review* 408

JIM HARRIS, 'Towards Principles of Overruling—When Should a Final Court of Appeal Second Guess?' (1990) 10 *Oxford Journal of Legal Studies* 135

HLA HART, 'Negligence, *Mens Rea* and Criminal Responsibility' in Hart (1968), also in Guest (ed) (1961)

HLA HART, *Punishment and Responsibility: Essays in the Philosophy of Law* (Oxford, Clarendon Press, 1968)

Her Majesty's Commissioners for Revising and Consolidating the Criminal Law (appointed 1845), Fourth Report (1848), *Parliamentary Papers* (1847–8) XXVII, 1

PADDY HILLYARD, 'Invoking Indignation: Reflections on Future Directions of Socio-legal Studies' (2002) 29 *Journal of Law and Society* 645

LORD HOFFMAN, 'The Influence of the European Principle of Proportionality upon UK Law' in Ellis (ed) (1999)

Home Office, *Stalking—The Solutions: A Consultation Paper* (London, Home Office, 1996)

JEREMY HORDER, 'Cognition, Emotion, and Criminal Culpability' (1990) 106 *Law Quarterly Review* 469

JEREMY HORDER, 'Criminal Culpability: The Possibility of a General Theory' (1993) 12 *Law and Philosophy* 193

JEREMY HORDER, 'Intention in the Criminal Law—A Rejoinder' (1995) 58 *Modern Law Review* 678

JEREMY HORDER, 'Criminal Law: Between Determinism, Liberalism, and Criminal Justice' (1996) *Current Legal Problems* 159

JEREMY HORDER, 'Crimes of Ulterior Intent' in Simester and Smith (eds) (1996)

JEREMY HORDER, 'Two Histories and Four Hidden Principles of Mens Rea' (1997) 113 *Law Quarterly Review* 95

JEREMY HORDER, 'Gross Negligence and Criminal Culpability' (1997) 47 *University of Toronto Law Journal* 495

JEREMY HORDER (ed), *Oxford Essays in Jurisprudence, Fourth Series* (Oxford, Clarendon Press, 2000)

JEREMY HORDER, 'Criminal Law and Legal Positivism' (2002) 8 *Legal Theory* 221

DOUGLAS HUSAK, 'The Sequential Principle of Relative Culpability' (1995) 1 *Legal Theory* 493

GRANT HUSCROFT and PAUL RISHWORTH (eds), *Litigating Rights: Perspectives from Domestic and International Law* (Oxford, Hart Publishing, 2002)

ELIZABETH IGLESIAS, 'Latcrit Theory: Some Preliminary Notes towards a Transatlantic Dialogue' (2000) 9 *University of Miami International and Comparative Law Review* 1

International Chamber of Commerce, *Uniform Customs and Practices for Documentary Credits* (UCP 500) (Paris, International Chamber of Commerce, 1993)

LORD IRVINE, 'Judges and Decision-makers: The Theory and Practice of Wednesbury Review' [1996] *Public Law* 59

DAVID JABBARI, 'Reason, Cause and Principle in Law: The Normativity of Context' (1999) 19 *Oxford Journal of Legal Studies* 203

DAVID JABBARI, 'Radical Particularism: A Natural Law of Context' (1999) 50 *Northern Ireland Legal Quarterly* 454

SUSAN JAMES and STEPHANIE PALMER (eds), *Visible Women: Essays on Feminist Legal Theory and Political Philosophy* (Oxford, Hart Publishing, 2002)

CATHERINE JONES FINER and MIKE NELLIS (eds), *Crime and Social Exclusion* (Oxford, Blackwell Publishing, 1998)

JUSTINIAN, *Institutes*, JB Moyle (ed) (5th edn, Oxford, Clarendon Press, 1912)

MARK KELMAN, 'Interpretive Construction in the Substantive Criminal Law' (1981) 33 *Stanford Law Review* 591

MARK KELMAN, *A Guide to Critical Legal Studies* (Cambridge, MA, Harvard University Press, 1987)

DUNCAN KENNEDY, *A Critique of Adjudication* (Cambridge, MA, Harvard University Press, 1997)

DUNCAN KENNEDY, 'The Critique of Rights in Critical Legal Studies' in Brown and Halley (eds) (2002)

Kenny's *Outlines of Criminal Law*—see Turner

GEORGE KLIPPERT, 'The Juridical Nature of Unjust Enrichment' (1980) 30 *University of Toronto Law Journal* 356

MORDECHAI KREMNITZER, Preface (1996) 30 *Israel Law Review* 1

ITZHAK KUGLER, *Direct and Oblique Intention in the Criminal Law: An inquiry into degrees of blameworthiness* (Aldershot, Ashgate, 2002)

NICOLA LACEY, 'A Clear Concept of Intention: Elusive or Illusory?' (1993) 56 *Modern Law Review* 621

NICOLA LACEY, 'In(de)terminable Intentions' (1995) 58 *Modern Law Review* 692

NICOLA LACEY, 'Contingency, Coherence, and Conceptualism: Reflections on the Encounter between "Critique" and "the Philosophy of the Criminal Law"' in Duff (ed) (1998)

NICOLA LACEY, 'General Principles of Criminal Law? A Feminist View' in Nicolson and Bibbings (eds) (2000)

NICOLA LACEY, 'Violence, Ethics and Law: Feminist Reflections on a Familiar Dilemma' in James and Palmer (eds) (2002)

NICOLA LACEY and CELIA WELLS, *Reconstructing Criminal Law: Critical Perspectives on Crime and the Criminal Process* (2nd edn, London, Butterworths, 1998); (3rd edn with Oliver Quick, 2003)

Law Commission No 143 (HC 270, 1985), *Codification of the Criminal Law*

Law Commission No 177 (HC 299, 1989), *A Criminal Code for England and Wales*

Law Commission No 237 (HC 171, 1996), *Legislating the Criminal Code: Involuntary Manslaughter*

Law Commission, LCCP No 155 (1999), *Legislating the Criminal Code: Fraud and Deception*

Law Commission No 274 (HC 227, 2001), *Eighth Programme of Law Reform*

Law Commission No 276 (Cm 5560, 2002), *Fraud*

SIR JOHN LAWS, 'Law and Democracy' [1995] *Public Law* 72

SIR JOHN LAWS, 'The Limitations of Human Rights' [1998] *Public Law* 254

SIR JOHN LAWS, 'Judicial Review and the Meaning of Law' in Forsyth (ed) (2000)

LH LEIGH, 'Some Remarks on Appropriation in the Law of Theft after *Morris*' (1985) 48 *Modern Law Review* 167

LH LEIGH, 'Recklessness after *Reid*' (1993) 56 *Modern Law Review* 208

LH LEIGH, 'Liability for Inadvertence: A Lordly Legacy?' (1995) 58 *Modern Law Review* 457

IAN LOVELAND, *Constitutional Law, Administrative Law and Human Rights: A Critical Introduction* (3rd edn, London, Butterworths, 2003)

NEIL MACCORMICK, 'Reconstruction after Deconstruction: A Response to CLS' (1990) 10 *Oxford Journal of Legal Studies* 539

NEIL MACCORMICK, *Legal Reasoning and Legal Theory* (rev edn, Oxford, Clarendon Press, 1994)

CATHERINE MACKINNON, 'Towards Feminist Jurisprudence' (1982) 34 *Stanford Law Review* 703

SIR HENRY MAINE, *Ancient Law* (10th edn with Introduction and Notes by Sir Frederick Pollock, London, John Murray, 1920)

BASIL MARKESINIS, *Comparative Law in the Courtroom and in the Classroom: The Story of the Last Thirty-Five Years* (Oxford, Hart Publishing, 2003)

FINBARR MCAULEY and J PAUL MCCUTCHEON, *Criminal Liability: A Grammar* (Dublin, Round Hall Sweet & Maxwell, 2000)

SHAUN MCVEIGH and PETER RUSH, 'Cutting our Losses: Criminal Legal Doctrine' in McVeigh, Rush and Young (eds) (1997)

SHAUN MCVEIGH, PETER RUSH and ALISON YOUNG (eds), *Criminal Legal Doctrine* (Aldershot, Ashgate, 1997)

BARRY MITCHELL, 'Culpably Indifferent Murder' (1996) 25 *Anglo-American Law Review* 64

MICHAEL MOORE, *Placing Blame: A General Theory of the Criminal Law* (Oxford, Clarendon Press, 1997)

MAYO MORAN, *Rethinking the Reasonable Person: An Egalitarian Reconstruction of the Objective Standard* (Oxford, OUP, 2003)

COLIN MUNRO, *Studies in Constitutional Law* (2nd edn, London, Butterworths, 1999)

DANA NEASCU, 'CLS Stands for Critical Legal Studies, If Anyone Remembers' (2000) 8 *Journal of Law and Policy* 415

DAVID NELKEN, 'Critical Criminal Law' (1987) 14 *Journal of Law and Society* 105, also in Fitzpatrick and Hunt (eds) (1987)

JASON NEYERS, MITCHELL MCINNES and STEPHEN PITEL (eds), *Understanding Unjust Enrichment* (Oxford, Hart Publishing, 2004)

DONALD NICOLSON and LOIS BIBBINGS (eds), *Feminist Perspectives on Criminal Law* (London, Cavendish Publishing, 2000)

ALAN NORRIE, *Law, Ideology and Punishment: Retrieval and Critique of the Liberal Idea of Criminal Justice* (Dordrecht, Kluwer Academic Publishers, 1991)

ALAN NORRIE, 'Subjectivism, Objectivism and the Limits of Criminal Recklessness' (1992) 12 *Oxford Journal of Legal Studies* 45

ALAN NORRIE, 'Legal and Moral Judgment in the "General Part"' in McVeigh, Rush and Young (eds) (1997)

ALAN NORRIE, '"Simulacra of Morality"? Beyond the Ideal/Actual Antinomies of Criminal Justice' in Duff (ed) (1998)

ALAN NORRIE, *Punishment, Responsibility, and Justice: A Relational Critique* (Oxford, OUP, 2000)

ALAN NORRIE, *Crime, Reason and History: A Critical Introduction to Criminal Law* (2nd edn, London, Butterworths, 2001)

ALAN NORRIE, 'From Criminal Law to Legal Theory: The Mysterious Case of the Reasonable Glue Sniffer' (2002) 65 *Modern Law Review* 538

CHRISTOPHER NORRIS, *Deconstruction and the Interests of Theory* (London, Pinter Publishers, 1988)

VF NOURSE, 'Hearts and Minds: Understanding the New Culpability' (2002) 6 *Buffalo Criminal Law Review* 361

MARTHA NUSSBAUM, 'Skepticism about Practical Reason in Literature and the Law' (1994) 107 *Harvard Law Review* 714

FRANCES OLSEN, 'Statutory Rape: A Feminist Critique of Rights Analysis' (1984) 63 *Texas Law Review* 387

DAVID ORMEROD, 'A Bit of a Con? The Law Commission's Consultation Paper on Fraud' [1999] *Criminal Law Review* 789

Oxford English Dictionary (2nd edn prepared by JA Simpson and ECS Weiner, Oxford, Clarendon Press, 1989)

DENNIS PATTERSON, 'Introduction' in Patterson (ed) (1994)

DENNIS PATTERSON (ed), *Postmodernism and Law* (Aldershot, Dartmouth, 1994)

DENNIS PATTERSON (ed), *A Companion to Philosophy of Law and Legal Theory* (Oxford, Blackwell Publishers, 1996)

DENNIS PATTERSON, 2002 Quinlan Lecture, 'What is at Stake in Jurisprudence?' (2003) 28 *Oklahoma City University Law Review* 173

DENNIS PATTERSON, 'From Postmodernism to Law and Truth' (2003) 26 *Harvard Journal of Law and Public Policy* 49

GEORGE PAVLICH, 'The Art of Critique or How Not to be Governed Thus' in Wickham and Pavlich (eds) (2001)

A PHILLIPS GRIFFITHS (ed), *Philosophy and Practice* (Cambridge, Cambridge University Press, 1985)

SAMUEL PILLSBURY, *Judging Evil: Rethinking the Law of Murder and Manslaughter* (New York, NY, New York University Press, 1998)

PLATO, *Republic*, Loeb edition with translation by Paul Shorey (London, William Heinemann, 1935)

Gerald Postema, 'Philosophy of the Common Law' in Coleman and Shapiro (eds) (2002)

JIRI PRIBAN, 'Sharing the Paradigms? Critical Legal Studies and the Sociology of Law' in Banakar and Travers (eds) (2002)

PETER PUGH, *Is Guinness Good for You?* (London, Financial Training Publications, 1987)

LEON RADZINOWICZ, 'The Waltham Black Act: A Study of the Legislative Attitude towards Crime in the Eighteenth Century' (1945) 9 *Cambridge Law Journal* 56

LEON RADZINOWICZ, *A History of English Criminal Law and its Administration from 1750, 1: The Movement for Reform* (London, Stevens & Sons, 1948)

RICHARD REVESZ, 'Ideology, Collegiality, and the D.C. Circuit: A Reply to Chief Judge Harry T. Edwards' (1999) 85 *Virginia Law Review* 805

PAUL ROBERTS, 'Philosophy, Feinberg, Codification, and Consent: A Progress Report on English Experiences of Criminal Law Reform' (2001) 5 *Buffalo Criminal Law Review* 173

PAUL ROBINSON, 'A Brief History of Distinctions in Criminal Culpability' (1980) *Hastings Law Journal* 815

PAUL ROBINSON, 'Should the Criminal Law Abandon the *Actus Reus-Mens Rea* Distinction?' in Shute, Gardner and Horder (eds) (1993)

PAUL ROBINSON, *Structure and Function in Criminal Law* (Oxford, Clarendon Press, 1997)

PAUL ROBINSON, 'In Defense of the Model Penal Code: A Reply to Professor Fletcher' (1998) 2 *Buffalo Criminal Law Review* 25

PAUL ROBINSON, MICHAEL CAHILL and USMAN MOHAMMAD, 'The Five Worst (and Five Best) American Criminal Codes' (2000) 95 *Northwestern University Law Review* 1

RICHARD ROBINSON, *Definition* (Oxford, Clarendon Press, 1954)

MICHEL ROSENFELD, 'Deconstruction and Legal Interpretation, Conflict, Indeterminacy and the Temptations of the New Legal Formalism' in Cornell, Rosenfeld and Carlson (eds) (1992)

KATHERYN RUSSELL, 'A Critical View from the Inside: An Application of Critical Legal Studies to Criminal Law' (1994) 85 *Journal of Criminal Law and Criminology* 222

ANDREW RUTHERFORD, 'Criminal Policy and the Eliminative Ideal' (1997) 31 *Social Policy and Administration* 116, also in Jones Finer and Nellis (eds) (1998)

ANDREW SANDERS, Review of Alldridge's *Relocating Criminal Law* (2002) 65 *Modern Law Review* 151

FREDERICK SCHAUER, *Playing by the Rules: A Philosophical Examination of Rule-Based Decision Making in Law and in Life* (Oxford, Clarendon Press, 1991)

ELIZABETH SCHNEIDER, 'Equal Rights to Trial for Women: Sex Bias in the Law of Self-Defense' (1980) 15 *Harvard Civil Rights-Civil Liberties Law Review* 623

LOUIS SCHWARTZ, 'With Gun and Camera Through Darkest CLS-Land' (1984) 36 *Stanford Law Review* 413

SIR STEPHEN SEDLEY, 'Human Rights: a Twenty-First Century Agenda' [1995] *Public Law* 386

SIR STEPHEN SEDLEY, *Freedom, Law and Justice* (London, Sweet & Maxwell, 1999)

SEXTUS EMPIRICUS, *Against the Logicians* in the Loeb edition, *Sextus Empiricus* II, with translation by RG Bury (London, William Heinemann, 1935)

EMILY SHERWIN, 'A Defense of Analogical Reasoning in Law' (1999) 66 *University of Chicago Law Review* 1179

STEPHEN SHUTE, 'Appropriation and the Law of Theft' [2002] *Criminal Law Review* 445

STEPHEN SHUTE, JOHN GARDNER and JEREMY HORDER, 'Introduction: The Logic of Criminal Law' in Shute, Gardner and Horder (eds) (1993)

STEPHEN SHUTE, JOHN GARDNER and JEREMY HORDER (eds), *Action and Value in Criminal Law* (Oxford, Clarendon Press, 1993)

STEPHEN SHUTE and AP SIMESTER (eds), *Criminal Law Theory: Doctrines of the General Part* (Oxford, OUP, 2002)

STEPHEN SILBER, 'The Law Commission, Conspiracy to Defraud and the Dishonesty Project' [1995] *Criminal Law Review* 461

RAIMO SILTALA, *A Theory of Precedent: From Analytical Positivism to a Post-Analytical Philosophy of Law* (Oxford, Hart Publishing, 2000)

AP SIMESTER, 'Can Negligence be Culpable?' in Horder (ed) (2000)

AP SIMESTER and ATH SMITH (eds), *Harm and Culpability* (Oxford, Clarendon Press, 1996)

NE SIMMONDS, 'Bluntness and Bricolage' in Gross and Harrison (eds) (1992)

KENNETH SIMONS, 'Rethinking Mental States' (1992) 72 *Boston University Law Review* 463

KENNETH SIMONS, 'Dimensions Of Negligence in Criminal and Tort Law' (2002) 3 *Theoretical Inquiries in Law (Online Edition)* No 2 Article 2

KENNETH SIMONS, 'Does Punishment for "Culpable Indifference" Simply Punish for "Bad Character"? Examining the Requisite Connection Between Mens Rea and Actus Reus' (2002) 6 *Buffalo Criminal Law Review* 219

ATH SMITH, 'On Actus Reus and Mens Rea' in Glazebrook (ed) (1978)

ATH SMITH, 'Judicial Lawmaking in the Criminal Law' (1984) 100 *Law Quarterly Review* 46

ATH SMITH, *Property Offences* (London, Sweet & Maxwell, 1994)

ATH SMITH, 'Offences Against Property' in Feldman (ed) (2004)

JOHN SMITH, Comment on *Caldwell* [1981] *Criminal Law Review* 393

JOHN SMITH, Comment on *Morris* [1983] *Criminal Law Review* 815

JOHN SMITH, Comment on *Dobson* [1990] *Criminal Law Review* 273

JOHN SMITH, Comment on *Buzalek and Schiffer* [1991] *Criminal Law Review* 130

JOHN SMITH, Comment on *O'Connell* [1991] *Criminal Law Review* 771

JOHN SMITH, Comment on *R v R* [1992] *Criminal Law Review* 207

JOHN SMITH, Comment on *Gallasso* [1993] *Criminal Law Review* 459

JOHN SMITH, 'Reforming the Theft Acts' (1996) 28 *Bracton Law Journal* 27

SIR JOHN SMITH, *The Law of Theft* (8th edn, London, Butterworths, 1997); (6th edn, 1989)

SIR JOHN SMITH, 'The Sad Fate of the Theft Act 1968' in Swadling and Jones (eds) (1999)

SIR JOHN SMITH, Smith and Hogan's *Criminal Law* (10th edn, London, Butterworths, 2002)

KEITH SMITH, *Lawyers, Legislators and Theorists: Developments in English Criminal Jurisprudence 1800–1957* (Oxford, Clarendon Press, 1998)

LAWRENCE SOLUM, 'On the Indeterminacy Thesis: Critiquing Critical Dogma' (1987) 54 *University of Chicago Law Review* 54

JOHN STANNARD, 'Subjectivism, Objectivism, and the Draft Criminal Code' (1985) 101 *Law Quarterly Review* 540

SIR JAMES FITZJAMES STEPHEN, *A History of the Criminal Law of England* (London, Macmillan & Co, 1883; reprinted New York, NY, Burt Franklin, 1973)

SIR JAMES FITZJAMES STEPHEN, *A Digest of the Criminal Law (Crimes and Punishments)* (3rd edn, London, Macmillan & Co, 1883)

NADINE STROSSEN, 'Liberty and Equality: Complementary, Not Competing, Constitutional Commitments' in Huscroft and Rishworth (eds) (2002)

DON STUART, 'Supporting General Principles for Criminal Responsibility in the Model Penal Code with Suggestions for Reconsideration: A Canadian Perspective' (2000) 4 *Buffalo Criminal Law Review* 13

GR SULLIVAN, 'Intent, Subjective Recklessness and Culpability' (1992) 12 *Oxford Journal of Legal Studies* 380

GR SULLIVAN, 'Is Criminal Law Possible?' (2002) 22 *Oxford Journal of Legal Studies* 747

CASS SUNSTEIN, 'On Analogical Reasoning' (1993) 106 *Harvard Law Review* 741

CASS SUNSTEIN, *Legal Reasoning and Political Conflict* (New York, NY, OUP, 1996)

WILLIAM SWADLING and GARETH JONES (eds), *The Search for Principle: Essays in Honour of Lord Goff of Chieveley* (Oxford, OUP, 1999)

VICTOR TADROS, 'Recklessness and the Duty to Take Care' in Shute and Simester (eds) (2002)

VICTOR TADROS, 'The system of the criminal law' (2002) 22 *Legal Studies* 448

COLIN TAPPER (ed), *Crime, Proof and Punishment: Essays in Memory of Sir Rupert Cross* (London, Butterworths, 1981)

CHARLES TAYLOR, *Sources of the Self: The Making of the Modern Identity* (Cambridge, Cambridge University Press, 1989)

CHARLES TAYLOR, *The Ethics of Authenticity* (Cambridge, MA, Harvard University Press, 1992)

JENNIFER TEMKIN, 'Rape and Criminal Justice at the Millenium' in Nicolson and Bibbings (eds) (2000)

JENNIFER TEMKIN, *Rape and the Legal Process* (2nd edn, Oxford, OUP, 2002)

JENNIFER TEMKIN, 'Sexual History Evidence—Beware the Backlash' [2003] *Criminal Law Review* 217

EP THOMPSON, *Whigs and Hunters: The Origin of the Black Act* (London, Allen Lane, 1975)

ROSY THORNTON, 'Dishonest Assistance: Guilty Conduct or a Guilty Mind?' (2002) 61 *Cambridge Law Journal* 524

RICHARD TUR, 'Dishonesty and the Jury: a Case Study in the Moral Content of Law' in Phillips Griffiths (ed) (1985)
RICHARD TUR, 'Subjectivism and Objectivism: Towards Synthesis' in Shute, Gardner and Horder (eds) (1993)
JWC TURNER (ed), *Kenny's Outlines of Criminal Law* (16th edn, Cambridge, Cambridge University Press, 1952); (1st edn, 1902)
MARK TUSHNET, 'Critical Legal Studies: A Political History' (1991) 100 *Yale Law Journal* 1515
MARK TUSHNET, Review of Schauer's *Playing with the Rules* (1992) 90 *Michigan Law Review* 1560
MARK TUSHNET and JENNIFER JAFF, 'Critical Legal Studies and Criminal Procedure' (1986) 35 *Catholic University Law Review* 361
WILLIAM TWINING and DAVID MIERS, *How To Do Things With Rules* (4th edn, London, Butterworths, 1999)
WILLIAM TWINING, WARD FARNSWORTH, STEFAN VOGENAUER and FERNANDO TESÓN, 'The Role of Academics in the Legal System' in Cane and Tushnet (eds) (2003)
ROBERTO UNGER, 'The Critical Legal Studies Movement' (1983) 96 *Harvard Law Review* 561
ROBERTO UNGER, *The Critical Legal Studies Movement* (Cambridge, MA, Harvard University Press, 1986)
RC VAN CAENEGEM, *Judges, Legislators and Professors: Chapters in European Legal History* (Cambridge, Cambridge University Press, 1987)
GRAHAM VIRGO, 'Back to Basics—Reconstructing Manslaughter' (1994) 53 *Cambridge Law Journal* 44
ANDREW VON HIRSCH and ANDREW ASHWORTH (eds), *Principled Sentencing: Readings on Theory and Policy* (2nd edn, Oxford, Hart Publishing, 1998)
CELIA WELLS, 'Swatting the Subjectivist Bug' [1982] *Criminal Law Review* 209
CELIA WELLS, 'Codification of the Criminal Law: Restatement or Reform?' [1986] *Criminal Law Review* 314
CELIA WELLS, 'Stalking: The Criminal Law Response' [1997] *Criminal Law Review* 463
ROBIN WEST, 'Re-Imagining Justice' (2002) 14 *Yale Journal of Law and Feminism* 333
ROBIN WEST, *Re-Imagining Justice: Progressive Interpretations of Formal Equality, Rights, and the Rule of Law* (Aldershot, Ashgate, 2003)
PETER WESTEN and JAMES MANGIAFICO, 'The Criminal Defense of Duress: A Justification, Not an Excuse—And Why it Matters' (2003) 6 *Buffalo Criminal Law Review* 833
ALAN WHITE, *Grounds of Liability: An Introduction to the Philosophy of Law* (Oxford, Clarendon Press, 1985)
ALAN WHITE, *Misleading Cases* (Oxford, Clarendon Press, 1991)
GARY WICKHAM and GEORGE PAVLICH, *Rethinking Law, Society and Governance: Foucault's Bequest* (Oxford, Hart Publishing, 2001)
GLANVILLE WILLIAMS, *Criminal Law: The General Part* (2nd edn, London, Stevens & Sons, 1961)
GLANVILLE WILLIAMS, *The Mental Element in Crime* (Jerusalem, Magnes Press, 1965)
GLANVILLE WILLIAMS, 'Recklessness Redefined' (1981) 40 *Cambridge Law Journal* 252
GLANVILLE WILLIAMS, *Textbook of Criminal Law* (2nd edn, London, Stevens & Sons, 1983)

GLANVILLE WILLIAMS, 'The Lords and Impossible Attempts, or *Quis Custodiet Ipsos Custodes?*' (1986) 45 *Cambridge Law Journal* 33

GLANVILLE WILLIAMS, 'The *Mens Rea* for Murder: Leave It Alone' (1989) 105 *Law Quarterly Review* 387

WILLIAM WILSON, 'Murder and the Structure of Homicide' in Ashworth and Mitchell (eds) (2000)

WILLIAM WILSON, *Central Issues in Criminal Theory* (Oxford, Hart Publishing, 2002)

LUDWIG WITTGENSTEIN, *Philosophical Investigations*, GEM Anscombe (transl) (2nd edn, Oxford, Basil Blackwell, 1958)

DAVID WOOD and ROBERT BERNASCONI (eds), *Derrida and* Différance (Coventry, Parousia Press, 1985; republished, Evanston, IL, Northwestern University Press, 1988)

LORD WOOLF, 'Droit Public—English Style' [1995] *Public Law* 57

RS WRIGHT (C 1893, 1877), *Drafts of a Criminal Code and a Code of Criminal Procedure for the Island of Jamaica with an Explanatory Memorandum*

STANLEY YEO, *Fault in Homicide: Towards a Schematic Approach to the Fault Elements for Murder and Involuntary Manslaughter in England, Australia and India* (Annandale, NSW, The Federation Press, 1997)

MICHAEL ZANDER, 'What precedents and other source materials do the courts use?' (2000) 150 *New Law Journal* 1790

Index